# HIKING CANYONLANDS AND ARCHES

## NATIONAL PARKS

2012 eclipse in Arches
National Park
NPS/NEAL HERBERT

# HIKING
# CANYONLANDS
# AND ARCHES
## NATIONAL PARKS

### FOURTH EDITION

Published in partnership with the National Park Service
and Canyonlands Natural History Association

## Bill Schneider

**FALCON**GUIDES

GUILFORD, CONNECTICUT

# FALCONGUIDES®

An imprint of Globe Pequot

Falcon and FalconGuides are registered trademarks and Make Adventure Your Story is a trademark of Rowman & Littlefield.

Distributed by NATIONAL BOOK NETWORK

Copyright © 2017 Rowman & Littlefield

Photos by Bill Schneider unless otherwise noted.

Topo maps copyright 2017 National Geographic Partners, LLC. All Rights Reserved.

Maps by Alena Pearce © Rowman & Littlefield

British Library Cataloguing-in-Publication Information available

**Library of Congress Cataloging-in-Publication Data available**

ISBN 978-1-4930-2739-2 (paperback)
ISBN 978-1-4930-2738-5 (e-book)

∞™ The paper used in this publication meets the minimum requirements of American National Standard for Information Sciences—Permanence of Paper for Printed Library Materials, ANSI / NISO Z39.48-1992.

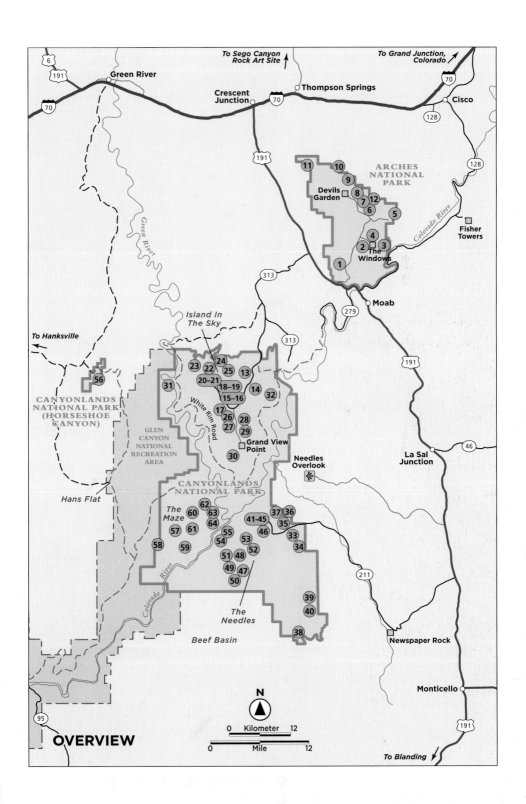

# THE HIKES

## Canyonlands National Park: The Needles

## Canyonlands National Park: The Maze, Orange Cliffs, and Horseshoe Canyon

## THE HIKES

# MEET YOUR GUIDE

**BILL SCHNEIDER** has spent a half century hiking trails all across America. It all started in college in the late-1960s when he landed a job that paid him to hike, working on the trail crew in Glacier National Park. He spent the 1970s publishing *Montana Outdoors* magazine for the Montana Department of Fish, Wildlife & Parks and covering as many miles of trails as possible on weekends and holidays. In 1979 Bill and his partner, Mike Sample, founded Falcon Publishing and gradually built the company for the next 20 years. Along the way,

Bill Schneider at the confluence of the Colorado and Green Rivers
MARNIE SCHNEIDER

Bill wrote twenty-one books and hundreds of magazine articles on wildlife, outdoor recreation, and conservation issues. For twelve years he taught classes on bicycling, backpacking, zero-impact camping, and hiking in bear country for the Yellowstone Institute, a nonprofit educational organization in Yellowstone National Park.

In 2000 Bill retired from his position as president of Falcon Publishing (now part of Rowman & Littlefield) after it had grown into the premier publisher of outdoor recreation guidebooks with more than 800 titles in print. During the early twenty-first century, he stayed in the publishing game for six more years by working as a consultant and acquisition editor for the Lyons Press and FalconGuides imprints and as Travel and Outdoor editor for NewWest.net, a regional online magazine, where he wrote a weekly *Wild Bill* column devoted to what he called "outdoor politics."

He now lives in Helena, Montana, with his wife, Marnie, works as little as possible, and spends almost every day hiking, bicycling, or fishing.

## 5 HIKING TIPS FROM BILL

**1.** Be sure to carry plenty of drinking water. You need more than you think and won't find any along the trail. **2.** Hike early in the day when it's cooler and there's less chance of a thunderstorm. **3.** Instead of shorts and a tank top, wear proper desert hiking clothing: "light and white" long pants, long sleeves, and a wide-brimmed hat. It's better than sunscreen. **4.** Buy a separate map to use in addition to the small maps in this guidebook. **5.** Read up on symptoms of hyperthermia so you can recognize it before it's too late.

# HOW TO USE THIS BOOK

This guide won't answer all the questions you have concerning your hiking vacation to Arches or Canyonlands National Parks, but it should answer a lot of them.

## DISTANCES

In this guide most road distances came from odometer readings or from National Park Service (NPS) signs and brochures. However, in some cases estimates were made.

When hiking the trails, you may notice slight variations in stated mileages between trail signs, park maps, and Trails Illustrated maps, but in most cases the variations are insignificant. The trail distances used in this book mirror those on the Trails Illustrated maps, which are the most current mileages provided by the NPS. The Trails Illustrated maps are slightly ahead of the NPS's process of updating park maps and signs, which will eventually be corrected to match the mileages on the Trails Illustrated maps.

Keep in mind that distance is less important than difficulty. A rocky, steep, 2-mile trail can take longer and require more effort (and water) than 4 miles on a well-contoured trail on flat terrain. Often the trails and roads in these parks are better measured in hours instead of miles.

## RATINGS

Difficulty ratings for trails serve as a general guide only, not the final word. What is difficult to one hiker may be easy to the next. In this guidebook, difficulty ratings consider both how long and how strenuous the route is. Here are general definitions of the ratings:

**Easy:** Suitable for any hiker, including small children, without serious elevation gain, hazardous sections, or places where the trail is hard to follow.

**Moderate:** Suitable for hikers who have some experience and at least an average fitness level, but probably not suitable for small children. The hike may have some short sections where the trail is difficult to follow and often includes some hills.

**Difficult:** Suitable for experienced hikers with an above-average fitness level. These hikes often have sections that are difficult to follow and require knowledge of route-finding with topo map and compass or GPS, sometimes with serious elevation gain, and possibly some hazardous conditions.

## ROADS

In the back of this book you'll find an appendix on backcountry roads. To help you plan your trip, each road description in this section includes vehicle recommendations. Vehicle ratings for backcountry roads came from experience in driving the roads and from NPS recommendations. These recommendations are, admittedly, on the conservative side. Play it safe and take a high-clearance, four-wheel-drive vehicle with low-range gearing to safely cover any road in the park. Such a vehicle is required for all backcountry roads in the Needles and the Maze.

## TYPES OF TRIPS

Suggested hikes have been split into the following categories:

**Loop:** Starts and finishes at the same trailhead, with no (or very little) retracing of your steps. This includes "lollipop" loops.

**Shuttle:** A point-to-point trip that requires two vehicles (one left at the other end of the trail) or an arrangement where hikers are picked up at a designated time and place. The best way to manage the logistical problems of shuttles is to arrange for another party to start at the other end of the trail. When the two parties meet at a predetermined point, they trade keys. When finished, they drive each other's vehicle home. The NPS does not provide shuttle service in Arches or Canyonlands National Parks.

**Out and Back:** Traveling to a specific destination, then retracing your steps back to the trailhead.

# Map and Icon Legends

## ICON LEGEND

 BEST
FOR PHOTOS

 HIKES FOR
FAMILIES

 HIKES FOR
WATERFALLS

 FINDING
SOLITUDE

## NOTES ON MAPS

Topographic maps are an essential companion to the activities in this guide. Falcon has partnered with National Geographic to provide the best mapping resources. Each activity is accompanied by a detailed map and the name of the National Geographic TOPO! map (USGS), which can be downloaded for free from natgeomaps.com.

If the activity takes place on a National Geographic Trails Illustrated map it will be noted. Continually setting the standard for accuracy, each Trails Illustrated topographic map is crafted in conjunction with local land managers and undergoes rigorous review and enhancement before being printed on waterproof, tear-resistant material. Trails Illustrated maps and information about their digital versions, which can be used on mobile GPS applications, can be found at natgeomaps.com.

## MAP LEGEND

| | | | |
|---|---|---|---|
|  70 | Interstate Highway | – – – | Recreation Area |
| 6 | US Highway |  | Bridge |
| 46 | State Highway | Campground | Campground |
| | Local Road | | Campsite |
| – – – – | Gravel Road | P | Parking |
| – – – – | Unimproved Road | ▲ | Peak |
|  | Featured Route on Trail | | Picnic Area |
|  | Featured Route on Paved Trail | □ | Point of Interest |
|  | Featured Route on Road | | Ranger Station/Park Office |
| – – – – – | Trail | | Restroom |
| | Paved Trail |  | Scenic View |
| ·········· | Off-Trail Route |  | Tower |
| | Small River or Creek | 1 | Trailhead |
| | Intermittent Stream | ? | Visitor/Information Center |
|  | Body of Water | | |
| | National Park | | |

# PREFACE

Geographically, the Canyonlands is a section of southeastern Utah, some of it embodied in two magnificent national parks, Arches and Canyonlands. But geography is only a small part of the story. Naturally, the Canyonlands, or Abbey Country, as it has been called, is much more.

It's a rugged piñon pine growing out of solid slickrock—and the beautiful blue piñon jay screaming at you from it.

It's the stealthy mountain lion stalking the understandably skittish mule deer, or the seldom-seen bobcat getting fat on the foolish young of the desert cottontail. You rarely see the desert cats, but they leave their story in the sand.

It's those little whiptail and fence lizards darting away as you walk down the trail. I wonder if some scientist knows how these little lizards can run so fast on centimeter-long legs and could tell me how they do it?

It's those amazingly hardy desert plants. After being out in the Canyonlands heat for a few days, you grow to really appreciate their toughness and special adaptations and longevity. Stepping on a desert plant is like cutting down a big tree in the rain forest—except the desert plant is probably older, and tougher than nails to make a living in this harsh environment. If desert plants were human, they'd be ninjas or extreme cage fighters. I also like the way they give each other space. I imagine they could grow closer to each other, but instead they prefer to keep their distance from their neighbors. Sound familiar?

It's all that blackbrush, everywhere, like oceans of tumbleweeds that haven't blown away yet, growing on the harshest sites where only the hardiest plants could survive. Individual plants live for hundreds of years on almost nothing, and the desert bighorn will never go hungry.

It's a whole lot of slickrock, everywhere you look. Even when you aren't standing on it, you get the feeling it's only a few inches down. Since lots of names get changed and shortened as time goes by, I suspect that slickrock is really a shortened version of slick-when-wet-rock.

It's those little potholes in the slickrock that evolve into microhabitats and then into stone-ringed "pothole gardens," like bonsai gardens with all plants aged but dwarfed.

It's deep canyons dropping suddenly out of the desert and winding aimlessly through the plateau and majestic arches highlighting so many skylines, along with awesome sandstone spires and cliffs everywhere, and, of course, it's those "Canyonlands mushrooms"—multihued, mushroom-shaped sandstone formations.

It's the light, that wonderfully clear light. The light can change colors on the cliffs and highlight the gorgeous deep green of emerging buckthorn leaves against the reddish sandstone, especially on a rare overcast day or after a rain.

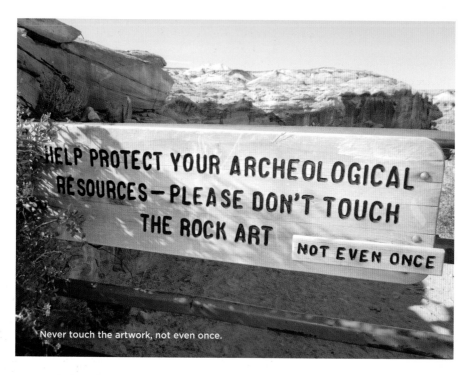

Never touch the artwork, not even once.

It's the quiet. I don't know why, but canyons always seem so quiet—at least compared to the forest or the beach or the prairie. The wind can unexpectedly whip up and threaten the stillness, but it doesn't seem to work. When there is a sound, you really hear it. When you sneeze, it echoes around for several seconds and you feel like saying, "Excuse me, Mother Nature." If you're lucky enough to get caught by an afternoon storm, you can hear the quiet burst suddenly, with thunderclaps pounding up and down the canyon walls like a drum roll loud enough to shake off the desert varnish.

It's a classroom for prehistory—ancient rock art on canyon walls and adobe ruins under sandstone overhangs left by long-gone cultures. We have to paint our houses every few years, but these cultures painted their life story on desert rocks, and it has lasted 2,000 years.

It's getting caught in a desert rain and sitting in an alcove to watch the plants turn a gorgeous deep green an artist couldn't duplicate and the water system start to work—little rivulets following slickrock curves, merging, getting bigger and bigger. Those stark, dry pour-overs become elegant waterfalls right before your eyes, and you can walk beside the head of the newly born stream as it inches its way down the dry wash. The rain washes the dust off the plants, and awash in their new vivid green, they seem to almost want to stand up and stretch like we do at the start of a new day. And they all seem to be smiling.

It's that awesome flash flood that I haven't seen . . . yet. But I've seen the tracks a flash flood leaves, and I've talked to a few people fortunate enough to experience a flash flood ripping down a canyon. I'll keep coming back, hoping to see one.

Recreationally, the Canyonlands is a mecca for outdoor sports, but it's the natural wonders that make the hiking, bicycling, four-wheeling, camping, and river running so great. And all this fun fuels an economy almost completely based on outdoor recreation. Where else does that happen?

Perhaps most of all, however, the Canyonlands is a place to relax, take a deep breath, let your nails grow. Or as Edward Abbey used to do, enjoy a cold beer after a hard day of cloud watching. That works for a hard day of hiking, too, incidentally.

Do yourself a favor and don't hurry through the Canyonlands, seeing only a few arches and then moving on to the next national park. Instead, take your time and let the nature of the Canyonlands sneak up on you and take root in your heart. This can become quite a burden, though—you'll become so attached to the place that you'll have to return again and again and again.

Turret Arch at sunset
COURTESY BRAD WAGNER/
IMPACT PHOTOGRAPHICS

# BEFORE YOU HIT THE TRAIL

If you're going to **ARCHES OR CANYONLANDS NATIONAL PARKS** for the first time, the first question is usually, where do you go?

It depends on how you like to enjoy your outdoors. Mountain bikers, for example, might like the areas contiguous to the parks, where they have more options. Ditto for four-wheel-drive fans. But here, unlike most national parks, you can also find opportunities for mountain biking and four-wheeling within park boundaries.

If you're a hiker, you have lots of choices, depending on how much time you have, your physical capabilities, and your appetite for adventure. For the seriously adventurous, it's the Maze, and for the beginner, it's Arches. For the casual tourist who wants to see some fantastic scenery without working up a sweat, it's the Island in the Sky or Arches. For the intermediate to serious hiker, it's the Needles.

The following suggestions will make planning easier, but to get more help with your decision on where to go, refer to the overview sections in each of the four major areas covered in this book—Arches National Park and the Needles, Island in

Abbey Country, Arches
National Park
COURTESY BRAD WAGNER/
IMPACT PHOTOGRAPHICS

the Sky, and Maze Districts of Canyonlands National Park. (The Orange Cliffs Unit of Glen Canyon National Recreation Area is included in the Maze District.)

Wherever you go, however, you aren't likely to be disappointed.

## PLANNING YOUR TRIP

Getting to Canyonlands or Arches National Parks isn't a short drive for many people. It usually takes a major effort to get there, so plan your trip so you won't get stressed out or disappointed by some snafu that could have been avoided with advance planning.

Back in 1995 the National Park Service (NPS) launched a reservation system for backcountry permits. You don't have to get a permit until you get to the park, but if you want to be sure you can actually camp in the campsite you've preselected, you should use the advance reservation system to ensure a permit for that site. Demand for permits continues to increase, especially during spring and fall and at popular sites, so take advantage of the new system to avoid disappointment. Arches National Park is not covered by the backcountry management plan.

Before you apply for permits, digest as much information as you can about the area you plan to visit. Study the map and read whatever information you can get on the area. For starters, carefully review the wealth of information on the park service's official websites, www.nps.gov/cany and www.nps.gov/arch. Doing your advance research saves you and the NPS a lot of time and frustration.

If you plan to go to the visitor centers, check the websites for the hours they are open, which vary by the season.

## GETTING A BACKCOUNTRY PERMIT

Canyonlands National Park requires permits for backpacking, backcountry vehicle sites, mountain-bike camping in all vehicle campsites, and day use in three areas in the Needles District (Salt Creek, Horse Canyon, and Lavender Canyon). The park also requires free day-use permits for driving or bicycling on the White Rim Road in the Island in the Sky District and the Elephant Hill, Lavender Canyon, and Salt Creek Roads in the Needles District. When this revision was published (2017), these day-use permits were free, but you still have to pay the park entrance fee. For all other roads and trails, however, no permit is required for day use.

To start planning your trip, go to the park's excellent website, www.nps.gov/cany. There you'll find most of the information you need. You can make backcountry camping reservations up to four months in advance through the park's website. You can also call the park reservation office and request a backcountry trip-planning guide, a free handout that will answer most of your questions.

Then, as far in advance of your trip start date as possible (months, if possible), request your reservations by mail or fax (you can't make online reservations). If you plan a trip on the White Rim Road, you should make your reservation at least six months in advance. You can't make reservations over the phone, but you can call for help. All requests for advance reservations must include the name, address, and phone numbers of the trip leader, dates and campsites or zones desired with alternatives for both, number of people in the group, number of vehicles in the group (vehicle campers only), and the nonrefundable permit fee.

A granary on the Aztec Butte Trail
NPS/NEAL HERBERT

You can pay for your permit with Visa or MasterCard or with a personal check or money order made payable to the National Park Service. If faxing your reservation information, use a credit card to pay. Please don't send cash. Send a detailed itinerary with alternative sites and a check, money order, or your credit card number and expiration date to pay for the permit. Send the request to:

Reservation Office
Canyonlands National Park
2282 Resource Blvd.
Moab, UT 84532
Phone: (435) 259-4351
Fax: (435) 259-4285
E-mail: canyinfo@nps.gov
Website: www.nps.gov/cany

The NPS will respond to both phone and mail requests and send a written confirmation. This confirmation is not your permit. You must pick up the permit at the visitor center in the district where the trip begins. If you have to cancel or change your trip, please notify the Reservation Office as soon as possible so the campsite(s) can be made available to other park visitors.

If the campsite you want has already been reserved, the NPS will try to get as close to your route as possible by reserving alternative sites. If you send your alternatives, it makes it easier for the NPS to schedule something close to the trip you have planned. If you're already in the park, you can apply for your permit in person and pay the fee at that time. However, in some cases the area you want to see might not have permits available, especially during peak seasons.

## RESERVATION FEES

Fees for reserving campsites change from time to time, so check the park website for current amounts. Reservation fees don't go into the general fund in Washington, DC. These fees stay in Canyonlands National Park and pay for the operation of the backcountry reservation system. The fees cover the expense of salaries, phone lines, office supplies, postage, publication of a trip planner, and maintenance of the computer system. Without these fees the reservation system would be impossible, and permits would be issued on a first-come, first-served basis.

## OTHER CAMPING OPTIONS

If you want to stay in developed campgrounds, you can try the following:

Devils Garden Campground, Arches National Park: The campground has fifty-two individual sites, each of which can accommodate up to ten people. All individual

Turret Arch as seen through
the North Window at the
first light of the day
NPS/JACOB W. FRANK

campsites may be reserved through Recreation.gov for nights between March 1 and October 31. Reservations must be made no less than 4 days and no more than 240 days in advance. To make a reservation, visit www.recreation.gov or phone (877) 444-6777. *Note:* Due to a one-year, temporary, but major construction project, the Devils Garden Campground will be completely closed until October 31, 2017. For more info, visit nps.gov/arch/planyourvisit/camping.htm.

Squaw Flat Campground, Needles District: Twenty-six sites plus three group sites, drinking water available mid-March through October, maximum group size ten people per site with the exception of the group sites.

Willow Flat Campground, Island in the Sky District: Twelve sites, no water, maximum group size ten people per site.

In peak seasons these three national park campgrounds fill up fast, and with the exception of Devils Garden's sites in March through October and the group sites, which can be reserved, spaces go on a first-come, first-served basis. The ranger on duty at the entrance station often can tell you how full the campgrounds are, and during peak seasons they're usually full. The nominal camping fees are subject to change without notice.

Dead Horse Point State Park, near the Island in the Sky District, has a twenty-one-site campground. You can reserve a site in advance by calling Utah State Parks at (800) 322-3770.

If you can't find a spot in one of the national park campgrounds, you can often find a place outside of the parks on public land managed by the Bureau of Land Management and the USDA Forest Service. To get more information on these camping alternatives, call the following phone numbers:

Bureau of Land Management Offices
Moab Office (outside Island in the Sky): (435) 259-2100
San Juan Resource Area (outside Needles): (435) 587-1500
Hanksville Resource Area (outside the Maze): (435) 542-3461
USDA Forest Service Offices (Moab): (435) 259-7155
USDA Forest Service Offices (Monticello): (435) 587-2041
Grand County Travel Council (Moab/Green River): (800) 635-6622
San Juan County Travel Council (Monticello/Blanding): (800) 574-4386

## FINDING DRINKING WATER

When hiking in Arches and Canyonlands National Parks, bring plenty of water with you (to be safe, as much as 1 gallon per person per day, stored in multiple containers). You can find water in the parks at these locations:

**Arches National Park:** Visitor Center and Devils Garden Campground
**Island in the Sky District:** Visitor Center
**Needles District:** Visitor Center and Squaw Flat Campground
**Maze District:** No water available in the Maze

## FINDING MAPS

Be sure to get park maps at the entrance stations or off the park websites. In addition to the NPS maps, get more detailed maps for any backcountry excursion. For safety reasons, you need maps for route-finding and for "staying found." For non-safety reasons, you would not want to miss out on the joy of whittling away hours staring at a topo map and wondering what it really looks like here and there.

For trips into the Canyonlands and Arches National Parks, you have two good choices for maps—US Geological Survey (USGS) topo maps and Trails Illustrated maps. Well-prepared wilderness travelers take both. You can find these maps at the following locations:

Trails Illustrated maps—Check at the national park visitor centers when you get to the parks or at gift shops and bookstores in the local area. Trails Illustrated publishes one map for each of Arches and Canyonlands National Parks and individual maps for each of the three districts (Island in the Sky, Maze, and Needles) in Canyonlands. If you're only going to one district, the map for that district might be your best choice. You can also find them at natgeomaps.com.

USGS maps—These maps are also available at national park visitor centers and sporting goods stores in the local area. Again, if you would like the maps in advance,

The art of the Great Gallery
in Horseshoe Canyon

write directly to the USGS at the following address: Map Distribution, US Geological Survey, Box 25286, Federal Center, Denver, CO 80225. USGS topo maps can also be downloaded at www.usgs.gov. You can also buy software programs to print your own topo maps, and you can do the same from several websites.

## DRIVING BACKCOUNTRY ROADS: 4WD VERSUS AWD

One persistent problem faced by rangers in Arches and Canyonlands National Parks is visitors who incorrectly believe they have the skills and the vehicle suited for the rough backcountry roads in the parks. There seems to be a common misconception that "all-wheel-drive" is the same as "four-wheel-drive," when it certainly is not. To drive many of these roads, you need a true high-clearance, four-wheel-drive vehicle with low-range gearing.

Even if you have the correct vehicle, you need the skills and experience necessary to navigate rough roads. If not, you might be looking at a dangerous and expensive rescue operation. In other words, don't rent a jeep for the first time and assume you can drive these roads.

If you have any doubts about the suitability of your vehicle or the skills required, discuss it with rangers at the visitor centers.

## MINIMUM VEHICLE REQUIREMENTS FOR UNPAVED ROADS

| | 2WD-LC | 2WD-HC | 4WD-LC | 4WD-HC |
|---|---|---|---|---|
| Arches | Salt Valley | | Willow Flats | Four-Wheel-Drive Road |
| Island in the Sky | Green River Overlook | | | Shafer Trail, Taylor Canyon, White Rim Road, Lathrop Canyon |
| Needles | Cave Spring | Elephant Hill (to trailhead) | | Colorado Overlook, Salt Creek, Horse Canyon, Lavender Canyon, Elephant Hill, Devils Lane |
| Maze | Gordon Flats | Horseshoe Canyon, Waterhole Flat, Hite | | Doll House, Millard Canyon, Maze Overlook, North Point, Panorama Point, Cleopatra's Chair, Big Ridge, Sunset Pass, Golden Stairs |

Definitions: 2WD (two-wheel drive), 4WD (four-wheel drive), HC (high clearance), LC (low clearance)

## FOR MORE INFORMATION

The best source of more information on vehicle requirements is the NPS's information-packed websites. If you can't find what you need there, you can get the information at the following addresses and phone numbers:

Arches National Park
PO Box 907
Moab, UT 84532
Phone: (435) 719-2299
E-mail: archinfo@nps.gov
Website: www.nps.gov/arch

Canyonlands National Park
2282 South West Resource Blvd.
Moab, UT 84532
Phone: (435) 719-2313
E-mail: canyinfo@nps.gov
Website: www.nps.gov/cany

Outstanding desert scenery lines the White Rim Road.

| | BEST PHOTOS | FAMILY FRIENDLY | WATER FEATURES | FINDING SOLITUDE |
|---|:---:|:---:|:---:|:---:|
| **ARCHES NATIONAL PARK** | | | | |
| 1. Park Avenue | • | • | | |
| 2. Balanced Rock | • | • | | |
| 3. Windows Primitive Loop | • | • | | |
| 4. Double Arch | • | • | | |
| 5. Delicate Arch | • | • | | |
| 6. Sand Dune Arch | • | • | | |
| 7. Broken Arch | • | • | | |
| 8. Skyline Arch | • | • | | |
| 9. Landscape Arch | • | • | | |
| 10. Devils Garden Primitive Loop | • | | | • |
| 11. Tower Arch | • | • | | • |
| 12. Fiery Furnace | • | | | • |
| **CANYONLANDS NATIONAL PARK: ISLAND IN THE SKY** | | | | |
| 13. Neck Spring | • | • | | |
| 14. Lathrop | • | | | • |
| 15. Mesa Arch | • | • | | |
| 16. Aztec Butte | • | | | |
| 17. Wilhite | • | | | • |
| 18. Alcove Spring | • | | | |
| 19. Whale Rock | • | • | | |
| 20. Upheaval Dome Overlook | • | | | |
| 21. Syncline Loop | • | | | • |
| 22. Crater Spur Trail | • | | | • |
| 23. Upheaval Canyon | • | • | | |
| 24. Moses | • | • | | |

| | BEST PHOTOS | FAMILY FRIENDLY | WATER FEATURES | FINDING SOLITUDE |
|---|---|---|---|---|
| **CANYONLANDS NATIONAL PARK: ISLAND IN THE SKY (CONTINUED)** | | | | |
| 25. Alcove Spring / Syncline Loop | • | | | • |
| 26. Murphy Point | • | • | | |
| 27. Murphy Loop | • | | | • |
| 28. Gooseberry | • | | | |
| 29. White Rim Overlook | • | • | | |
| 30. Grand View | • | • | | |
| 31. Fort Bottom | • | • | | |
| 32. Gooseneck | • | • | | |
| **CANYONLANDS NATIONAL PARK: THE NEEDLES** | | | | |
| 33. Roadside Run | • | • | | |
| 34. Cave Spring | • | • | | |
| 35. Pothole Point | • | • | | |
| 36. Slickrock Foot Trail | • | • | | • |
| 37. Confluence Overlook | • | | | • |
| 38. Upper Salt Creek | • | | | • |
| 39. Castle Arch | • | • | | |
| 40. Fortress Arch | • | • | | |
| 41. Peekaboo | • | | | • |
| 42. Lost Canyon | • | • | | |
| 43. Lost Canyon/ Elephant Canyon | • | | | • |
| 44. Squaw Canyon / Big Spring Canyon | • | • | | |
| 45. Big Spring Canyon / Elephant Canyon | • | | | • |
| 46. Elephant Hill to Squaw Flat | • | • | | |
| 47. Druid Arch | • | | | |

| | BEST PHOTOS | FAMILY FRIENDLY | WATER FEATURES | FINDING SOLITUDE |
|---|---|---|---|---|
| **CANYONLANDS NATIONAL PARK: THE NEEDLES (CONTINUED)** | | | | |
| 48. Chesler Park / Devils Kitchen | • | | | • |
| 49. The Joint Trail | • | • | | |
| 50. Druid Arch West | • | | | • |
| 51. Chesler Park Loop | • | • | | |
| 52. Devils Pocket Loop | • | • | | |
| 53. The Big Needles Loop | • | | | • |
| 54. Lower Red Lake | • | | | • |
| 55. The Tumbleweed Loop | • | • | | |
| **CANYONLANDS NATIONAL PARK: THE MAZE, ORANGE CLIFFS, AND HORSESHOE CANYON** | | | | |
| 56. The Great Gallery | • | • | | |
| 57. The North Trail | • | | | • |
| 58. Happy Canyon | • | • | | |
| 59. The Golden Stairs | • | • | | |
| 60. Maze Overlook | • | | | |
| 61. Harvest Scene | • | | | • |
| 62. Colorado / Green River Overlook | • | • | | |
| 63. Spanish Bottom | • | | | |
| 64. The Granary | • | • | | |

# MANAGING THE BACKCOUNTRY

The management plan for Canyonlands National Park, which doesn't include Arches National Park, established a set of regulations to preserve the fragile high desert environment. The plan:

- Establishes nineteen backcountry zones for backpacking. Only three—Island in the Sky / Syncline, Needles / Upper Salt Creek, and Needles / Needles Trails—have designated campsites. The remaining zones allow at-large camping.
- Limits the total number of backcountry permits to sixty-three.
- Establishes a backcountry permit reservation system.
- Establishes a user fee to fund the backcountry reservation system and maintain backcountry facilities.
- Limits the length of backcountry stays to seven to ten days in any zone and establishes a limit of fourteen consecutive days per trip.
- Limits backpacking group size to seven per party in the Needles and Island in the Sky and five per party in the Maze.
- Establishes vehicle group size at ten for the Needles, fifteen for Island in the Sky, and nine for the Maze.
- Closes two sensitive areas to all entry.
- Prohibits all wood fires and wood gathering throughout the backcountry.
- Closes sections of some roads by converting them to hiking trails.
- Removes all garbage cans from the backcountry.
- Sets acceptable noise levels.
- Prohibits all pets in the backcountry.
- Limits stock use (horses, mules, and burros) in the backcountry and prohibits llamas and goats.
- Requires use of pelletized feed for stock 48 hours before and during any trip to the backcountry.
- Allows caches under some circumstances.

Delicate Arch. Better at night?
NPS/JACOB W. FRANK

## SPECIAL REGULATIONS FOR BACKCOUNTRY USE

Canyonlands and Arches National Parks have strict regulations to protect the fragile environment. Under these regulations you may not:

- Take pets, with or without a leash, into the backcountry.
- Drive vehicles off established roads.
- Collect, destroy, or deface any mineral, plant, wildlife, or natural feature.
- Swim or bathe in any water source with the exception of the Colorado and Green Rivers and along the Salt Creek backcountry road.
- Have a wood fire or gather wood.
- Go into the backcountry without an overnight permit.

## WHAT IS AT-LARGE BACKPACKING?

In many areas in Canyonlands National Park—such as Lavender Canyon and Lower Salt Creek in the Needles District, along the White Rim Road in the Island in the Sky District, and in most of the Maze District—the NPS allows what's called "at-large" backpacking or at-large camping. All vehicle camping in these areas is restricted to designated backcountry camps, but backpackers can choose their own low-impact sites. However, you must follow the regulations listed below and camp at least 1 mile from and out of sight of roads and trailheads. This doesn't mean you can drive partway up a backcountry road, stop at a convenient point and carry your pack a mile away from the road and spend the night. You must park your vehicle at a trailhead, not along the road.

The only place you can leave your vehicle overnight is at an official vehicle camp (if you have a permit for that site) or at a trailhead for either a road or a trail. For example, you can at-large backpack in Lavender Canyon or Salt Creek in the Needles, but you must leave your vehicle at the locked gate for these areas.

In Arches National Park backpacking is allowed 0.5 mile from trails and 1 mile from roads, with a few other restrictions.

Most backpacking permits in the three districts of Canyonlands National Park (but not in Arches National Park) are for at-large campsites. This means you can camp anywhere subject to the following regulations. All at-large campsites must be:

- 300 feet from any water source, including seeps, potholes, springs, and streams, not including the Green and Colorado Rivers.

- 300 feet from any archaeological site, including alcoves, rock art, surface scatters of lithics or ceramics, and partial or complete structures or ruins.

- At least 1 mile from a trailhead or road, including backcountry roads.

- Within the zone for which the permit is issued.

- In an area open to at-large camping.

- Left with the least possible evidence of use and environmental impact.

- Accessed by the least-impacting route, using washes or rock surfaces to reach the campsite.

- Located on rock surfaces, previously disturbed sites, or surfaces without cryptobiotic soil crusts or vegetation.

## BACKPACKING PERMITS BY ZONE

| AREA | ZONE NAME | NUMBER OF PERMITS |
|---|---|---|
| Island in the Sky | Taylor Canyon | 4 |
| | Syncline | 1* |
| | Upper West Basins | 3 |
| | Lower Basins | 2 |
| | Gooseberry/Lathrop | 3 |
| | Murphy Point | 1 |
| Needles | Davis and Lavender | 2 |
| | Upper Salt Creek | 4* |
| | Salt Creek/Horse Canyon | 4 |
| | Butler/West Side Canyons | 2 |
| | Red Lake/Grabens | 5 |
| | Needles North | 1 |
| Maze | Maze Area | 11 |
| | Orange Cliffs | 1 |
| | High Spur | 3 |

\* Designated backcountry campsites

For detailed backcountry camping information, visit the official Canyonlands National Park website at www.nps.gov/cany. For excellent maps of the backcountry zones, visit www.nps.gov/cany/maps.

# HIKING THE HIGH DESERT

The Canyonlands are high desert country, so come prepared for the climate. Have the right equipment and clothing, and be mentally and physically prepared.

For starters, make one major attitude adjustment: It's very likely the only water you'll drink is the water you carry. This differs significantly from most hiking areas, where you can bank on filtering or purifying water from a stream or lake along the way. This is actually a difficult adjustment for many people accustomed to hiking in non-desert climates.

## WHEN TO HIKE

In northern climates most hiking occurs during the summer months, particularly July and August. But summer might be the worst time to hike in Arches and Canyonlands. Instead, choose one of the "shoulder seasons"—spring (March, April, or May), when the fabulous desert wildflowers bloom, or fall (September, October, or November), when the weather is more pleasant. Spring and fall temperatures usually make hiking much more enjoyable than in summer.

To get extra enjoyment out of hiking the high desert, take advantage of the early morning or late evening. The desert light is the purest early and late in the day, when the temperature usually drops to a more comfortable level. Plus, you stand a better chance of seeing desert wildlife. Some desert fauna is nocturnal, and even diurnal species often remain inactive during midday but come out at dawn and dusk.

## THE WATER DILEMMA

Hiking in the high desert, simply put, provides more exercise than hiking in moist climates. You can't go lightweight because you must carry water. Experts recommend taking 1 gallon of water per person per day for long day hikes and even more for backpacking trips. Water weighs 8.35 pounds per gallon, so for many people this essentially limits the length of the trip. That means, for example, that a four-person group on a three-day trip (two nights out) would have to carry 100 pounds of water.

If you're planning a longer trip and the weight of your pack is stretching your physical abilities, reduce your load, but don't reduce your water supply. For example, abandon optional equipment such as extra camera gear or clothing, or at least invest in lightweight gear. You'll live if you have to wear the same underwear two days in a row, but running short on water can kill you. It might be tempting to leave your tent home to save weight, but a tent can be a lifesaver if bad weather blows in. However,

Cairns show the way on many Canyon Country trails.

you can take a lightweight three-season tent, or a four-person group can use a light-weight four-person tent instead of two smaller tents.

Food presents a special challenge. The lightest food (premade freeze-dried meals or dehydrated foods such as pasta, rice, and oatmeal) requires water to prepare. This means you have to use precious drinking water for cooking. This might seem like heresy to backpacking gourmands, but one alternative is to take the no-cooking option. Prepare evening meals in advance in leakproof containers or make sand-wiches and snack for breakfast and lunch. This might seem radical, but you save weight in two ways: You use less water and need less gas for your stove. You could, actually, leave your stove and gas at home if you're sure of the weather forecast and have no chance of running into cold weather.

## THE DESERT SUN

Although water presents the biggest challenge for hikers, the intense sun also requires special preparation. Three pieces of equipment that might be optional elsewhere—a wide-brimmed hat, sunglasses, and sunscreen—are essential for desert hiking.

Don't underestimate the power of the desert sun, even on a cool day. You might think you have a tan and don't need sunscreen, but you're almost always wrong. If you're still lily-white from your winter hibernation, start hiking with sunscreen protection rated SPF 25 to 30. Later, if you want a tan, move down to SPF 8 to 12. If you expose your skin without sunscreen, do it for only an hour or so per day. You'll be unpleasantly shocked by how fast you can burn, and in addition to being unhealthy, a sunburn can ruin your vacation.

Also pay attention to the clothing you wear. When choosing your wardrobe, go "light and white" and use natural fibers such as cotton whenever possible. A round, wide-brimmed hat with a drawstring keeps more sun off your neck and ears than a baseball cap, and will stay on. If the wind keeps blowing off your hat, you might not wear it and could get fried. Add a lightweight Buff for even more protection or drape a bandanna from the back of your hat to prevent you from becoming a "redneck." Long pants and long-sleeve shirts reduce the amount of skin exposed to the sun. The sun isn't the only reason to wear long pants, however. If you're going cross-country or on a rough trail, you should definitely wear long pants. If you don't, the desert flora (many species armed with spines) will constantly take little nicks out of your legs.

Another piece of equipment essential for enjoying the desert is good footwear. You don't need the extra-heavy boots mountain climbers wear, but you need sturdy boots. Running or cross-training shoes might suffice for easier trips on well-defined trails, but anything long and rough calls for sturdier boots, even more so than in forested hiking areas in temperate-zone mountain ranges.

## FAINT TRAILS

Most of the short, frequently used trails in Arches and Canyonlands National Parks are well defined and marked, and few people have problems following them. However, some trails receive infrequent use and can be difficult to find in places. Plus, terrain such as slickrock and canyon washes makes construction and maintenance of permanent trails nearly impossible, so the NPS uses cairns to mark these routes.

If you get in a situation where you can't see the trail, don't panic. Usually you can look ahead to see where the trail goes. Even if you can't, don't worry about being off the trail for a short distance. Some trails simply follow canyon washes with an occasional cairn to remind you that you're still on the correct route. In a narrow canyon the trail can rarely go anywhere but between the canyon walls. However, if you've gone a long way without seeing a cairn, you might be in the wrong canyon and need to backtrack to the last cairn. Again, don't panic. Get out the topo map or GPS unit and figure out where you went wrong.

Most trails in these parks are marked with cairns, but cairns can be knocked down or blown away. Also, hikers have been known to put up unofficial cairns to mark a route back to their camp or to an off-trail destination.

## SHARING

Each of us wants our own private wilderness area, but that only happens in our dreams. Many people use the national parks. To give everybody an equal chance at a great experience, all of us must work at politely sharing the wilderness. In some places in Canyonlands, for example, hikers, mountain bikers, and four-wheelers share the same backcountry road. Every situation is different, but safety and courtesy should always dictate who yields. In most cases hikers should yield to mountain bikers or vehicles, and mountain bikers should yield to vehicles.

Although stock use is rare in Canyonlands and Arches, hikers occasionally share trails with backcountry horsemen. Keep in mind that horses and other stock animals are much less maneuverable than hikers, so it becomes the hiker's responsibility to yield. If possible, step off the trail on the downhill side and stand quietly while the stock party passes.

Choosing a campsite also requires polite sharing. If you get to a popular at-large camping area late in the day and all good campsites are taken, don't crowd another camper. These sites rightfully go on a first-come, first-served basis. If you're late, you have the responsibility to move on or take a less desirable site a respectable distance away from other campers. In some backcountry zones designated campsites have multiple tent sites. Try to pick one as far away from other campers as possible.

## LEAVE NO TRACE

Going into a national park is like visiting a famous museum. You obviously don't want to leave your mark on an art treasure in the museum. If everybody going through the museum left one little mark, the piece of art would be quickly destroyed—and of what value is a big building full of trashed art? The same goes for pristine wildernesses such as Canyonlands and Arches National Parks, which are as magnificent as any masterpiece by any artist. If we all left just one little mark on the landscape, the wilderness would soon be despoiled.

A wilderness can accommodate a lot of human use if everybody behaves. But a few thoughtless or uninformed visitors can ruin it for everybody who follows. The need for good manners applies to all wilderness users, not just hikers. We all must leave no clues of our passing.

Most of us know better than to litter. Be sure you leave nothing, regardless of how small it is, along the trail or at the campsite. This means you should pack out everything, including orange peels, flip tops, cigarette butts, and gum wrappers. Also pick up trash others left behind.

Follow the main trail. Avoid cutting switchbacks and walking on vegetation beside the trail. In the desert the terrain can be very fragile, so if possible, stay on the trail. If you're hiking off-trail, try to hike on slickrock or in canyon washes.

Don't pick up "souvenirs" such as rocks, antlers, or wildflowers. The next person wants to see them, too, and collecting such souvenirs violates park regulations.

Avoid making loud noises that may disturb others. Remember, sound travels easily to the other side of the canyon. Be courteous.

Carry a lightweight trowel and bury human waste 6 to 8 inches deep and pack out used toilet paper. Keep waste at least 300 feet away from any water source.

Finally, and perhaps most important, strictly follow the pack-in/pack-out rule. If you carry something into the backcountry, consume it or carry it out.

For more information on keeping our national parks clean, visit www.LNT.org.

## ENDANGERED DIRT

Some advocates of zero-impact recreation suggest you "leave only footprints," but in the high desert this is bad advice. One footprint can destroy decades of growth.

Cryptobiotic crust is the foundation of life in the high desert. It provides a seedbed for the desert plant community and serves as a sponge, retaining the precious moisture of a dry climate. The crust is also the primary source for fixation of nitrogen, which is crucial to all life in the desert. This crust is a complex community of microorganisms, the most important of which are called cyanobacteria.

When mature, cryptobiotic soil has a lumpy, black-tinged crust. In earlier stages the crust is almost invisible. If you step on it, ride on it, or drive on it, it blows away and erodes, and then it takes many years, if not decades, to recover.

This is a prime reason to stay on trails and roads. If you have to hike off-trail, try to stay on slickrock or in canyon washes to prevent stepping on cryptobiotic crust.

When somebody says "Watch your step," he or she often has safety in mind, but in Canyonlands, this can mean the preservation of the high desert environment.

Never step on the cryptobiotic crust.

Off-trail hiking—for experienced hikers only
NPS/JACOB W. FRANK

## MAKE IT A SAFE TRIP

The Boy Scouts have been guided for decades by what's perhaps the best single piece of safety advice—be prepared! For starters, this means carrying survival and first-aid materials, proper clothing, a compass and/or GPS unit, and a topographic map—and knowing how to use them.

Perhaps the second-best piece of safety advice is to tell somebody where you're going and when you plan to return. Pilots file flight plans before every trip, and anybody venturing into a blank spot on the map should do the same. File your "flight plan" with a friend or relative before taking off.

Close behind filing your flight plan and being prepared with proper equipment is physical conditioning. Being fit not only makes wilderness travel more enjoyable, it also makes it safer. To whet your appetite for more knowledge of wilderness safety and preparedness, here are a few more tips:

- Check the weather forecast. Be careful not to get caught at high altitude by a bad storm or in a narrow canyon by a flash flood. Watch cloud formations closely so you don't get stranded on a ridgeline during a lightning storm. Avoid traveling during prolonged periods of cold weather.

- Avoid traveling alone in the wilderness.

- Keep your group together.

- Know preventive measures, symptoms, and treatment of hypothermia, the silent killer.

- Study basic survival and first aid before leaving home.

- Don't eat wild plants.

- Before you leave for the trailhead, find out as much as you can about the route, especially the potential hazards.

- Don't exhaust yourself or other members of your group by traveling too far or too fast. Let the slowest person set the pace.

- Don't wait until you're confused to look at your maps. Follow them as you go along, from the moment you start moving up the trail, so you have a continual fix on your location.

- If you get lost, don't panic. Sit down and relax for a few minutes while you carefully check your topo map and take a reading with your compass or GPS. Confidently plan your next move. It's often smart to retrace your steps until you find familiar ground, even if you think it might lengthen your trip. Lots of people get temporarily lost in the wilderness and survive—usually by calmly and rationally dealing with the situation.

- Stay clear of all wild animals, and never feed them or leave food unattended. Never let a wild animal get a food reward and become conditioned to human food.

- Take a first-aid kit that includes, at a minimum, the following: sewing needle, snakebite kit, pain reliever/anti-inflammatory tablets, antibacterial ointment, two antiseptic swabs, two butterfly bandages, adhesive tape, four adhesive strips, four gauze pads, two triangular bandages, two inflatable splints, moleskin, one roll of 3-inch gauze, rubber gloves, and lightweight first-aid instructions.

- Take a survival kit that includes, at a minimum, the following: compass, whistle, matches in a waterproof container, cigarette lighter, candle, signal mirror, fire starter, aluminum foil, water purification tablets, space blanket, and flare.

- Last but not least, don't forget that the best defense against unexpected hazards is knowledge.

## YOU MIGHT NEVER KNOW WHAT HIT YOU

The high desert environs of Canyonlands are prone to sudden thunderstorms, especially in spring and summer months. If you get caught by a lightning storm, take special precautions. Remember:

- Lightning can travel far ahead of the storm, so be sure to take cover before the storm hits.

The famous Windows in Arches
NPS/NEAL HERBERT

- Don't try to make it back to your vehicle. Instead, seek shelter, even if it's only a short way back to the trailhead. Trying to make it is not worth the risk. Lightning storms usually don't last long, and from a safe vantage point, you might enjoy the sights and sounds.

- Be especially careful not to get caught on an exposed ridge; under large, solitary trees; in the open; or near standing water.

- Seek shelter in a low-lying area, ideally in a dense stand of small, uniformly sized trees.

- Stay away from anything that might attract lightning, such as metal tent poles, trekking poles, or pack frames.

- Get in a crouched position and place both feet firmly on the ground.

- If you have a pack (without a metal frame) or a sleeping pad with you, put your feet on it for extra insulation against shock.

- Don't huddle together. Instead, sit at least 50 feet apart, so if somebody gets hit by lightning, others in your party can give first aid.

- If you're in a tent, stay there, in your sleeping bag with your feet on your sleeping pad.

## HYPOTHERMIA AND HYPERTHERMIA

These are two things you never want to experience. Trust me; I've had both.

In most hiking areas hypothermia, or the silent killer, as it's called, is the biggest threat to backcountry travelers. In desert environs, however, hyperthermia, especially the most serious form, heat stroke, can be equally dangerous.

And you can get both while hiking Canyon Country.

Hypothermia, a condition in which the body's internal temperature drops below normal, can—and way too often does—lead to mental and physical collapse and death. It's caused by exposure to cold and is aggravated by wetness, wind, exhaustion, and dehydration. The moment you begin to lose heat faster than your body produces it, you're suffering from exposure. Your body starts involuntary exercise, such as shivering, to stay warm and makes involuntary adjustments to preserve normal temperature in vital organs, restricting blood flow in the extremities. Both responses drain your energy reserves. The only way to stop the drain is to reduce the degree of exposure.

With full-blown hypothermia, as energy reserves are exhausted, cold reaches the brain, depriving you of good judgment and reasoning power. You won't be aware that it's happening. You lose control of your hands. Your internal temperature slides downward. Without treatment this slide leads to stupor, collapse, and death.

To defend against hypothermia, stay dry. When clothes get wet they lose about 90 percent of their insulating value. Wool loses relatively less heat; cotton, down, and some synthetics lose more. Some new synthetic materials can help prevent heat loss. Take good rain gear that covers the head, neck, body, and legs and protects against wind-driven rain. Most hypothermia cases develop in air temperatures between 30 and 50 degrees Fahrenheit, but hypothermia can develop in warmer temperatures.

If your party is exposed to wind, cold, and wet, automatically think hypothermia. Watch yourself and others for these symptoms: uncontrollable fits of shivering; vague, slow, slurred speech; memory lapses; incoherence; immobile or fumbling hands; frequent stumbling or a lurching gait; drowsiness (to sleep is to die); apparent exhaustion; and inability to get up after a rest. When a member of your party has hypothermia, he or she may deny any problem. Believe the symptoms, not the victim. Even mild symptoms demand treatment, as follows:

- Protect the victim from wind and rain.

- Remove all wet clothing and keep the victim dry.

- Get the victim into warm clothes and a dry sleeping bag.

- Place well-wrapped water bottles filled with heated water close to the victim, especially next to the neck, chest, and groin.

- Try to get the victim to ingest warm liquids, but don't force it.

- Attempt to keep the victim awake.

Hyperthermia can manifest itself in several forms—heat cramps, heat exhaustion, and heat stroke, the most serious and life-threatening form and a definite medical emergency.

Your body normally generates heat, especially during vigorous physical exercise, and dissipates that heat through the skin or by evaporation of sweat. When hiking in intense heat under the sun, especially if you're dehydrated, the body may not be able to dissipate enough heat and the body temperature rises—not a good thing.

The advanced form of hyperthermia, heat stroke, is life-threatening. A person with heat stroke usually has a body temperature above 104 degrees Fahrenheit. Other symptoms include confusion, combativeness, bizarre behavior, faintness, staggering, strong and rapid pulse, and possible delirium or coma.

Heat stroke is often preceded by heat exhaustion, which is a warning sign that the body is getting too hot. Symptoms include acute thirst, weakness, lack of coordination, nausea, profuse sweating, and cold, clammy skin.

To treat heat stroke, seek emergency assistance as soon as possible. In the meantime:

- Get the victim out of the sun and into a cool place, if possible.

- Encourage drinking water or other fluids, but nothing with alcohol or caffeine.

- Immerse the victim in water, if possible, or sponge off the victim with cool water, again if possible.

- Urge the person to lie down and rest, preferably in a cool place.

To prevent heat exhaustion and heat stroke and other forms of hyperthermia, avoid dehydration by drinking a lot of water during your hike, especially at the beginning of the hike when you aren't thirsty and don't think you need fluids.

Neck Spring, an oasis in the desert
NPS/NEAL HERBERT

# ARCHES NATIONAL PARK

Compared to many national parks, **ARCHES** is small (73,379 acres), but it's very scenic and very popular. It was designated a national monument in 1929 and then expanded and designated a national park in 1971.

The trail to Delicate Arch is perhaps the busiest hiking trail in Canyon Country.

One small sample of the scenic splendor of Arches National Park
COURTESY BRAD WAGNER/IMPACT PHOTOGRAPHICS

Water, wind, extreme temperatures, and other geologic forces have created the greatest diversity of arches in the world at Arches National Park, along with many other multihued, finely sculpted rock formations. Delicate Arch, perhaps the park's most famous feature, shows up in an endless array of videos, postcards, posters, books, and magazines. However, the numerous arches along the Devils Garden hike, the cathedralesque columns of Park Avenue, the cavern-like canyons of Fiery Furnace, and many other spectacular features rival the Delicate Arch (and just about everything else in nature!) for awesome beauty.

A hole in a rock has to have an opening of at least 3 feet to be officially listed as an arch and be given a name. Arches National Park has more than 2,000 arches, a preponderance of arches that makes the park unique. In fact, there is no place on Earth even remotely like it.

Arches National Park is not well suited for the serious hiker. Instead, it's a better fit for the visitor who doesn't mind seeing most scenery from the car window and on short walks. The trails offer spectacular scenery but, with one exception, are all short day hikes. Unlike Canyonlands National Park, Arches offers limited opportunities to the four-wheeler, with only three short backcountry road sections.

The park is open 24 hours a day, seven days a week. The visitor center is open every day, but hours are shorter in the off-season. In the prime season (May through September), it's open from 7:30 a.m. to 6 p.m. Check the park's website (www.nps .com/arch) for exact hours during the off-season (October through April), but it's open at least from 9 a.m. to 4 p.m.

The park has a fifty-two-site campground at Devils Garden. During the prime season (March through October), camping sites must be reserved online at www .recreation.gov or by calling (877) 444-6777. In the off-season, sites go on a first-come, first-served basis.

To avoid long lines at the entrance station, try to arrive earlier or later in the day, which can be the best time to view the park's features with the early or late light of the day. If you arrive mid-morning to early afternoon, expect a long line at the entrance station.

## GETTING TO ARCHES NATIONAL PARK

Arches National Park is located 25 miles south of I-70 and 5 miles north of Moab on US 191. The starting points for hikes and drives are referenced from the entrance station.

# 1. PARK AVENUE

## WHY GO?
A scenic stroll in the shadow of nature's skyscrapers

### THE RUNDOWN

**Start:** Park Avenue Parking Area

**Distance:** 1 mile; shuttle

**Difficulty:** Easy

**Nat Geo Trails Illustrated Map:**
Arches National Park

**Nat Geo TOPO! Map (USGS):**
Arches National Park

### FINDING THE TRAILHEAD

The Park Avenue Parking Area is on your left 2.5 miles from the entrance station. The Courthouse Towers Parking Area is on your right 3.7 miles from the entrance station in the shadow of massive Courthouse Towers.

**GPS coordinates:** 38° 37′ 27.653″ N / 109° 35′ 58.132″ W

## WHAT TO SEE

The Park Avenue Trail is most aptly named for New York City's famous street. Early travelers noticed a similarity between these sandstone spires and the famous skyscrapers along New York's Park Avenue, and the name stuck. The main difference, of course, is that nature, not mankind, sculpted the "skyscrapers" of Arches National Park.

Although you can start at either end of this shuttle trail, starting at the south end results in a totally downhill hike, but the slope is very gradual. However, if you want to arrange your own shuttle (not provided by NPS), start at the north end and have somebody pick you up at the south end. If you don't have access to two vehicles and can't arrange a shuttle, this hike is still definitely worth taking, even with double the mileage (only 2 miles) by going out and back.

You'll really be missing something if you leave Arches without taking this short hike. You can see the Courthouse Towers, Tower of Babel, Three Gossips, the Organ, and other grand "skyscrapers" from the road, but if you don't take this hike, you'll miss the truly stimulating experience of walking among them.

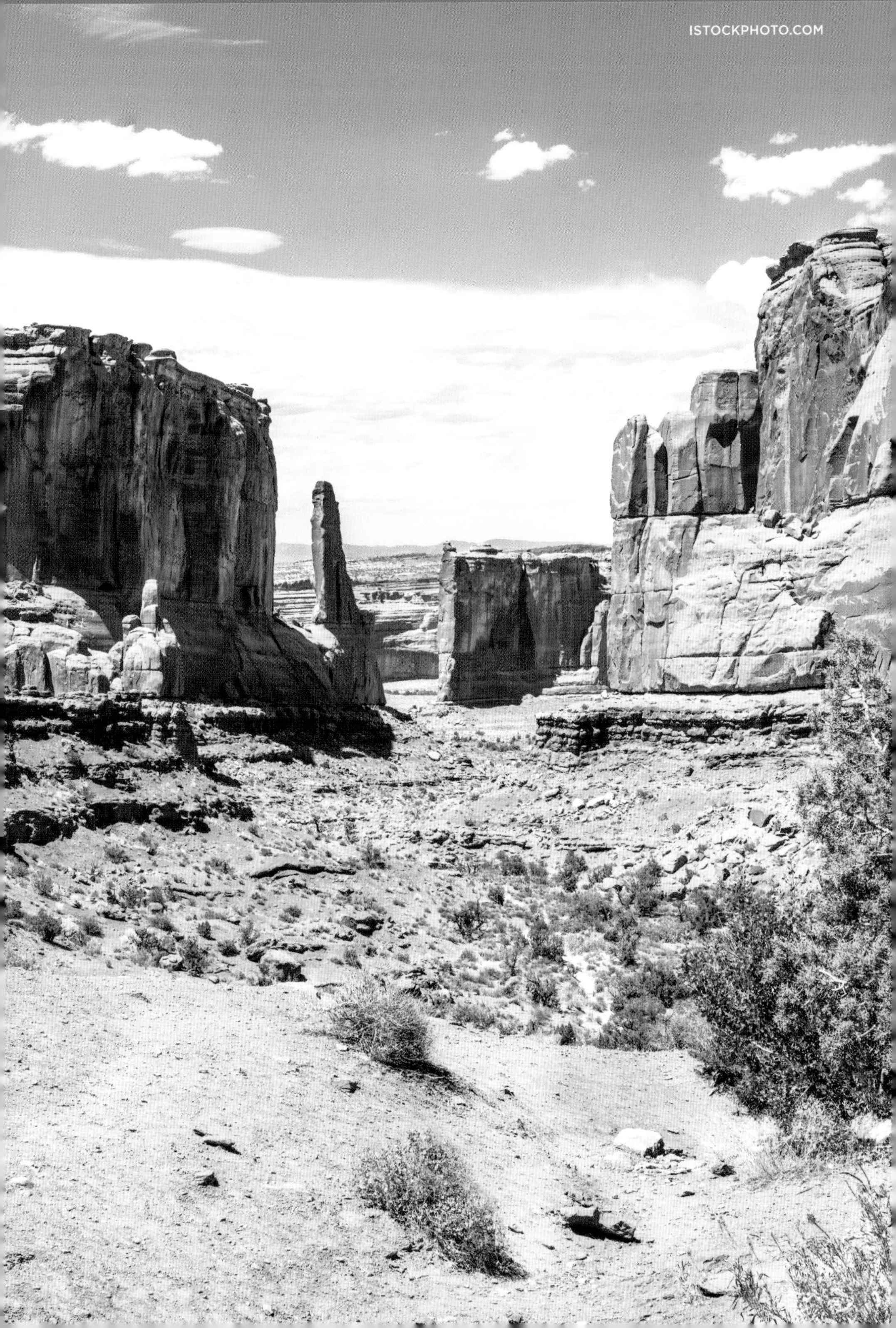

ISTOCKPHOTO.COM

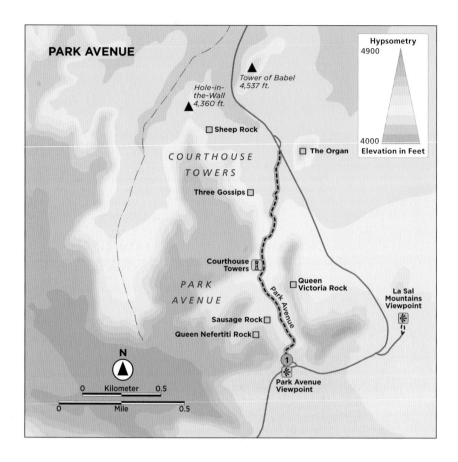

PARK AVENUE

Tower of Babel
4,537 ft.

Hole-in-
the-Wall
4,360 ft.

Sheep Rock

COURTHOUSE
TOWERS

The Organ

Three Gossips

Courthouse
Towers

Queen
Victoria Rock

PARK

AVENUE

Sausage Rock

Queen Nefertiti Rock

La Sal
Mountains
Viewpoint

Park Avenue

N

1

Park Avenue
Viewpoint

0    Kilometer    0.5

0         Mile         0.5

Hypsometry
4900

4000
Elevation in Feet

From the south the trail starts out as a concrete path leading to a scenic overlook about 100 yards from the trailhead. From here a well-defined trail goes through juniper and cactus until it melts into a slickrock dry wash, marked by an occasional cairn, and stays there until just before you return to the main road. The trail disappears at times, but there's no chance of getting lost. Stay in the dry wash and follow well-placed cairns to the Courthouse Towers Parking Area.

# 2. BALANCED ROCK

## WHY GO?

A very easy walk to the base of a fragile, picturesque rock formation

### THE RUNDOWN

**Start:** Balanced Rock Parking Area

**Distance:** 0.3 mile; loop

**Difficulty:** Easy

**Nat Geo Trails Illustrated Map:** Arches National Park

**Nat Geo TOPO! Map (USGS):** Arches National Park

## FINDING THE TRAILHEAD

The Balanced Rock Parking Area is on the east side of the main park road 9 miles from the entrance station. **GPS coordinates:** 38° 42' 6.332" N/109° 33' 57.780" W

Balanced Rock, a must-see feature in Arches National Park
NPS

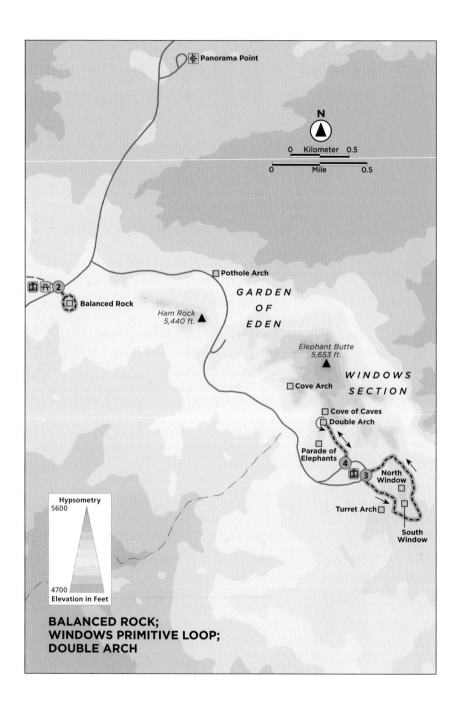

Panorama Point

N

0    Kilometer    0.5

0    Mile    0.5

Pothole Arch

GARDEN
OF
EDEN

Balanced Rock

Ham Rock
5,440 ft.

Elephant Butte
5,653 ft.

Cove Arch

WINDOWS
SECTION

Cove of Caves
Double Arch

Parade of
Elephants

North
Window

Turret Arch

South
Window

Hypsometry
5600

4700
Elevation in Feet

**BALANCED ROCK;
WINDOWS PRIMITIVE LOOP;
DOUBLE ARCH**

## WHAT TO SEE

This is a short hike, perfect for travelers who would like to stretch their legs without working up a big sweat. You can see Balanced Rock and read about it on an interpretive display at the parking area, but it's more impressive up close. The trail makes a short loop around Balanced Rock and returns to the parking area.

The forces of nature sculpted Balanced Rock out of Entrada sandstone. Technically this is called a "caprock" of the harder Slick Rock Member (part of Entrada sandstone) perched on a pedestal of softer Dewey Bridge Member (part of the Carmel Formation). The pedestal erodes more quickly than the more resistant caprock. The entire Balanced Rock formation is 128 feet high, and the rock itself measures 55 feet.

Balanced Rock used to have a companion called Chip-Off-the-Old-Block, but it toppled during the winter of 1975–76. You can still see its pedestal on the south side of Balanced Rock.

You can get up close to Balanced Rock with a short walk.

# 3. WINDOWS PRIMITIVE LOOP

## WHY GO?
Three fantastic arches along a short, scenic trail

### THE RUNDOWN

**See map on page 38.**

**Start:** Windows Parking Area

**Distance:** 1 mile; loop

**Difficulty:** Easy

**Nat Geo Trails Illustrated Map:**
Arches National Park

**Nat Geo TOPO! Map (USGS):**
Arches National Park

**FINDING THE TRAILHEAD**

Drive 9.2 miles north into the park on the main road until it forks. Take a right (east) and drive 3 miles to the Windows Parking Area. **GPS coordinates:** 38° 41' 13.680" N / 109° 32' 11.880" W

## WHAT TO SEE

The scenery is sensational on this short hike, but don't expect to have it to yourself. Almost everybody who comes to the park hikes up to see these spectacular arches. When you hear somebody talking about overcrowding in the national parks, the

Ranger-led hike in Arches, the famous Windows in the background
NPS/ANDREW KUHN

Moonrise over Turret Arch
NPS/NEAL HERBERT

Windows section of Arches often comes to mind. Consider taking this short hike early or late in the day when the crowds are somewhat diminished and you have a better chance of scoring a parking place.

Although it seems like it should be the other way around, the trail goes to the North Window first and then to the South Window. On the way back to the parking lot, take a short side trip to the right (south) to see Turret Arch. The Windows are sometimes called the Spectacles, and you can see why. If you hike the primitive loop around the back of the arches, you can see the "nose" on which the spectacles rest.

It's fairly easy to go off-trail and climb up right under North Window and Turret Arch. Do not attempt to climb into South Window. Several people have fallen while trying or have gotten stranded here. Be careful not to fall on or damage any vegetation or natural features. Also, hang onto your hat. The strong winds in the area tend to blow it off as soon as you reach either arch.

After you finish marveling at the Windows and Turret Arch, continue along the well-defined loop trail from the viewpoint of South Window. It makes a small circle around the Windows, giving you another great view of North Window. It also offers a glimpse at the native vegetation of the area. The primitive loop trail hits the parking lot about 50 yards north of the main trailhead.

For a shorter hike (0.7 mile), go to the South Window, turn around and retrace your steps back to the parking lot.

# 4. DOUBLE ARCH

## WHY GO?
A short walk to and under a spectacular arch

### THE RUNDOWN

See map on page 38.

**Start:** Double Arch Parking Area

**Distance:** 0.8 mile; out and back

**Difficulty:** Easy

**Nat Geo Trails Illustrated Map:**
Arches National Park

**Nat Geo TOPO! Map (USGS):**
Arches National Park

## FINDING THE TRAILHEAD

Drive 9.2 miles north into the park on the main road until it forks. Take the right fork for 3 miles to the Windows Parking Area and keep going around a loop in the parking area for about a quarter mile. Park in the Double Arch Parking Area on your right (north). **GPS coordinates:** 38° 41' 17.880" N/109° 32' 18.120" W

Taking a short hike to get up close to Double Arch

Stargazing through the Double Arch
NPS/JACOB W. FRANK

## WHAT TO SEE

The short, mostly flat hike to Double Arch goes through scattered junipers and oaks. In the spring you might see Utah's state flower, the sego lily, a large, single, cream-colored flower. The trail is well defined and easy to follow all the way. Along the way, off to your left, you can see the series of buttes called the Parade of Elephants.

Double Arch looks sort of average from the parking area, but as you approach, its massiveness starts to sink in. Then, when you get there (and especially if you can climb up right under the arches), the imposing size of the arch becomes absolutely clear. It's the third-largest arch opening in the park.

You can lengthen your trip by climbing up under Double Arch, but be careful not to disturb vegetation or natural features. If each person visiting this area left only a tiny mark, it wouldn't take long for the impact to be devastating.

# 5. DELICATE ARCH

## WHY GO?

A moderately difficult and very heavily used route to the world's most famous arch

### THE RUNDOWN

**Start:** Wolfe Ranch Parking Area

**Distance:** 3 miles; out and back

**Difficulty:** Moderate

**Nat Geo Trails Illustrated Map:**
Arches National Park

**Nat Geo TOPO! Map (USGS):**
Arches National Park

### FINDING THE TRAILHEAD

 Drive 11.7 miles north into the park on the main road until you see the right-hand turn to Delicate Arch and Wolfe Ranch. Turn right and drive another 1.2 miles to the parking area on your left (north). Look to your right for a lot for oversize vehicles. **GPS coordinates:** 38° 44' 7.703" N/109° 31' 14.941" W

## WHAT TO SEE

If you've ever seen a postcard or poster of Arches National Park, you've probably seen Delicate Arch. This amazing arch has become the symbol of Arches National Park, which is somewhat surprising because it's barely visible from the road.

Try to get here early. The temperature will be more pleasant, and you might even find a parking spot. The trailhead has a Walmart-sized parking lot, but it's often full after 9 a.m.

You have three options for viewing this magnificent natural feature. You can take a 1.5-mile trail (3 miles round-trip) that goes right under the arch; you can go to the Delicate Arch Viewpoint; or you can take a 5-minute walk to a closer viewpoint. If you choose the hiking option, be aware that the trail to Delicate Arch is not a stroll. This is a real hike, and you should be prepared. Bring extra water; wear good hiking shoes; and try to avoid the midday heat. You're often walking on slickrock following cairns much of the way, and there's little shade along the route. The NPS describes the trail as "strenuous," and it truly can be for the inexperienced, poorly conditioned hiker, especially on a hot summer day. So be prepared.

If you decide to see the famous arch from the viewpoint instead of taking the hike, you have to drive past the Wolfe Ranch Trailhead for another 1.2 miles to the Delicate Arch Viewpoint Parking Area.

Rock art on the Delicate Arch Trail

At the Wolfe Ranch Trailhead, you can see the remains of the historic Wolfe Ranch, settled in 1888 and sold by John Wolfe in 1910. Shortly after leaving the trailhead, you cross over Salt Wash on a sturdy new bridge. Right after the bridge you might notice a large pile of "green stuff" on your right. This is volcanic ash with a high iron content that has gone through a chemical process that gives it this greenish cast.

Just after the bridge you can take a short side trip to the left to a Ute petroglyph panel. This is well worth adding a quarter mile to your trip.

During the first part of the hike, watch for collared lizards. These large lizards can run on their hind feet when chasing prey.

For the first half mile or so, you hike on a wide, well-defined, mostly level trail, probably the best trail you've ever been on. Then the excellent trail disappears, and you start a gradual ascent to Delicate Arch. Most of the rest of the trip is on slickrock, so be alert. You have to follow cairns and a few strategically located signs the rest of the way, and sometimes the "cairns" are only one rock. Don't worry about getting lost, though. You can almost always see a string of hikers ahead of you.

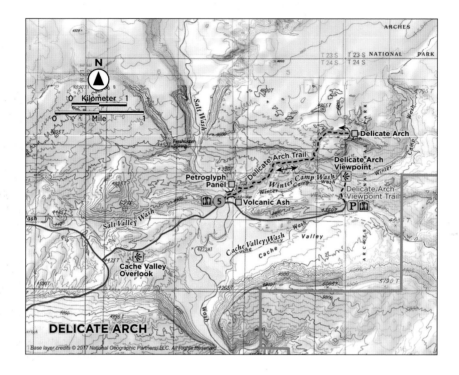

As you get closer to Delicate Arch, you can see Frame Arch off to your right (south). This arch forms a perfect "frame" for a photograph of Delicate Arch. If you decide to climb up this short, steep slope to get that photograph, be careful.

Just before you get to Delicate Arch, the trail goes along a ledge for about 200 yards. This section of trail was blasted out of the cliff, and you can still see the bore holes in the rock. If you have children with you, watch them carefully in this section. Just after the ledge ends, you see Delicate Arch with its huge opening (33 feet wide and 45 feet high). You can take an awe-inspiring walk down to right below the arch, but you might ruin somebody's photo. A shot of Delicate Arch with the often-snowcapped La Sal Mountains as a backdrop must be one of those photos every professional photographer has to have in his or her file, so shutterbugs are usually setting up tripods for the grand view.

When you finally come around the corner and see the full breadth of Delicate Arch, you'll know why this is such a classic hike, perhaps the best in Arches National Park. It's definitely one of the most popular. Many thousands of people take this hike every year.

If you prefer the less-strenuous option for seeing Delicate Arch, drive past the Wolfe Ranch Parking Area for another 1.2 miles. From the parking area take one of two short walks—a 0.5-mile trail to the top of a small ridge where you can look north for

Delicate Arch, as seen on many thousands of postcards and covers

a good view of Delicate Arch or an even shorter trail to a different viewpoint. These views don't quite compare with being right there, but they're still awe inspiring.

The first part of the longer viewpoint trail is well defined, but the last part goes over slickrock marked by cairns. There is no sign marking the end of the trail, but you'll know when to stop. At the end of the trail, you're at the edge of a steep cliff that drops down into Winter Camp Wash. You can't hike to the arch from this point.

# 6. SAND DUNE ARCH

## WHY GO?

A very short, sandy route to one of the park's most famous arches

### THE RUNDOWN

**Start:** Broken Arch/Sand Dune Arch Parking Area

**Distance:** 0.3 mile; out and back

**Difficulty:** Easy

**Nat Geo Trails Illustrated Map:** Arches National Park

**Nat Geo TOPO! Map (USGS):** Arches National Park

### FINDING THE TRAILHEAD

Drive north into the park on the main road for 17.5 miles and park in the Broken Arch/Sand Dune Arch Parking Area. **GPS coordinates:** 38° 45' 52.860" N/109° 35' 0.780" W

Sand Dune Arch
NPS/NEAL HERBERT

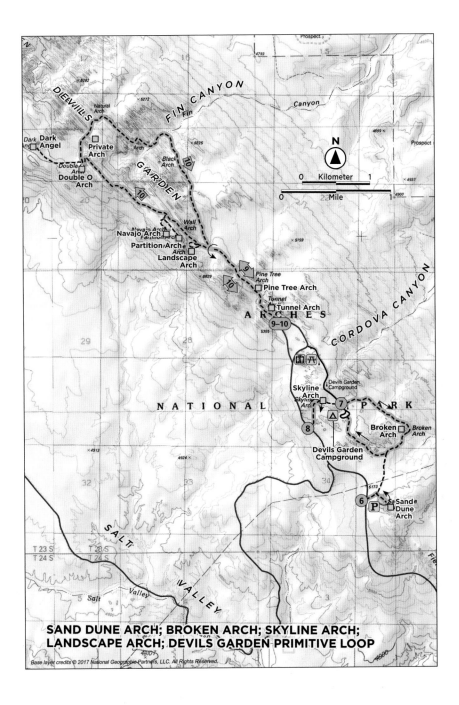

**SAND DUNE ARCH; BROKEN ARCH; SKYLINE ARCH;
LANDSCAPE ARCH; DEVILS GARDEN PRIMITIVE LOOP**

## WHAT TO SEE

Sand Dune Arch is an easy, short walk nicely suited for groups with children. Even on a hot day, kids will love this place.

Shortly after leaving the trailhead, you hit a junction with the left-hand trail going to Broken Arch. Go to the right to Sand Dune Arch. Until the junction the trail is well defined. After the junction you enter a narrow canyon (actually the gap between two sandstone fins) and stay there until you see Sand Dune Arch off to your right.

The reason for this arch's name becomes obvious along the way. You walk through deep sand, which can make footing difficult and progress slow. The trail ends right at the arch. Below the arch the sand has collected in a huge "sandbox" that kids love. The area usually stays shaded and coolish, even on a hot summer day. It might be tempting to climb to the top of the arch, but please resist the urge. Rangers frequently have to rescue people who injured themselves when falling or jumping from the arch.

# 7. BROKEN ARCH

## WHY GO?
A short loop trail through a big arch

### THE RUNDOWN

**See map on page 49.**

**Start:** Devils Garden Campground across from campsite No. 40

**Distance:** 2 miles; loop

**Difficulty:** Easy

**Nat Geo Trails Illustrated Map:** Arches National Park

**Nat Geo TOPO! Map (USGS):** Arches National Park

## FINDING THE TRAILHEAD

Drive north into the park on the main road for 19 miles and turn into the Devils Garden Campground. Go to the end of the campground and park along the small loop near the trailhead. **GPS coordinates:** 38° 46' 23.87" N/109° 35' 13.42" W

Broken Arch
NPS/NEAL HERBERT

## WHAT TO SEE

The trail goes through sand dunes and slickrock on its way to Broken Arch. In places the trail isn't well defined, but well-placed cairns make it easy to follow all the way. The trail goes right through Broken Arch—a nice place to take a break and study a great piece of nature's art. *Option:* To shorten your route, you can retrace your steps back to the trailhead from here for an out-and-back hike of 1.3 miles.

Continue through the arch and return to the campground at campsite No. 51. Along the way you'll see a trail coming in from Sand Dune Arch. If you're interested in adding a half mile to your hike, you can take this trail out and back to Sand Dune Arch before completing the loop.

At the end of the loop, you have to walk about a quarter mile on the paved campground road back to your vehicle.

# 8. SKYLINE ARCH

## WHY GO?
A very easy walk to a large arch

---

### THE RUNDOWN

**See map on page 49.**

**Start:** Skyline Arch Parking Area

**Distance:** 0.4 mile; out and back

**Difficulty:** Easy

**Nat Geo Trails Illustrated Map:**
Arches National Park

**Nat Geo TOPO! Map (USGS):**
Arches National Park

---

### FINDING THE TRAILHEAD

 Drive north into the park on the main road for 18.5 miles and park in the Skyline Arch Parking Area. If you see the Devils Garden Campground or Trailhead, you've driven just past the Skyline Arch Parking Area.
**GPS coordinates:** 38° 46' 19.200" N / 109° 35' 27.180" W

Skyline Arch

ISTOCKPHOTO.COM

## WHAT TO SEE

This is a very easy walk, only 0.2 mile, to Skyline Arch on a flat, well-defined trail.

True to its name, Skyline Arch dominates the horizon for most of the trip. When you get there, you can see where a mammoth boulder fell out of the arch on a cold November night in 1940, greatly enlarging the size of the opening. This essentially doubled the size of the arch.

At the base of the arch, it looks as though a trail goes off to your left (north), but this isn't an official trail and doesn't go anywhere. This is a good example of why the NPS encourages hikers to stay on official trails. In the area around Skyline Arch, hikers who should have stayed on the official trail have created several well-defined "social trails."

# 9. LANDSCAPE ARCH

## WHY GO?

A short stroll to the longest arch in the park, plus a short side trip to two more large arches

### THE RUNDOWN

**See map on page 49.**

**Start:** Devils Garden Trailhead Parking Area

**Distance:** 1.6 miles; out and back

**Difficulty:** Easy

**Nat Geo Trails Illustrated Map:** Arches National Park

**Nat Geo TOPO! Map (USGS):** Arches National Park

**FINDING THE TRAILHEAD**

Drive north into the park on the main road for 19 miles and park in the large parking area at the Devils Garden Trailhead. The trailhead is at the end of the road where it makes a small loop. Be sure to stay on the loop instead of turning into the Devils Garden Campground. **GPS coordinates:** 38° 46′ 58.354″ N/109° 35′ 41.986″ W

## WHAT TO SEE

The hike to Landscape Arch is akin to the trip to Delicate Arch. It's one of those must-see features of Arches National Park.

Landscape Arch has an opening spanning an incredible 306 feet, which may make it the longest stone span in the world. On the geologic time scale, Landscape Arch is a senior citizen among arches in the park. It's also famous for the extreme slenderness of its stone span.

And don't wait too long to see it. Geologically speaking, it's likely to collapse any day.

This is a "super trail"—flat, easy, double-wide all the way—and usually heavily populated with hikers.

About a quarter mile from the trailhead, the trail splits. To go to Landscape Arch, take the left-hand fork. The right-hand fork takes you on a short spur trail down to Pine Tree and Tunnel Arches, both well worth adding 0.4 mile to your hike. If you take this spur trail, it splits again at the bottom of a small hill. Go left to Pine Tree Arch and right to Tunnel Arch. After checking out these two large arches, head back to the main trail and on to Landscape Arch.

Just before you see Landscape Arch and as you descend a series of steps, you come

Landscape Arch, the longest arch in Arches National Park

to the junction with the Devils Garden Primitive Loop Trail. Stay left here, and continue for about another quarter mile for your chance to marvel at the incredible Landscape Arch.

# 10. DEVILS GARDEN PRIMITIVE LOOP

## WHY GO?
The longest, most difficult hike in Arches National Park

### THE RUNDOWN

**See map on page 49.**

**Start:** Devils Garden Trailhead Parking Area

**Distance:** 7.2 miles; loop

**Difficulty:** Difficult

**Nat Geo Trails Illustrated Map:** Arches National Park

**Nat Geo TOPO! Map (USGS):** Arches National Park

### FINDING THE TRAILHEAD

Drive north into the park on the main road for 19 miles and park in the large parking area at the Devils Garden Trailhead. The trailhead is at the end of the road where it makes a small loop. Be sure to stay on the loop instead of turning into the Devils Garden Campground. **GPS coordinates:** 38° 46′ 58.354″ N / 109° 35′ 41.986″ W

## WHAT TO SEE

If you take the Primitive Loop Trail and all short spur trails to nearby arches and other features, this becomes the longest maintained trail in Arches National Park. It's also one of the most spectacular hikes you can take in any national park.

You can hike the entire loop in 3 to 4 hours, but you could—and probably should—spend an entire day checking out the area and relaxing along the way. In any case, carry extra water. Also, you might want to get up early to start this hike to beat the heat—and to have a better shot at finding a parking spot in the large but often packed parking area.

About a quarter mile from the trailhead, the trail splits. To go to Landscape Arch and Double O Arch and complete the entire loop, take the left-hand fork. The right-hand fork takes you on a short spur trail down to Pine Tree and Tunnel Arches, definitely worth adding 0.4 mile to your hike. If you take this spur trail, it splits again at the bottom of a small hill. Go left to Pine Tree Arch and right to Tunnel Arch. After checking out these two large arches, head back to the main trail.

Tunnel Arch

Just before you see Landscape Arch and as you descend a series of steps, you can see where the Primitive Loop Trail starts. You can take the loop either way, of course, but this description covers the clockwise route, so take a left at this junction and continue to Landscape Arch.

The hike to Landscape Arch is, along with Delicate Arch, one of those must-see features of Arches National Park. This first part of the Devils Garden hike is a "super trail"—flat, easy, double-wide—and usually heavily populated with hikers.

Landscape Arch has an opening spanning an incredible 306 feet, which may make it the longest stone span in the world. On the geologic time scale, Landscape Arch is a senior citizen among arches in the park. The arch is also famous for the extreme slenderness of its stone span. Don't wait too long to see Landscape Arch. Geologically speaking, it's likely to collapse any day.

After Landscape Arch the trail gets less defined and stays that way, and the NPS considers it "strenuous" the rest of the way until the Primitive Loop Trail rejoins the main trail to Landscape Arch. In fact, right after Landscape Arch the trail gets primitive for a short stretch, where it climbs over the ends of fins and is marked with cairns. It's still easy to follow, though, and the trail all the way to Double O Arch gets lots of use. In this section you used to pass by Wall Arch on your right, but no more. It collapsed in August 2008.

Another quarter mile or so up the trail, you'll see a short spur trail going off to the left to Partition and Navajo Arches. Partition Arch is the arch you can see in the background when you're looking at Landscape Arch. Yes, Partition Arch has a partition, and the spur trail goes right up under the arch and ends, a great place to relax and soak in the view. The spur trail to Navajo Arch also stops right under the arch, another great place for a break. This arch is shaded and perhaps an even better place than Partition Arch to stop and relax before continuing to Double O Arch.

When you get back on the main trail from Navajo Arch, go another half mile or so to Double O Arch on a fairly rough trail that is mostly on slickrock and somewhat difficult to follow at times. Double O Arch is most unusual, with one arch on top of another.

Just after Double O Arch, you hit a junction with a spur trail heading to the left to Dark Angel. Taking this spur trail adds nearly a mile to your trip, but it's worth it to get a close look at this blackish sandstone spike jutting out of the desert landscape.

Also right after Double O Arch, the Primitive Loop Trail heads off to the right. The NPS has marked it Caution, Primitive Trail, Difficult Hiking, and the loop section of this hike is even more difficult than the section between Landscape and Partition Arches, which you have already hiked. In winter some sections can be wet or icy, making footing quite slick. If you turn back at this point, you will have seen most of the famous features of the Devils Garden Trail.

About a half mile farther up the Primitive Loop Trail, watch for a short spur trail going off to the right to Private Arch, the last arch you see on this loop. From here, instead of going from arch to arch as on the first part of this trip, the loop trail traverses a beautiful desert environment where you can study the flora and fauna—and probably have it all to yourself. Even though thousands of hikers take the first part of this loop trip, most people choose to retrace their steps on a better trail rather than brave the Primitive Loop route.

## MILES AND DIRECTIONS

0.0   Start at Devils Garden Trailhead.

0.25 Spur trail to Tunnel and Pine Tree Arches.

0.8   Landscape Arch, junction with Primitive Loop Trail; turn left.

1.0   Ruins of Wall Arch.

1.4   Navajo Arch.

1.5   Partition Arch.

2.0   Double O Arch.

2.1   Junction with Primitive Loop Trail; turn right.

2.5   Junction with spur trail to Dark Angel.

2.9   Private Arch.

6.4   Junction with main trail; turn left.

7.2   Arrive back at Devils Garden Trailhead.

# 11. TOWER ARCH

## WHY GO?
A moderate hike to one of the remotest arches in the park

---

### THE RUNDOWN

**Start:** Tower Arch Trailhead

**Distance:** 3.4 miles; out and back

**Difficulty:** Moderate

**Nat Geo Trails Illustrated Map:**
Arches National Park

**Nat Geo TOPO! Map (USGS):**
Arches National Park

---

### FINDING THE TRAILHEAD

Turn left (west) onto Salt Valley Road, which leaves the main road 16 miles beyond the entrance station. You can take any vehicle on this road, but the NPS recommends staying off it when it's wet, so don't get caught in a thunderstorm. Follow the road for 7.1 miles until you see a junction with a sign pointing to a left turn to Klondike Bluffs. Take this road for 1.1 miles until it ends at the Tower Arch Trailhead. (At this junction be sure to take the second left turn to Klondike Bluffs Road, not the first left, a primitive four-wheel-drive road to Balanced Rock.) **GPS coordinates:** 38° 47' 32.780" N / 109° 40' 30.389" W

## WHAT TO SEE

Tower Arch is a short but rugged hike, or as indicated by the sign at the trailhead, a primitive trail, and the NPS considers it "strenuous." To avoid an afternoon thunderstorm, which makes the Salt Valley Road impassable, start early.

The trail immediately starts to climb to the top of the bluff, up a steep but short incline. After this brief climb the trail continues up and down until you see massive Tower Arch surrounded by a maze of spectacular sandstone spires. Along the way you get great views of the Marching Men rock formation on your left and the austere Klondike Bluffs on your right.

Part of the trail is on slickrock, so always be watching ahead for the next cairn. The roughest part of the trail, however, goes through two stretches of loose sand near the end of the hike that make hiking uphill difficult. It's easier coming back, though.

You can climb up under the arch and get a great view while taking a deserved rest stop. In spring you'll see the magnificent, snowcapped La Sal Mountains to the east through the arch opening.

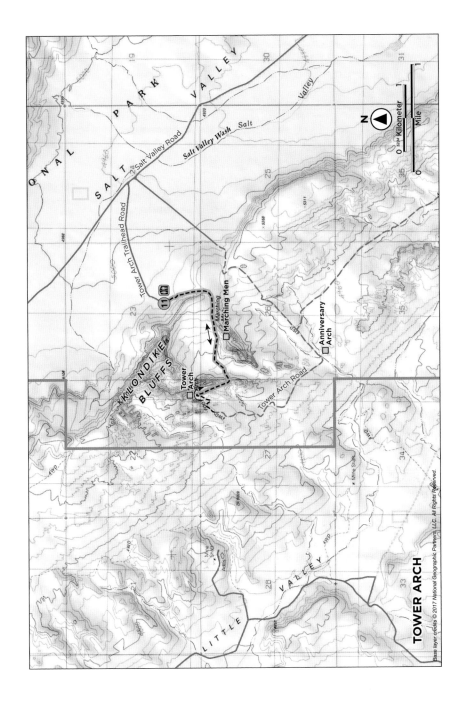

TOWER ARCH

Base layer credits © 2017 National Geographic Partners, LLC. All Rights Reserved.

Desert cottontail
NPS/ANDREW KUHN

While you're at Tower Arch, you might see a vehicle just to the east. That's because you can drive around on a rough four-wheel-drive road, but those who do miss out on a great hike.

The return hike is noticeably easier than the way in. When driving back, you're treated to a nice view of Skyline Arch from the last part of the Salt Valley Road.

# 12. FIERY FURNACE

## WHY GO?
A ranger-guided tour of a rare desert environment

### THE RUNDOWN

**No map available for this hike**

**Start:** Fiery Furnace Parking Area

**Distance:** 2 miles; loop

**Difficulty:** Moderate

**Nat Geo Trails Illustrated Map:**
Arches National Park

**Nat Geo TOPO! Map (USGS):**
Arches National Park

## FINDING THE TRAILHEAD

Drive north into the park on the main road for 14.5 miles and turn right (east) at well-signed Fiery Furnace Road (just after the Salt Valley Overlook). Park in the Fiery Furnace Parking Area, which is a short drive from the main road. **GPS coordinates:** 38° 44' 34.544" N / 109° 33' 56.599" W

Hiking through a tight spot
in the Fiery Furnace
NPS/ANDREW KUHN

## WHAT TO SEE

To see the Fiery Furnace area of Arches National Park, you should take a ranger-led tour. You can explore the area by yourself with a hiking permit obtained at the park's visitor center, but I highly recommend signing up for the guided tour, where you'll learn ten times more than you would on your own, and you won't get lost. Also, you will have much less impact on this fragile desert environment.

You can reserve a spot in the morning tours through Recreation.gov, but for afternoon tours and for tours anytime during the shoulder seasons, you have to sign up in person at the visitor center. Because of the rough terrain, the NPS only allows hikers over 5 years old. For current information on Fiery Furnace tours, follow the links on the park's website at www.nps.gov/arch.

The Fiery Furnace isn't named for its average temperature. Actually, it belies its name and remains fairly cool even in midsummer due to the many shady canyons. Instead, the area was named for the reddish glow it often takes on at sunset, which resembles a furnace.

After a brief orientation talk, a ranger leads the guided tour down one of the faint trails leaving the parking area. Three hours later you return to the parking area on another trail. As you walk along the 2-mile loop, the ranger explains the incredible natural history of the area and points out rare plants and semi-concealed arches. As with any desert hike, be sure to take water.

The Fiery Furnace has suffered from its popularity. As a result, the NPS imposed special restrictions in 1994 in an attempt to curb a disturbing amount of damage to the fragile resources of the area. If you elect to go exploring on your own, you must talk to a ranger, who will help you understand the problems of overuse and discuss getting a permit. The area is a labyrinth of narrow sandstone canyons, and there are no marked trails, making it difficult to stay oriented.

Two defined trails leave the trailhead, but they soon melt away into a fascinating puzzle of crevasses, fins, and boulders. This maze of canyons may be one of the most difficult areas to hike in the park, but it's also one of the most remarkable. The scenery, especially the steep-sided canyons and weird-shaped rocks, along with several arches and bridges, is unforgettable. You can also find a totally quiet place in the Fiery Furnace to help you forget the stress in your life.

The Fiery Furnace also provides critical habitat for many rare plant species, such as the Canyonlands biscuitroot, so please be intensely careful not to step on black-crusted cryptobiotic soil (desert topsoil) or delicate plant communities. Try to walk on rock or in sandy washes.

The NPS charges a nominal fee for both ranger-led tours and permits in the Fiery Furnace area.

Because of sensitive and threatened vegetation and the fact that it's easy to get lost in this area, the NPS prefers that no map of the route be included with this hike description.

# CANYONLANDS NATIONAL PARK: ISLAND IN THE SKY

**ISLAND IN THE SKY** is a high mesa wedged between the Colorado and Green Rivers like a natural observation platform. Vistas rival those found anywhere. This district of **CANYONLANDS NATIONAL PARK** is also the darling of the mountain biker, and mountain-biking tours on the White Rim Road have become intensely popular. During peak seasons campsites along the road are always full, having been reserved many months in advance. The NPS has long required backcountry permits for overnight stays on the White Rim Road, but now the agency also requires permits for day use.

Interpretive display on the Upheaval Dome Overlook (Hike 20)

However, those without a mountain bike need not worry. Island in the Sky has lots to offer hikers. The trail system is not as extensive as in the Needles District, but hikers may choose from a variety of well-maintained trails. Trails dropping off the mesa and going to the White Rim Road are for the serious hiker, but the area also has easy and moderate hiking opportunities.

Many four-wheelers enjoy the White Rim Road (free day-use permit required) and side roads, but these roads might not present a serious challenge for experts. Tourists with only a day or two to spend here can view some fantastic scenery from the main paved roads in the park. They can supplement their brief visit with several excellent short hikes on the mesa (Grand View, White Rim Overlook, Mesa Arch, Aztec Butte, Whale Rock, or Upheaval Dome Overlook).

Rangers at the Island in the Sky Visitor Center (on your right about a mile past the entrance station) can answer your questions about the natural features and recreational opportunities found in the Island in the Sky District of Canyonlands National Park.

## GETTING TO ISLAND IN THE SKY

From Moab drive north on US 191 10 miles to UT 313. To reach the same point from farther north, drive 22 miles south from I-70. Once on UT 313 drive southwest 25 miles to the Island in the Sky entrance station.

# 13. **NECK SPRING**

## WHY GO?

A popular day hike and one of the few loop routes in Island in the Sky

### THE RUNDOWN

**Start:** Neck Spring Trailhead at Shafer Canyon Overlook

**Distance:** 6 miles; loop

**Difficulty:** Moderate

**Nat Geo Trails Illustrated Map:** Island in the Sky

**Nat Geo TOPO! Map (USGS):** Musselman Arch

### FINDING THE TRAILHEAD

 Drive 0.2 mile south of the Island in the Sky Visitor Center and turn left (east) into the Shafer Canyon Overlook Parking Area. **GPS coordinates:** 38° 27' 8.626" N / 109° 49' 13.597" W

## WHAT TO SEE

The Neck has historical significance. Here the Island in the Sky plateau narrows to about 40 feet with sheer cliffs dropping off on both sides. This natural phenomenon allowed early ranchers who ran livestock in the area (before the park was created) to control the entire 43-square-mile mesa with one 40-foot fence across this narrow spot, later named the Neck. Nature is also making a play at the Neck. Erosion is gradually wearing away the already narrow entrance to Island in the Sky. Sometime in the future Island in the Sky might really be an island.

The Neck Spring Trail is one of the few loops in the Island in the Sky where most trails are out and backs or shuttles. This trail description follows the counterclockwise route. For more information you can get a small brochure on the Neck Spring area at the visitor center.

For hikers looking for a moderate, half-day hike, this trail is ideal. It's well defined the entire way, with good footing (only a few small slickrock sections) and minor elevation gain. There are a few confusing spots where social trails can be as defined as the main trail, but the main trail is always marked with cairns. Parts of the trail parallel the main road, but you're far enough away that you hardly notice. You will notice, however, the panoramic views from the trail.

Up-close view of Neck Spring
NPS/NEAL HERBERT

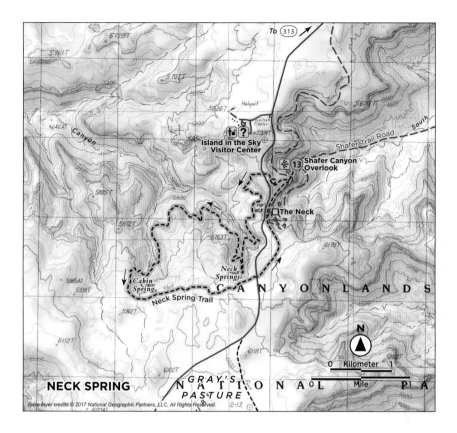

The Neck Spring area allows hikers to experience a wide variety of high desert habitats in a small area. In spring the area often turns into a wildflower garden, so wildflower buffs will love this trail.

After leaving the trailhead, immediately cross the main road and continue on the trail on the other side of the highway. The first part of the trail is actually an old road built by ranchers who used Neck Spring as a water source. Along this section of trail, you'll notice signs of past ranching activities, such as pipes and water troughs.

The trail then drops in elevation and angles to the left toward Neck Spring, but not directly to the spring. You can easily see it, however. It's tempting to bushwhack over to the spring, but please enjoy it from a distance. This trail gets heavy use, and this is an extremely fragile area.

From the trail you'll notice a change in the vegetation with species such as Gambel oak and maidenhair fern able to exist in this area with its extra moisture and shade. Also watch for hummingbirds, deer, and other wild animals frequenting the area.

After Neck Spring the trail climbs slightly as you head toward the second major water source in the area, Cabin Spring. At this spring you see the same type of vegetative change as Neck Spring—and a few aging signs of past ranching activity. Shortly after Cabin Spring, you face a short but steep climb up to the Island in the Sky mesa. The trail gets a little rough here, some of it on slickrock. At the top you get a grand vista of Upper Taylor Canyon and the Henry Mountains off in the distance.

The last part of the trail follows the rim of the plateau directly above Cabin Spring and Neck Spring and through Gray's Pasture, a grassy bench used for cattle grazing until 1975. With no livestock grazing, the area's native grasses have begun to recover and now provide food for native species only. After passing by the top of Neck Spring, cross the main road again and follow the old road cut about a half mile back to the parking area. Be careful crossing and walking along the road.

# 14. LATHROP

## WHY GO?
A long day hike or overnighter across Island in the Sky plateau, down to White Rim Road, and on to the Colorado River

### THE RUNDOWN

**Start:** Lathrop Trailhead

**Distance:** 13.6 miles to White Rim Road; out and back

**Difficulty:** Difficult; White Rim Road to Colorado River, moderate

**Nat Geo Trails Illustrated Map:** Island in the Sky

**Nat Geo TOPO! Map (USGS):** Musselman Arch and Monument Basin

### FINDING THE TRAILHEAD

Drive 2.2 miles south of the Island in the Sky Visitor Center and park in the turnoff on the left (east) side of the road at the Lathrop Trailhead sign.
**GPS coordinates:** 38° 24' 6.183" N / 109° 47' 38.525" W

## WHAT TO SEE

The Lathrop Trail is significantly different from the other trails that leave Island in the Sky for White Rim Road. The trail goes 2.5 miles on top of the mesa before it heads down toward the White Rim, and the climb back up is more gradual than the Wilhite, Gooseberry, and Murphy Trails.

The hike starts out through flat grassland of peppergrass and ricegrass (both native species) with meadowlarks singing in the background and not even a juniper to break up the grassy sea. After a mile you leave the sea of grass and head off, mostly over slickrock with a few stretches of loose sand, dropping gradually in elevation until you reach the canyon rim. Here you get a grand view of Lathrop Canyon and a glimpse of the mighty Colorado River far below. You can also see White Rim Road and the well-named Airport Tower, a dominant landmark off to your right.

The trail doesn't drop directly off the rim into a series of switchbacks (as other trails from the mesa do). Instead it angles off to the right (south) on a ledge and then starts switchbacking gradually down a side canyon to Lathrop Canyon. You can see the trail far below as you gradually drop down to it.

The trail heads east on a little ridge between two canyons for about a half mile and then drops into a dry wash, which is where you stay for the last half mile or so

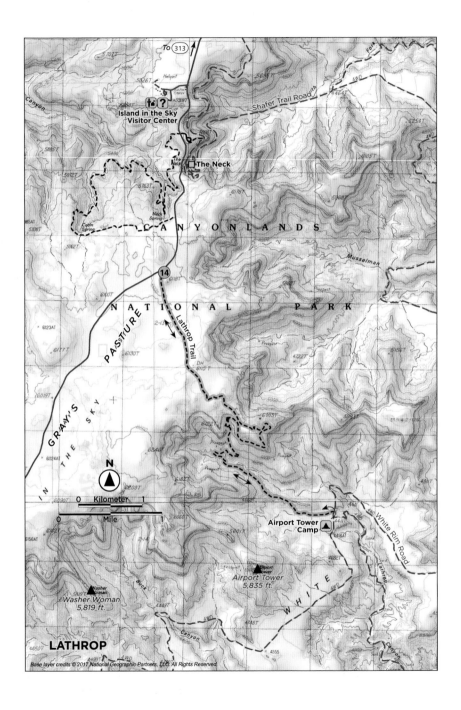

Gopher snake
NPS/NEAL HERBERT

to White Rim Road. When you get there, find a nice rock to sit on and marvel at the awesome Airport Tower and the beautiful cliffs you just came down—and, of course, start thinking about climbing back up. **Options:** For a nice, flat, easy day hike, go only as far as the canyon rim—a 5-mile out and back. After you take a break and enjoy the view, return to the trailhead.

If you're very persuasive and prefer a hike of 6.8 miles, try to talk someone into picking you up on White Rim Road to avoid the climb back up to the mesa.

Backpacking is not allowed above White Rim Road in the Lathrop and Gooseberry areas, but you can camp below the road in Lathrop Canyon (ask a ranger about the specifics of this backpacking zone and get a permit at the visitor center in advance). If you camp overnight, you might consider the moderate hike down to the Colorado River the next day. It's 4 miles from this point on the White Rim Road for a 21.5-mile round-trip from the Lathrop Trailhead. (Walk on the four-wheel-drive Lathrop Canyon Road, not on the White Rim Road.) There's a great place to take a long break at the river—a picnic area with three tables and a vault toilet all nestled under a grove of willows and cottonwoods. The road is easy walking after you drop below the cliffs at the top of the road.

Even though you might be tempted, you can't camp at the end of the Lathrop Canyon Road near the picnic tables. This violates park regulations, and since it's in a big wash, it can be dangerous too. Don't be too daunted at the cliffs as you walk back. Remember how easy the descent was, which means the ascent is not too strenuous.

# 15. MESA ARCH

## WHY GO?
A very short walk to a magnificent arch with a spectacular view

### THE RUNDOWN
**Start:** Mesa Arch Trailhead

**Distance:** 0.5 mile; loop

**Difficulty:** Easy

**Nat Geo Trails Illustrated Map:** Island in the Sky

**Nat Geo TOPO! Map (USGS):** Musselman Arch

### FINDING THE TRAILHEAD
 Drive 6.3 miles south of the Island in the Sky Visitor Center and turn left (east) into the Mesa Arch Parking Area. **GPS coordinates:** 38° 23' 21.028" N/109° 52' 5.339" W

Mesa Arch in Island in the Sky
NPS

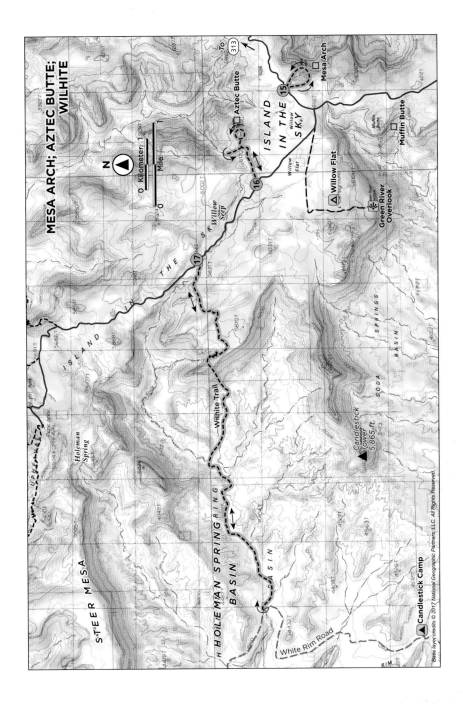

## MESA ARCH; AZTEC BUTTE; WILHITE

N

0 Kilometer 1
0 Mile 1

To 313

Mesa Arch
15

Aztec Butte

ISLAND IN THE SKY

Muffin Butte

Willow Flat

16

Willow Flat Campground

Green River Overlook

Willow Seep

17

ISLAND IN THE SKY

Wilhite Trail

SODA SPRINGS BASIN

STEER MESA

UPHEAVAL

Holeman Spring

HOLEMAN SPRING BASIN

Candlestick Tower 5,865 ft.

BASIN

Candlestick Camp

White Rim Road

ISTOCKPHOTO.COM

## WHAT TO SEE

This is a perfect trail for beginners. It's easy and short, and a detailed display at the trailhead explains how to hike the trail. Although the NPS manages this trail for beginners, it has something for everybody, and halfway along the short loop you're treated to spectacular Mesa Arch. The arch is right on the edge of a 500-foot cliff, part of a 1,200-foot drop into Buck Canyon. You can get a keyhole view of the White Rim country through the arch. If you step back a few steps, you can also frame the lofty La Sal Mountains (usually snow-topped in the spring) within the arch.

The trail is well marked and partly on slickrock. It's an easy hike, but if you have children along, watch them carefully around the arch. There is no fence to prevent a sure-to-be-fatal fall. Do not climb on the arch.

If you look carefully, you can also see another arch from Mesa Arch Overlook—Washer Woman Arch—off to the left (east) when facing the arch.

# 16. AZTEC BUTTE

## WHY GO?

A short but not easy climb to a scenic viewpoint of the Island in the Sky area

### THE RUNDOWN

**See map on page 75.**

**Start:** Aztec Butte Trailhead

**Distance:** 1.2 miles; out and back.

**Difficulty:** Moderate

**Nat Geo Trails Illustrated Map:** Island in the Sky

**Nat Geo TOPO! Map (USGS):** Musselman Arch and Upheaval Dome

### FINDING THE TRAILHEAD

Drive 6.5 miles south of the Island in the Sky Visitor Center and turn right (west) onto Upheaval Dome Road. Go another 0.8 mile and turn right (north) into the Aztec Butte Parking Area. **GPS coordinates:** 38° 23′ 36.581″ N / 109° 52′ 55.321″ W

Ancient ruins on Aztec Butte
NPS/NEAL HERBERT

ISTOCKPHOTO.COM

## WHAT TO SEE

This hike can be deceptively difficult. The first two-thirds of the trail is well defined and on packed sand, but near the end of the hike, you follow cairns as you climb about 200 feet up a difficult slickrock slope. The climb up the slickrock slope to the top of the butte is more difficult than ascending Whale Rock, and there are no handrails. Make sure you have appropriate shoes, and be careful.

Once on top you can see an Ancestral Puebloan structure—a two-room structure on the upper butte. Don't touch or enter any of these ruins. You can also enjoy some great vistas, particularly the view toward the headwall of massive Trail Canyon to the northwest.

On the way back you can climb up and around the top of a similar but smaller butte between Aztec Butte and the trailhead. If you want to take this option, watch for a trail veering off to the west (marked with a sign) just before you start going around the other, unnamed butte. On the top you can see two Ancestral Puebloan granaries. This adds 0.8 mile to your hike.

# 17. WILHITE

## WHY GO?
A long, strenuous day hike or overnighter

### THE RUNDOWN

**See map on page 75.**

**Start:** Wilhite Trailhead

**Distance:** 12.2 miles; out and back

**Difficulty:** Difficult

**Nat Geo Trails Illustrated Map:**
Island in the Sky

**Nat Geo TOPO! Map (USGS):**
Upheaval Dome

### FINDING THE TRAILHEAD

Drive 6.5 miles south of the Island in the Sky Visitor Center and turn right (west) onto Upheaval Dome Road. Go another 2.1 miles to the Wilhite Parking Area at the trailhead sign on the left (south) side of the road.
**GPS coordinates:** 38° 24' 15.464" N / 109° 53' 54.117" W

## WHAT TO SEE

Like other trails leaving Island in the Sky, the Wilhite hike includes a big hill. Although the Gooseberry Trail has the reputation of being the toughest climb in Island in the Sky, the Wilhite has more elevation change (1,600 feet, compared to 1,400 feet for Gooseberry). However, that elevation change is spread out over more miles of trail.

The first mile of the hike is easy walking on a nicely defined trail with a few short sections of loose sand and slickrock. Then the trail veers off to the right at the top of the headwall of Holeman Spring Canyon. As on other trails that drop over the "edge of the sky," the view can be somewhat daunting when you realize you have to climb down and then, ouch, back up the steep cliff. However, looks can be deceiving. The NPS has expertly routed the trail down the canyon wall to make it safe, and used stairs and switchbacks to minimize the steep grade. All the way down you get great views of expansive Holeman Spring Basin.

At the bottom of the big descent, the trail follows the blackbrush-dotted flats for about a half mile before angling off to the left toward awesome Candlestick Tower. The trail then follows the rim of a canyon for another half mile before dropping off the rim to the north toward Steer Mesa and then into the dry wash of a small, unnamed canyon. The trail follows the canyon bottoms the rest of the way. In some

Evening primrose
NPS/JACOB W. FRANK

sections cairns are scarce, but don't fret. The trail stays in the dry wash the entire last 2 miles to White Rim Road. If you're backpacking, you can easily find a campsite in this area, but be sure to camp out of the wash for your own safety.

When you hit the road, the dry wash you've been hiking turns into a beautiful slot canyon. If you have some energy left, hike down the slot canyon. It's cool down there, and you can usually find pools of water. If you're staying overnight in the area, this makes a great side trip.

On the way back don't fall asleep on your feet and get in the wrong canyon wash. The canyon the trail follows forks several times. Go left at the first two forks, right at the next two, and then left once more before climbing out of the dry wash. Each fork is clearly marked with cairns, but if you suddenly wake up and realize you haven't seen a cairn for a while, you could have taken a wrong turn. If so, backtrack to the last fork and watch for cairns. Also, be alert not to miss the last turn out of the canyon. The trail takes a sharp right, and it wouldn't be difficult to miss it and continue up the dry wash.

# 18. ALCOVE SPRING

## WHY GO?
A long day hike or overnighter with spectacular scenery

### THE RUNDOWN

**Start:** Alcove Spring Trailhead

**Distance:** 11.2 miles; out and back

**Difficulty:** Difficult

**Nat Geo Trails Illustrated Map:**
Island in the Sky

**Nat Geo TOPO! Map (USGS):**
Upheaval Dome

## FINDING THE TRAILHEAD

Drive 6.5 miles south of the Island in the Sky Visitor Center and turn right (west) onto Upheaval Dome Road. Go another 3.3 miles to the Alcove Spring Parking Area at the trailhead sign on the right (north) side of the road. **GPS coordinates:** 38° 25' 23.233" N / 109° 54' 31.556" W

## WHAT TO SEE

The Alcove Spring Trail starts dropping immediately, but not as steeply as the "big drops" of Wilhite, Murphy, and Gooseberry. The first mile of the trail down from Island in the Sky is a little rocky, but with lots of steps installed to make hiking down and climbing back up easier. The last 4 miles is easy "wash walking."

The trail gradually switchbacks down, with one long stretch along an absolutely massive cliff with an enormous, amphitheater-like alcove for which the trail is named. After about a mile the well-defined trail levels out, angling to the left before heading down into Trail Canyon. In another mile or so, the trail dips into the dry wash of Trail Canyon and stays there until you reach the turnaround at the end of Taylor Canyon Road. Trail Canyon is a big, broad valley with sensational cliffs on both sides.

Once you're in the dry wash, follow it the rest of the way. Some long stretches don't have cairns, but don't fret. The trail stays in the dry wash. During the last mile you get great views of Zeus and Moses and Aphrodite, awesome spires of rock on the north horizon—the darlings of rock climbers everywhere.

If you're backpacking, you won't have any trouble finding a good spot in Trail Canyon. You can also go up into Upper Taylor Canyon to camp.

Just as Trail Canyon merges with Taylor Canyon, the trail leaves the dry wash. This turn could be missed, so have your topo map out and watch for cairns at about two

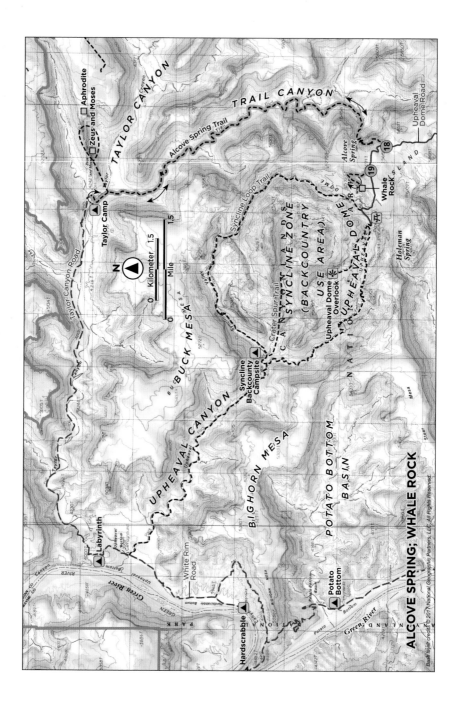

ALCOVE SPRING; WHALE ROCK

San Juan onion
NPS/JACOB W. FRANK

o'clock. From here it's only about a quarter mile on a defined trail to the Moses Trailhead. If you miss this turn, you'll come out at Taylor Camp, and you can walk back from there about a quarter mile to the trailhead.

From here retrace your route back to the Alcove Spring Trailhead. On the way back the point where you leave the dry wash is well marked with cairns, so you shouldn't miss it.

*Option:* You could turn this into a shuttle hike, assuming you can talk somebody into making a long, difficult drive to pick you up or leave a vehicle at the end of the Taylor Canyon Road. **GPS coordinates:** 38° 28' 31.29" N / 109° 55' 19.86" W

# 19. **WHALE ROCK**

## WHY GO?

A short climb onto one of the most prominent features in the Island in the Sky

### THE RUNDOWN

**See map on page 82.**

**Start:** Whale Rock Trailhead

**Distance:** 1 mile; out and back

**Difficulty:** Moderate

**Nat Geo Trails Illustrated Map:** Island in the Sky

**Nat Geo TOPO! Map (USGS):** Upheaval Dome

### FINDING THE TRAILHEAD

 Drive 6.5 miles south of the Island in the Sky Visitor Center and turn right (west) onto Upheaval Dome Road. Go another 3.9 miles to the Whale Rock Parking Area at the trailhead sign on the right (north) side of the road. **GPS coordinates:** 38° 25' 36.566" N / 109° 54' 49.982" W

## WHAT TO SEE

If you want a great view of the entire Island in the Sky area, take the short climb to the top of Whale Rock. From there you get a 360-degree panoramic look at the entire region. Plan on spending some extra time at the top to study all the interesting geological formations.

The trail goes over slickrock most of the way, but it's carefully marked with cairns. And yes, if you use a little imagination, this rock outcrop sort of resembles a big whale.

**Whale Rock in Island in the Sky**
NPS/NEAL HERBERT

# 20. UPHEAVAL DOME OVERLOOK

## WHY GO?

A short, steep hike to get the best view of perhaps the most interesting geological feature in Utah

### THE RUNDOWN

**Start:** Upheaval Dome Picnic Area

**Distance:** 1.6 miles; out and back

**Difficulty:** Moderate

**Nat Geo Trails Illustrated Map:** Island in the Sky

**Nat Geo TOPO! Map (USGS):** Upheaval Dome

### FINDING THE TRAILHEAD

Drive 6.5 miles south of the Island in the Sky Visitor Center and turn right (west) onto Upheaval Dome Road. Go another 4.8 miles to the Upheaval Dome Picnic Area at the end of the road. The trailhead is at the west end of the picnic area. **GPS coordinates:** 38° 25' 34.733" N/109° 55' 33.997" W

Cairns lead the way to the Upheaval Dome Overlook.

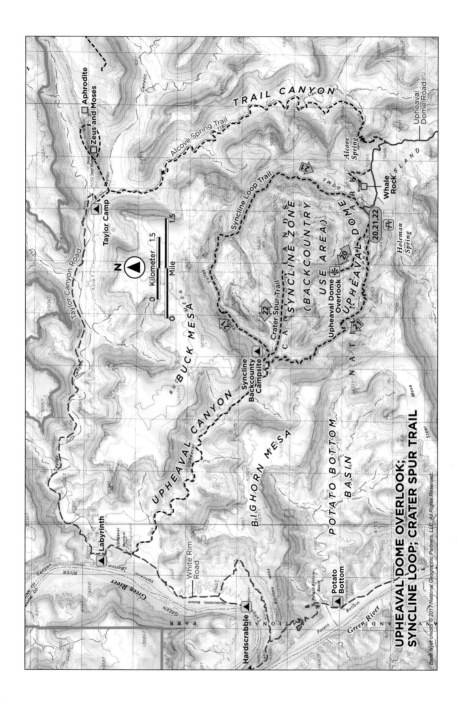

UPHEAVAL DOME OVERLOOK; SYNCLINE LOOP; CRATER SPUR TRAIL

ISTOCKPHOTO.COM

## WHAT TO SEE

This is a great way to observe and study the geological wonders of the Upheaval Dome area without taking the arduous 8.3-mile Syncline Loop. In fact, you get a better view of the mysterious crater from this short trail.

The entire Syncline area has a fascinating—and controversial—geological history. Some geologists call Upheaval Dome "the most peculiar structural feature in southeastern Utah." The origin of the dome is the source of endless debate. For some mysterious reason, rocks formerly buried a mile underground are now on the surface in the crater. The two most common theories—the salt dome theory and the meteorite impact theory—are explained in a brochure available at the visitor center.

About 100 yards up the trail from the parking lot, the loop trail breaks off to the left and right. Continue straight and climb, often on slickrock, for 0.3 mile to the first scenic viewpoint and an excellent interpretive display explaining the famous geology of the area.

The trail continues another 0.5 mile to a second slickrock viewpoint that gives you an even better look at the Upheaval Dome area. This increases the total length of the trip to 1.6 miles, but the hike between the first and second overlooks is only a gradual upgrade. The second overlook is fenced for your protection.

# 21. **SYNCLINE LOOP**

## WHY GO?

A long day hike or overnighter and perhaps the premier hike in Island in the Sky

### THE RUNDOWN

**See map on page 87.**

**Start:** Upheaval Dome Picnic Area

**Distance:** 8.3 miles; loop

**Difficulty:** Difficult

**Nat Geo Trails Illustrated Map:** Island in the Sky

**Nat Geo TOPO! Map (USGS):** Upheaval Dome

## FINDING THE TRAILHEAD

Drive 6.5 miles south of the Island in the Sky Visitor Center and turn right (west) onto Upheaval Dome Road. Go another 4.8 miles to the Upheaval Dome Picnic Area at the end of the road. The trailhead is at the west end of the picnic area. **GPS coordinates:** 38° 25' 34.733" N/109° 55' 33.997" W

## WHAT TO SEE

This trail is the best choice for a long loop in the Island in the Sky District. With two exceptions (Neck Spring and Murphy), all other long trails in the district are out-and-back or shuttle hikes. Try for an early start, especially if you plan to cover this trail all in one day. This can be a long, hot day hike in canyon country. The hike involves one very difficult section of rock scrambling, and the NPS has posted a sign at the trailhead warning hikers about how strenuous this hike can be. That would be doubly true on a hot summer day. In any case, bring plenty of water.

The entire Syncline area has a fascinating—and controversial—geological history. Some geologists call Upheaval Dome "the most peculiar structural feature in southeastern Utah." The origin of the dome is the source of endless debate. For some mysterious reason rocks formerly buried a mile underground are now on the surface in the crater. The two most common theories—the salt dome theory and the meteorite impact theory—are explained in a brochure available at the visitor center. This trail circles the mysterious crater.

About 100 yards up the trail, the Upheaval Dome Overlook Trail goes straight and the loop trails go to the left and right. If you're hiking the clockwise route, as described here, take a left. The first 1.5 miles of the trail is quite pleasant—flat, well

The Syncline Loop goes around the Upheaval Canyon crater.

defined, and easy walking. Then you start a steep descent into Upheaval Canyon. For the next mile the trail drops abruptly. Some sections are rocky and rough with short switchbacks, but it's still easy to follow. Most of the 1,300-foot elevation loss occurs in this mile.

When you reach the bottom, follow the canyon wash for about another mile to the junction with the Upheaval Canyon Trail, which takes a sharp left and heads off to the west toward the Green River. You take a right and head northeast up the Syncline Valley.

Immediately after the junction you climb a short but steep hill that gets you out of the Upheaval Canyon dry wash and onto a defined trail. Just before the hill the trail splits. The Crater Spur Trail (see Hike 22) goes off to the right, which makes an excellent side trip if you have the time, but to stay on the Syncline Loop Trail, go left and up the steep, stair-stepped hill. The Crater Spur Trail follows a dry wash for 1.6 miles (one-way) into the depths of the crater.

After you get to the top of the hill, the trail goes by the designated Syncline Backcountry Campsite and then stays nearly level for about a half mile as it follows a grassy bench along the streambed.

Then the trail drops into the dry wash of Syncline Valley and starts up a narrow canyon, with massive Upheaval Dome on the right and the cliffs leading up to Buck Mesa on the left. This is a beautiful canyon highlighted by large cottonwood trees. In the spring you might see intermittent pools of water.

For the next mile or so, you climb steeply and gain most of the elevation you lost a few miles back. Near the top of the canyon is one very steep stretch where the trail goes through a field of huge boulders and the effort can best be described as scrambling, not hiking.

After the short steep section, the trail keeps climbing, but gradually. You go through an area of lush and diverse vegetation, including a stand of tall trees. At about the 6.5-mile mark, the trail forks. A short spur trail goes off to the right to a spring coming out of an alcove—a great spot for a lunch break.

From here the trail continues to climb gradually all the way to the trailhead, sometimes following the canyon wash. In the last 1.5 miles, you go over some slick-rock sections, some of them moderately steep, so be careful.

## MILES AND DIRECTIONS

**0.0** Start at Upheaval Dome Trailhead.

**0.1** Junction with Upheaval Dome Overlook Trail; turn left.

**1.5** Start of steep descent.

**3.4** Junction with Upheaval Canyon Trail; turn right.

**3.5** Junction with Crater Spur Trail; turn left.

**3.7** Syncline Backcountry Campsite.

**6.5** Spring.

**8.3** Arrive back at Upheaval Dome Trailhead.

# 22. CRATER SPUR TRAIL

## WHY GO?

An extension of the Syncline Loop or the Upheaval Canyon Trail that takes hikers into the famous crater

### THE RUNDOWN

**See map on page 87.**

**Start:** Upheaval Dome Picnic Area

**Distance:** 10.2 miles; out and back

**Difficulty:** Moderate

**Nat Geo Trails Illustrated Map:**
Island in the Sky

**Nat Geo TOPO! Map (USGS):**
Upheaval Dome

### FINDING THE TRAILHEAD

Drive 6.5 miles south of the Island in the Sky Visitor Center and turn right (west) onto Upheaval Dome Road. Go another 4.8 miles to the Upheaval Dome Picnic Area at the end of the road. The trailhead is at the west end of the picnic area. **GPS coordinates:** 38° 25' 34.733" N / 109° 55' 33.997" W

## WHAT TO SEE

This trail takes you into the heart of the famous crater. While the route is moderate, it gets hot, so start early and carry plenty of water.

Shortly after leaving the trailhead, the Upheaval Dome Overlook Trail goes straight and the Syncline Loop Trail heads left and right. Turn to the left. Enjoy easy walking over the flat, well-defined portion of the hike. After 1.5 miles start a steep, rough, and rocky descent into Upheaval Canyon. The next mile drops precipitously with short switchbacks, but it's still easy to follow. Most of the 1,300-foot elevation loss occurs in this section.

At the bottom, follow the canyon wash for another mile to the intersection with Upheaval Canyon Trail, which takes a sharp left and heads off to the west toward the Green River. You go to the right and head northeast up the Syncline Valley.

Almost immediately a short, steep hill takes you out of the Upheaval Canyon dry wash and onto a defined trail. Just before the hill the trail splits; at the sign for the junction of the two trails, you'll see the Syncline Loop trail heading up a steep, stair-stepped hill. Head for it, but before you get there, the Crater Spur Trail heads off to your right (east).

Hiking into the Upheaval crater

The route follows a beautiful dry wash the entire distance. There aren't a lot of cairns, but if you don't see one ahead, don't worry. Just stay in the wash, with the exception of a couple of places where the trail briefly climbs out of the wash to your right to get around large boulders or drop-offs.

The NPS put up a sign marking the end of the official trail, but from here you can go off-trail and explore the fascinating geology of the crater.

## MILES AND DIRECTIONS

**0.0** Start at Upheaval Dome Parking Area.

**0.1** Junction with Upheaval Dome Overlook Trail; turn left.

**1.5** Start of steep descent.

**3.4** Junction with Upheaval Canyon Trail; turn right.

**3.5** Junction with Crater Spur Trail; turn right.

**5.1** Reach the crater. After exploring, retrace your steps on the Crater Spur Trail.

**6.7** Junction with Upheaval Canyon Trail; turn left.

**6.8** Junction with Upheaval Dome Trail; turn left.

**10.2** Arrive back at Upheaval Dome Parking Area.

The Sego Lily is the state flower of Utah and is found in Canyonlands. ISTOCKPHOTO.COM

**Option:** After touring the crater, continue clockwise all the way around the Syncline Valley loop for a change of scenery and a slightly longer hike of 11.5 miles. At mile 6.7, when you return to Upheaval Canyon Trail, turn right and proceed toward Syncline Backcountry Campsite. The hike involves one very difficult section of rock scrambling. NPS has posted a warning at the trailhead about how strenuous this hike can be. That would be doubly true on a hot summer day, but in any case, bring plenty of water.

# 23. UPHEAVAL CANYON

## WHY GO?

A moderate day hike or overnighter to the edge of the Upheaval Dome

### THE RUNDOWN

**Start:** Upheaval Canyon Trailhead on the White Rim Road (high-clearance, four-wheel-drive vehicle required)

**Distance:** 7 miles; out and back

**Difficulty:** Moderate

**Nat Geo Trails Illustrated Map:** Island in the Sky

**Nat Geo TOPO! Map (USGS):** Upheaval Dome

## FINDING THE TRAILHEAD

 From the entrance station drive White Rim Road for 69.1 miles and park at the parking area on the left (west) side of the road. You can also reach the trailhead from the north, 3.1 miles from the park boundary.

**GPS coordinates:** 38° 28' 3.248" N / 109° 59' 56.591" W

Collared lizard
NPS/CASEY HODNETT

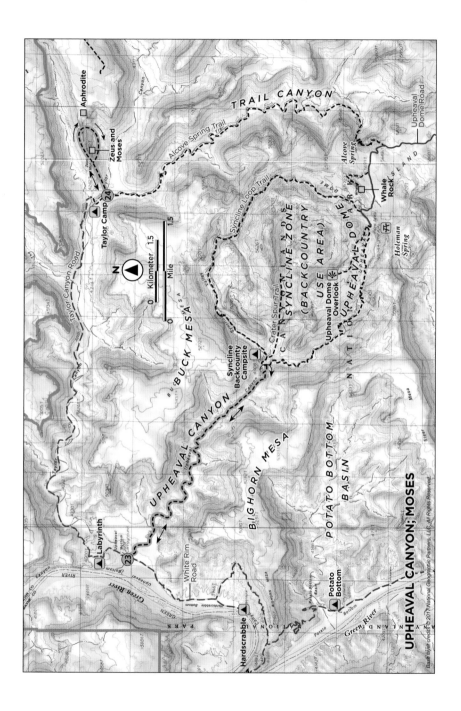

UPHEAVAL CANYON; MOSES

Base layer credit: © 2017 National Geographic Partners, LLC. All Rights Reserved.

## WHAT TO SEE

This is the longest hike on a trail accessed by White Rim Road. It's a great trail, mostly on packed sand. The first part of Upheaval Canyon is a broad open valley, and the trail cuts off the wide meanders. After the first mile or so, it drops into the dry wash. The broad valley you saw on the first part of the hike gradually becomes a narrow, twisting canyon just before you reach the junction with the Syncline Loop Trail.

This hike also makes a fairly easy overnighter, with a backcountry campsite located near the junction with the Syncline Loop Trail.

*Option:* Explore the crater itself by tacking on the 3.2-mile out-and-back Crater Spur Trail at the end of Upheaval Canyon Trail. The route follows a beautiful dry wash into the crater. There aren't a lot of cairns, but if you don't see one ahead, don't worry. Just stay in the wash, with the exception of a couple of places where the trail briefly climbs out of the wash to your right to get around large boulders or drop-offs. An NPS sign marks the end of the official trail, but from here you can go off-trail and explore the fascinating geology of the crater.

# 24. MOSES

## WHY GO?
A route developed by climbers to get to some of their favorite climbs, but also a nice hike for non-climbers

### THE RUNDOWN

**See map on page 96.**

**Start:** End of Taylor Canyon Road

**Distance:** 2 miles; lollipop loop

**Difficulty:** Moderate

**Nat Geo Trails Illustrated Map:** Island in the Sky

**Nat Geo TOPO! Map (USGS):** Upheaval Dome

## FINDING THE TRAILHEAD
You need a four-wheel-drive vehicle to reach this trailhead. To find Taylor Canyon Road, get on the White Rim Road, which turns off UT 313, 6.4 miles north of the Island in the Sky entrance station. Drive 18.2 miles to the park boundary and then another 2.5 miles to the junction with Taylor Canyon Road. Turn left (east) and drive to the end of Taylor Canyon Road, park in the parking area, and walk less than a quarter mile east to the point where both the Moses Trail and the Alcove Spring Trail start and end. **GPS coordinates:** 38° 28' 30.45" N / 109° 55' 8.5" W

## WHAT TO SEE
This trail climbs up and around the Zeus and Moses spires and then goes through the little pass between Moses and a smaller spire called Aphrodite (unnamed on the maps), all darlings of the rock-climbing fraternity. The route gets you up close and personal to these awe-inspiring formations.

It's a healthy climb to the base of the formations. Use caution hiking the loop around them, but if you start thinking this is risky, think of the people who climb all the way to the top. They make the official trail seem like a mall walk.

Star party over the Canyonlands
NPS/CHRIS WONDERLY

# 25. ALCOVE SPRING / SYNCLINE LOOP

## WHY GO?

A multiday backpacking trip, the longest in Island in the Sky

### THE RUNDOWN

**Start:** Alcove Spring Trailhead

**Distance:** 20.4 miles; loop

**Difficulty:** Difficult

**Nat Geo Trails Illustrated Map:** Island in the Sky

**Nat Geo TOPO! Map (USGS):** Upheaval Dome

### FINDING THE TRAILHEAD

Drive 6.5 miles south of the Island in the Sky Visitor Center and turn right (west) onto Upheaval Dome Road. Go another 3.3 miles to the Alcove Spring Parking Area at the trailhead sign on the right (north) side of the road. The Upheaval Dome Trailhead is another 1.5 miles down the paved road. **GPS coordinates:** 38° 25′ 23.233″ N / 109° 54′ 31.556″ W

### WHAT TO SEE

Regrettably, the Island in the Sky District doesn't have many long backpacking loops. Instead, most of the long hikes here are out and back. However, you can create one very nice loop trip by combining the Alcove Spring Trail, Upheaval Canyon Trail, and part of the Syncline Loop with Taylor Canyon Road and a short section of White Rim Road.

This loop requires a minimum of two nights out, but three nights would leave more time to enjoy the area. The loop can, of course, be taken in either direction, but this description covers the counterclockwise route.

From the Alcove Spring Trailhead, the trail drops, but not steeply, and the first mile is a little rocky with lots of steps installed to make hiking easier. The trail gradually switchbacks down, with one long stretch along an absolutely massive cliff with an enormous, amphitheater–like alcove for which the trail is named. After about a mile the well-defined trail levels out and angles to the left before heading down into Trail Canyon. In another mile or so, the trail dips into the dry wash of Trail Canyon and stays there until you reach the end of Taylor Canyon Road. Trail Canyon is a big, broad valley with sensational cliffs on both sides.

Sections of the Syncline Loop require some scrambling.

Some stretches of the dry wash don't have cairns, but don't fret. The trail stays in the wash. During the last mile you get great views of Moses, Zeus, and Aphrodite, awesome spires of rock on the north horizon, all darlings of rock climbers everywhere.

Just as Trail Canyon merges with Taylor Canyon, the trail leaves the dry wash. This turn could be missed, so watch for cairns at about two o'clock. From here it's only about a quarter mile on a defined trail to the Moses Trailhead. If you miss this turn, you'll come out at Taylor Camp, and you can walk back from there about a quarter mile to the trailhead.

From here (after taking a side trip up and around Moses), walk 4.7 miles down Taylor Canyon Road to White Rim Road. Turn left on the road, go another 0.6 mile along the road to the Upheaval Canyon Trailhead, and turn left (east) here.

After hiking the 3.5 miles up the canyon, you reach the junction with the Syncline Loop Trail. You can go left or right here, but I prefer taking a left. The north half of the Syncline Loop, albeit longer than the south half, seems more scenic. And it's probably more difficult, especially a short section where you must scramble over some huge boulders with your overnight pack. You can cut 1.2 miles off the trip and

Oasis along the Syncline Loop Trail

avoid the scramble by taking a right when you reach the Syncline Loop Trail, but you'll miss some outstanding scenery.

When you reach the Upheaval Dome Trailhead, elect somebody from your group to walk 1.2 miles on the paved road back to the Alcove Spring Trailhead to retrieve your vehicle while you relax and enjoy the afterglow of your incredible backpacking adventure.

If your party has two vehicles, you can also shorten the trip by leaving one at the Upheaval Dome Trailhead.

You have some great choices for both campsites and side trips. You can camp in several side canyons, but not at the designated vehicle campsites (Taylor Canyon or Labyrinth), which are reserved for vehicle campers. You can also camp at the Syncline Backcountry Campsite. Other options for overnight stays include camping in Trail Canyon, Upper Taylor Canyon, The Big Draw, Upheaval Bottom, and Upheaval Canyon.

A must-see side trip is to Moses, a short loop around the famous spire. Perhaps the best second choice is the 3.2-mile walk (round-trip) into the Upheaval Dome Crater on the Crater Spur Trail, which leaves from the junction of Syncline Loop and

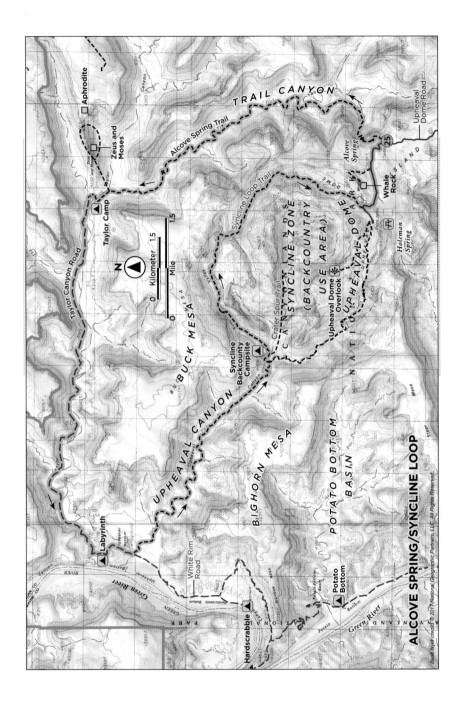

ALCOVE SPRING/SYNCLINE LOOP

Upheaval Canyon Trail. You can also take side trips up The Big Draw, into Upper Taylor Canyon, and along the Green River. See the chart following this entry for a few suggestions for your itinerary.

Refer to the Alcove Spring, Moses, Upheaval Canyon, Crater Spur Trail, and Syncline Loop descriptions for more details.

## MILES AND DIRECTIONS

**0.0** Start at the Alcove Spring Trailhead.

**5.3** Trail Canyon and Taylor Canyon merge.

**5.6** End of Taylor Canyon Road, Moses Trailhead, and Taylor Vehicle Campsite.

**6.4** The Big Draw.

**10.2** White Rim Road and Labyrinth Vehicle Campsite; turn left.

**10.8** Upheaval Canyon Trailhead; turn left.

**14.3** Syncline Loop Trail junction; turn left.

**14.4** Crater Spur Trail junction; turn left

**14.6** Syncline Backcountry Campsite.

**19.2** Upheaval Dome Trailhead.

**20.4** Arrive back at Alcove Spring Trailhead (on paved road).

| LENGTH OF TRIP | OVERNIGHT STAY | MILES PER DAY | SIDE TRIPS |
|---|---|---|---|
| TWO NIGHTS | 1—The Big Draw<br>2—Syncline Campsite | 1—6.4 miles<br>2—8.2 miles<br>3—5.8 miles | Moses<br>Crater Spur Trail |
| THREE NIGHTS | 1—The Big Draw<br>2—Upheaval Canyon<br>3—Syncline Campsite | 1—6.4 miles<br>2—4–5 miles<br>3—3–4 miles<br>4—5.8 miles | Moses<br>Along Green River<br>Crater Spur Trail |

# 26. MURPHY POINT

## WHY GO?
An easy, flat day hike or very easy overnighter with a stunning view

### THE RUNDOWN

**Start:** Murphy Trailhead

**Distance:** 3.6 miles; out and back

**Difficulty:** Easy

**Nat Geo Trails Illustrated Map:** Island in the Sky

**Nat Geo TOPO! Map (USGS):** Monument Basin and Turks Head

## FINDING THE TRAILHEAD

Drive 8.6 miles south from the Island in the Sky Visitor Center and park at the pullout at the Murphy Trailhead. **GPS coordinates:** 38° 21' 17.993" N/109° 51' 49.749" W

Giant desert hairy scorpion
NPS/ALICE DE ANGUERA

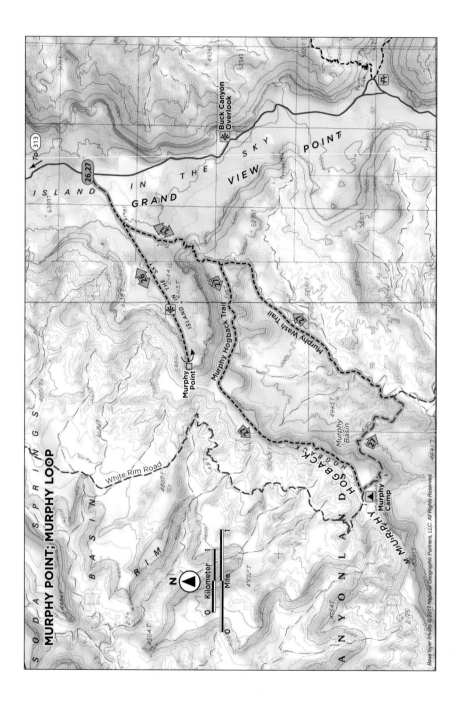

MURPHY POINT; MURPHY LOOP

**A view out toward the Green River** ISTOCKPHOTO.COM

## WHAT TO SEE

The Murphy Point Trail used to be Murphy Point Road, which went to within 0.2 mile of the overlook. In 1996 the NPS converted most of the road to a trail starting at the Murphy Trailhead. (Some older maps may still show it as a road.) This created a nice hike with an absolutely stunning view.

The trail is mostly flat as it stays on the same level as Island in the Sky. Because you're walking on what used to be a two-wheel-drive road, it's easy going. About 0.2 mile from the point, the trail reaches the spot where vehicles used to park. The rest of the way is on an easy trail with some slickrock sections.

From the point you get a breathtaking view of the White Rim country west of Island in the Sky, including the Green River slowly making its way to a grand meeting with the Colorado River a few miles later. Junction Butte dominates the southern horizon. You can see White Rim Road curving along the White Rim Sandstone far below. Plan on spending some extra time here relaxing and soaking in the incredible expansiveness of the Canyonlands.

You actually can spend the night on Murphy Point in an at-large camping area. Ask about getting a permit at the visitor center.

# 27. MURPHY LOOP

## WHY GO?
A nice lollipop loop, but long and difficult

### THE RUNDOWN

**See map on page 106.**

**Description:** A long, difficult day hike or overnighter from the Island in the Sky to the White Rim Road and back

**Start:** Murphy Trailhead

**Distance:** 10.8 miles; lollipop loop

**Difficulty:** Difficult

**Nat Geo Trails Illustrated Map:** Island in the Sky

**Nat Geo TOPO! Map (USGS):** Monument Basin and Turks Head

### FINDING THE TRAILHEAD

Drive 8.6 miles south from the Island in the Sky Visitor Center and park at the pullout at the Murphy Trailhead. **GPS coordinates:** 38° 21' 17.993" N / 109° 51' 49.749" W

## WHAT TO SEE

Unlike most trails in the Island in the Sky District, the hike into Murphy Basin is a nice lollipop loop instead of an out-and-back route. A pleasant mile-long walk on White Rim Road connects the Murphy Hogback Trail to the Murphy Wash Trail to complete the loop section of the route. This trail description follows the counterclockwise route, which allows you to walk down instead of up a hill on White Rim Road.

From the trailhead follow a recently abandoned road for about a half mile to the former trailhead and parking area and the junction with the Murphy Point Trail. Turn left (southwest) here. The trail stays on the flat mesa for less than a quarter mile before heading down a 1,000-foot descent into Murphy Basin. As with other such descents from Island in the Sky, the NPS has expertly routed and contoured the trail to make it safe and enjoyable walking. In one place a wooden bridge was installed to securely cross a short steep spot.

At the bottom of the mile-long descent the trail splits, with the right fork following the hogback and the left fork dropping into the dry wash. Take your pick on which way you want to do the 7-mile loop section of this trail. If you go right, you follow a flat, well-defined, packed-dirt trail all the way to White Rim Road. The trail stays on a small mesa and makes for pleasant walking.

When you reach White Rim Road, take a left (south). You'll see Murphy Vehicle Campsite and a vault toilet. Watching carefully to avoid vehicles, continue down White Rim Road for 1.3 miles until you see the sign for the Murphy Wash Trail, which heads up the dry wash. The trail stays in the dry wash until just before the big climb back up to Island in the Sky, where the Hogback Trail joins from the left. The climb looks even more daunting from below than it did from above. The cliff looks like sheer rock with no possibility of a safe trail, but at the top you'll probably say something to the effect that it wasn't half as hard as it looked.

## MILES AND DIRECTIONS

0.0   Start at the Murphy Trailhead.

0.5   End of abandoned road.

2.0   Junction with Murphy Wash Trail; turn right.

4.8   White Rim Road; turn left.

5.1   Murphy Vehicle Campsite.

6.1   Junction with Murphy Wash Trail; turn left.

8.8   Junction with Murphy Hogback Trail; turn right.

10.3 Junction with Murphy Point Trail; turn right.

10.8 Arrive back at Murphy Trailhead.

Candlestick Tower, a prominent feature along the White Rim Road and west-side trails of Island in the Sky District
NPS/NEAL HERBERT

# 28. GOOSEBERRY

## WHY GO?

A tough day hike from the Island in the Sky to the White Rim Road

### THE RUNDOWN

**Start:** Island in the Sky Picnic Area, Gooseberry Trailhead

**Distance:** 5.4 miles; out and back

**Difficulty:** Difficult

**Nat Geo Trails Illustrated Map:** Island in the Sky

**Nat Geo TOPO! Map (USGS):** Monument Basin

### FINDING THE TRAILHEAD

Drive 11.2 miles south from the Island in the Sky Visitor Center and turn left (east) into the picnic area. There is no trailhead sign on the main road. **GPS coordinates:** 38° 19' 22.274" N / 109° 50' 58.236" W

## WHAT TO SEE

When you look over the edge of Island in the Sky at the top of the Gooseberry Trail, you might think you forgot your parachute, because it looks like you're getting ready to jump off a cliff. At this point it's tempting to turn back, but you might be sorry if you do. This is a great hike, perfect for the person who has been confined to a car for several days of sightseeing and now really needs some serious cardiovascular exercise. If you're a nontechnical climber, you can also hike this trail and then tell everybody you climbed up to Island in the Sky—because that's exactly what you do on this hike.

The trail drops 1,400 feet over the span of 2.7 miles. That might not seem too bad until you look at the topo map and see that you lose 1,300 feet of that elevation in less than 1.5 miles. It looks deadly, but the NPS has done a superb job of constructing the trail to minimize the climb and make it as safe as possible.

The trail switchbacks down the steep side of the Island in the Sky formation and then drops into the dry wash for Gooseberry Canyon. While descending, watch your footing carefully—you can slip in the sections with loose sand. On the way down the hill, you get excellent views of White Rim country, and you can see the road ahead—perhaps with ant-size vehicles driving on it. In spring the white of the snowcapped La Sal Mountains merges nicely with the white of the White Rim Sandstone.

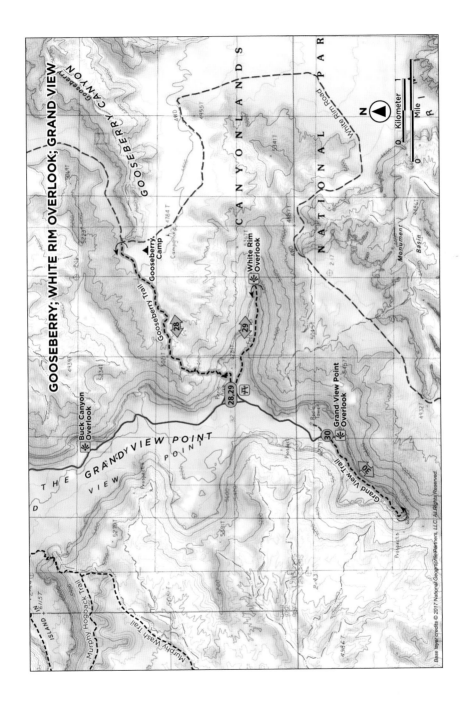

GOOSEBERRY; WHITE RIM OVERLOOK; GRAND VIEW

GOOSEBERRY CANYON

CANYONLANDS

NATIONAL PARK

White Rim Road

Gooseberry Trail

Gooseberry Camp

White Rim Overlook

Buck Canyon Overlook

THE GRANDVIEW POINT

VIEW POINT

Grand View Point Overlook

Grand View Trail

Murphy Hogback Trail

Murphy Wash Trail

ISLAND

N

Kilometer

Mile

**Northern sweetvetch**
NPS/JACOB W. FRANK

Once in the dry wash, it's easy, nearly flat hiking until you reach White Rim Road. When you get down to the road, you have to turn around and face the reality of climbing back up to the picnic area. It can be a daunting sight, but again, it isn't that bad for anybody in reasonable physical condition. Take it slowly, making frequent rest stops to check out the scenery. The trail is the steepest in the last half mile to the top.

When coming back up the arroyo for the first half of the return trip, watch for the trail to take a sharp left and stair-step up the side of Gooseberry Canyon. If you aren't alert, you could continue up the dry wash and then have to backtrack.

Try to do this hike in the morning when the sun is not shining directly on the trail. If you start early, you can do the entire climb in the shade.

# 29. WHITE RIM OVERLOOK

## WHY GO?

A short, flat walk with a great view of White Rim country

### THE RUNDOWN

**See map on page 111.**

**Start:** Island in the Sky Picnic Area, White Rim Lookout Trailhead

**Distance:** 1.8 miles; out and back

**Difficulty:** Easy

**Nat Geo Trails Illustrated Map:** Island in the Sky

**Nat Geo TOPO! Map (USGS):** Monument Basin

### FINDING THE TRAILHEAD

Drive 11.2 miles south from the Island in the Sky Visitor Center and turn left (east) into the picnic area. There is no trailhead sign on the main road. **GPS coordinates:** 38° 19′ 22.274″ N / 109° 50′ 58.236″ W

Watching the day disappear from Island in the Sky
NPS/KIRSTEN KEARSE

ISTOCKPHOTO.COM

## WHAT TO SEE

You can get a good view of the White Rim area from the parking lot, but a short, enjoyable walk gives you a really good view. The White Rim Overlook Trail starts at the right (south) side of the parking lot. It's flat and easy to follow the entire way. Some sections rely on well-placed cairns to show the route.

The trail stops at the end of a peninsula jutting out to the east from the Island in the Sky mesa. From the end of the trail, you can soak in an incredible panoramic view of the entire area. If it's near lunchtime, bring along a snack and a drink and have your lunch surrounded by the quiet beauty of the high desert before heading back to the parking lot.

# 30. GRAND VIEW

## WHY GO?
An easy day hike with a well-named view

### THE RUNDOWN

**See map on page 111.**

**Start:** Grand View Point Overlook

**Distance:** 2 miles; out and back

**Difficulty:** Easy

**Nat Geo Trails Illustrated Map:** Island in the Sky

**Nat Geo TOPO! Map (USGS):** Monument Basin

## FINDING THE TRAILHEAD

Drive south from the Island in the Sky Visitor Center for 12 miles all the way to the end of the main road. **GPS coordinates:** 38° 18' 38.702" N/109° 51' 23.777" W

Hiking the Grand View Trail
NPS/NEAL HERBERT

## WHAT TO SEE

The NPS has placed several wonderful interpretive signs at the Grand View Trailhead, including a panoramic sign that names many of the prominent features in the area such as the Totem Pole, the confluence of the Colorado and Green Rivers, and the White Rim Road winding its way around Island in the Sky.

This trail is flat all the way but poorly defined in spots, with lots of cairns showing the route. Be careful not to get too close to the cliffs: It's a long way down. If you have small children, watch them carefully.

At the end of the trail, you can sit and absorb a truly grand view, contemplating how nature transformed what was formerly a featureless plain into what you see today.

# 31. **FORT BOTTOM**

## WHY GO?
A day hike through the recent and not-so-recent history of the region

### THE RUNDOWN

**Start:** Fort Bottom Trailhead

**Distance:** 3 miles to the ruin or 4 miles to the cabin; out and back

**Difficulty:** Moderate

**Nat Geo Trails Illustrated Map:** Island in the Sky

**Nat Geo TOPO! Map (USGS):** Horsethief Canyon

### FINDING THE TRAILHEAD

From the entrance station drive White Rim Road in your high-clearance, four-wheel-drive vehicle for 66.1 miles and park at the parking area on the left (west) side of the road. You can also reach the trailhead from the north, 6.1 miles from the park boundary, if you have a four-wheel-drive vehicle.

**GPS coordinates:** 38° 26' 39.009" N / 110° 1' 3.046" W

## WHAT TO SEE
This interesting hike has two destinations. You can hike down to the bottomland where an old ranch building sits (a 4-mile round-trip), or you can climb up to the top of a small butte (3 miles out and back) to check out an intriguing structure built by Ancestral Puebloans.

The first part of the trail is a recently abandoned road, so it's very easy walking. About a mile from the trailhead, you go over a little divide made out of bentonite clay and then around the north side of the butte. Once on the other side, you can take a short side trip by taking a left at a junction there and climb up to the ruin (which you could see on the way down). After checking out the ruin, you can retrace your steps back to the trailhead, or if you have more time and energy, you can continue on down to the bottom, the site of a historic ranching operation.

If you opt to climb up to the top of the butte, the trail gets a little rough for about 100 yards, including two little cliffs you need to climb, but it's still safe. Once on top you can see the structure, but don't go in it or touch it. Tower structures are very common throughout the Southwest. This is the only known tower structure within Canyonlands National Park.

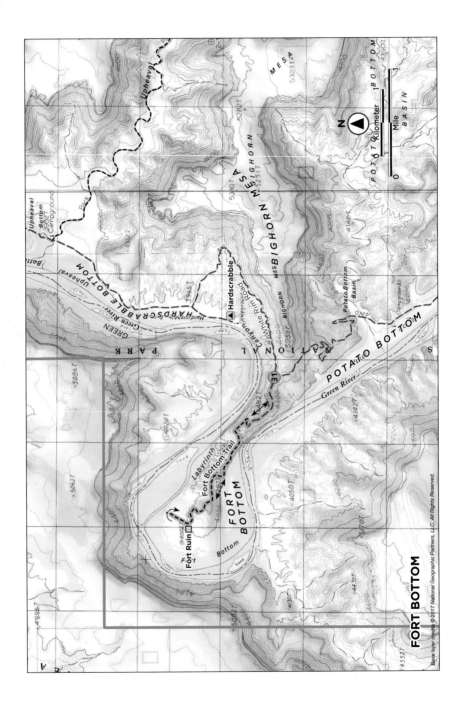

**FORT BOTTOM**

Green River from Fort Bottom
NPS/NEAL HERBERT

The trail down to the bottom is easier, so if you have children, this might be a better choice instead of climbing up to the top of the butte. When you get down there, you can see one old cabin and an area where a recent fire has destroyed some majestic old cottonwoods. The cabin was built in 1895 for people traveling the Green River and for people going to a planned tuberculosis sanitarium at the confluence of the Green and Colorado Rivers, which was never built.

You can also take a pleasant nap on the bank of the Green River.

# 32. GOOSENECK

## WHY GO?
A short walk with a scenic view that serves as a welcome relief from traveling the White Rim Road

### THE RUNDOWN

**Start:** Gooseneck turnoff on White Rim Road

**Distance:** 0.6 mile; out and back

**Difficulty:** Easy

**Nat Geo Trails Illustrated Map:** Island in the Sky

**Nat Geo TOPO! Map (USGS):** Musselman Arch

### FINDING THE TRAILHEAD
From the entrance station drive 6.4 miles on the White Rim Road and park at the parking area on the left (east) side of the road.
**GPS coordinates:** 38° 27' 17.843" N / 109° 46' 26.892" W

## WHAT TO SEE
At this point on White Rim Road, due east of the Island in the Sky Visitor Center, you'll have been bumping along on some of the rockiest sections of road, so a little hike might be just what you need. If so, the Gooseneck will be just right. This pleasant trail would also be a great diversion from your mountain bike or four-wheeler.

It's less than a half mile one-way. Enjoy a snack and relax for a few moments at this very scenic overlook.

Fishhook cactus

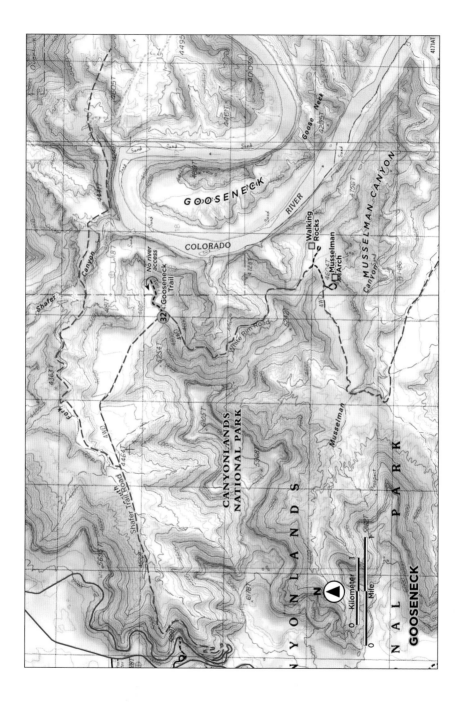

# CANYONLANDS NATIONAL PARK: THE NEEDLES

**THE NEEDLES DISTRICT OF CANYONLANDS NATIONAL PARK** is a high desert paradise. It is a jumbled landscape dominated by a series of distinctive sandstone spires called, of course, the Needles. Perhaps the other distinctive feature of the Needles District is an extensive trail system that offers nearly endless hiking options.

The Needles District has more hiking trails (about 74 miles) and a better variety of trails than the Island in the Sky and Maze Districts. In addition, this area is, in general, set up and managed for hikers, with lots of loop trails and a good selection of easy or moderate hiking options as well as backpacking opportunities. Most trails have sections of slickrock marked with cairns.

The following pages include many suggested hikes, but the Needles District has so many trails and hiking options that you can easily just get out the map and find additional options. Rangers at the Needles Visitor Center are most helpful in suggesting a hike that might be right for you.

For mountain bikers and four-wheelers, the Needles District has at least as much to offer as the Maze and Island in the Sky Districts, with several backcountry roads. Some have well-placed scenic campsites, so visitors with four-wheel-drive vehicles can base camp and day hike from their backcountry vehicle camp. In fact, some trailheads require a high-clearance, four-wheel-drive vehicle with low-range gearing and an experienced driver to access.

The Needles District has a great visitor center about a quarter mile past the entrance station. The Squaw Flat Campground has twenty-six campsites with picnic tables, fire rings (bring your own wood), a water supply (spring through fall), a dishwashing station, and two comfort stations with flush toilets. The campsites go on a first-come, first-served basis, and you'll be lucky to get one during the spring and fall peak seasons. The Needles District also has three group sites, which can be reserved in advance. Both individual sites in the campground and group sites have nominal fees.

The Needles District also has more water than other sections of Canyonlands National Park and Arches National Park. In spring you can often find flowing streams in several canyons. However, be sure to carry your own water instead of depending on unreliable desert water sources. In spring the entire area can be awash with wildflowers.

## FEAR THE NIGHT

The Needles District attracts thousands of hikers, some inexperienced. One fairly common—and serious—problem is that inexperienced hikers underestimate how much time it takes to complete a hike and get caught by nightfall, in many cases without a flashlight or headlamp.

Even with a flashlight or headlamp, following Needles trails at night can be challenging. Most trails have slickrock sections and go along canyon washes, making it easy to miss a cairn and get off the trail. Be extra careful not to underestimate the time a hike will take or overestimate your physical abilities, keeping in mind that summer heat can significantly slow you down.

## GETTING TO THE NEEDLES DISTRICT

From Moab take US 191 south for 40 miles and turn right (west) onto UT 211. Follow this paved road 35 miles to the Needles District entrance station. Be careful not to take Needles Overlook Road, which veers off a few miles before the correct junction. This road does not take you to Canyonlands National Park. Watch for the Canyonlands National Park sign before turning. From Monticello drive 14 miles north on US 191 and turn left (west) onto UT 211.

# 33. **ROADSIDE RUIN**

## WHY GO?

A very short walk and good opportunity to learn about local plant life and cultural history

### THE RUNDOWN

**Start:** Roadside Ruin Parking Area

**Distance:** 0.3 mile; loop

**Difficulty:** Easy

**Nat Geo Trails Illustrated Map:** Needles

**Nat Geo TOPO! Map (USGS):** The Loop

## FINDING THE TRAILHEAD

 Drive 0.6 mile from the Needles entrance station and park on the south side of the road in the well-signed Roadside Ruin Parking Area.
**GPS coordinates:** 38° 9′ 47.091″ N / 109° 45′ 45.376″ W

## WHAT TO SEE

This hike offers an easy introduction to the Canyonlands and its cultural history and plant life. At the trailhead, for a token fee, you can get a brochure for this self-guided interpretive trail.

Along the short, flat route, signs identify key native plant species, and the brochure describes these plants and how American Indians used them. Halfway around the loop, you can see a granary typical of the ancient Ancestral Puebloan structures found throughout the park, although few are as well preserved as this one.

# ROADSIDE RUIN; CAVE SPRING

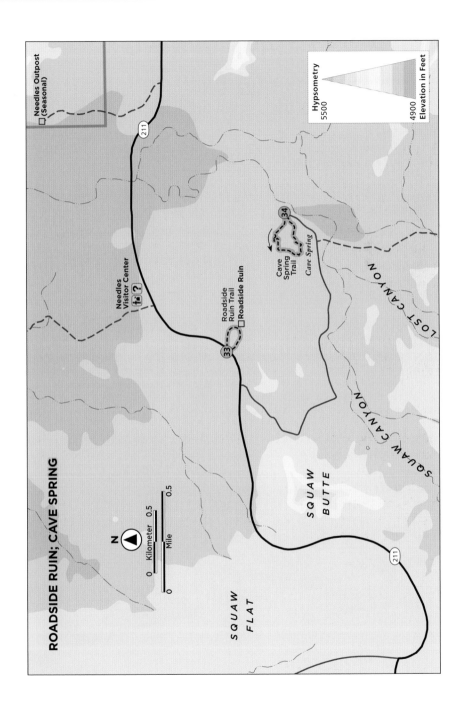

Needles Outpost
(Seasonal)

211

Needles
Visitor Center

Roadside
Ruin Trail
Roadside Ruin

33

Cave
Spring
Trail

34

Cave Spring

LOST CANYON

SQUAW CANYON

SQUAW
BUTTE

SQUAW
FLAT

211

N

0   Kilometer   0.5

0   Mile   0.5

Hypsometry
5500

4900
Elevation in Feet

# 34. CAVE SPRING

## WHY GO?

An opportunity to learn about the cultural history and desert plant life on a short hike

### THE RUNDOWN

**See map on page 125.**

**Start:** Cave Spring Parking Area

**Distance:** 0.6 mile; loop

**Difficulty:** Moderate

**Nat Geo Trails Illustrated Map:**
Needles

**Nat Geo TOPO! Map (USGS):**
The Loop

### FINDING THE TRAILHEAD

Drive 0.9 mile west from the Needles entrance station, take a left (south) onto a paved road (sign points to Salt Creek), and go 0.5 mile before taking another left (east) onto a dirt road. The unpaved road ends in 1.2 miles at the parking area and trailhead for the Cave Spring Trail.

**GPS coordinates:** 38° 9' 26.129" N/109° 45' 5.699" W

The Cave Spring loop trail

## WHAT TO SEE

If you're in the Needles area and have an extra hour, the Cave Spring hike is a pleasant way to spend it. The trailhead is conveniently located, and this short hike offers lots of diversity. At the trailhead, for a token fee, you can pick up a brochure that explains the area's history and plant life.

The small loop trail goes by ruins of historic ranching operations that were active here until 1975, when livestock grazing was abandoned in Canyonlands National Park. Please honor the barriers put up by the NPS to preserve this part of the area's history. Later the trail goes by Cave Spring and then passes by some rock art left by the Ancestral Puebloans who inhabited the area 1,000 years ago. Please don't touch these art treasures.

After you finish enjoying the signs of both recent and ancient history, hike around a large "Canyonlands mushroom" and climb a safety ladder to a slickrock flat. Here you get the experience of following cairns over slickrock and also get a great view of many of the area's main features, such as the Needles, North Six-shooter Peak, and South Six-shooter Peak.

Interpretive signs along the trail identify many of the high desert's most common plant species.

# 35. POTHOLE POINT

## WHY GO?
A short hike to learn about life in desert potholes

### THE RUNDOWN

**Start:** Pothole Point Parking Area

**Distance:** 0.6 mile; loop

**Difficulty:** Easy

**Nat Geo Trails Illustrated Map:**
Needles

**Nat Geo TOPO! Map (USGS):**
The Loop

### FINDING THE TRAILHEAD

From the Needles entrance station, drive 5.1 miles and park on the left (west) side of the road in the Pothole Point Parking Area.
**GPS coordinates:** 38° 10' 13.371" N / 109° 48' 22.982" W

Pothole Point

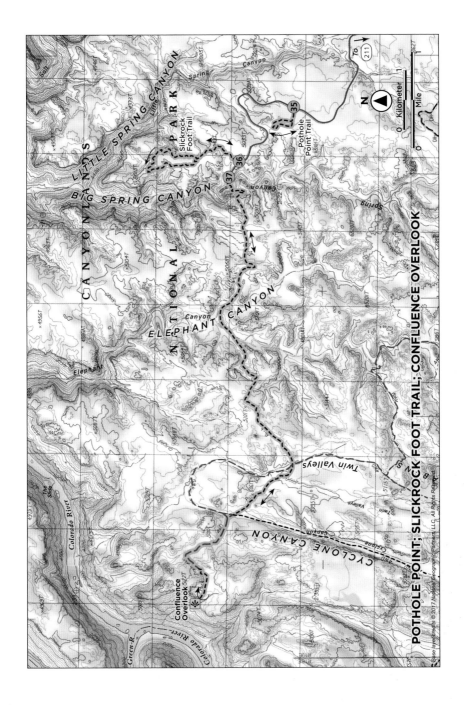

POTHOLE POINT; SLICKROCK FOOT TRAIL; CONFLUENCE OVERLOOK

## WHAT TO SEE

If you need a little exercise or want to take small children for an easy, safe hike where they might learn something about desert ecology, Pothole Point is an excellent choice. At the trailhead, for a token fee, you can buy a small brochure explaining the fascinating ecology of potholes.

Most of this hike follows a string of cairns over slickrock. The name Pothole Point comes from the numerous "potholes" that have formed in the slickrock along the trail. The potholes trap water after a desert rain. The rainwater is mildly acidic and ever so slowly enlarges the pothole. An intricate, symbiotic animal community featuring shrimp, worms, snails, and perhaps even a Great Basin spadefoot toad gradually develops in some potholes. If you're lucky enough to visit Pothole Point shortly after a rain, you can observe these tiny ecosystems.

Over time the wind continuously blows dirt, sand, and small bits of organic material into the potholes. Eventually plants take root in the thin layer of soil. The first sign of life in a pothole is often the cryptobiotic soil, which provides the foundation for growth of larger plants. The end result is a "pothole garden," a pocket of miniature, bonsai-like vegetation in a bowl of solid rock.

You can hike this short loop in either direction. Watch for a spur trail going to the top of some big boulders where you can get a great view of the surrounding terrain in either direction, including the area's namesake, the Needles.

# 36. **SLICKROCK FOOT TRAIL**

## WHY GO?
A scenic trip through the geology of the Canyonlands

---

### THE RUNDOWN

**See map on page 129.**

**Start:** Slickrock Foot Trail Parking Area

**Distance:** 2.4 miles; lollipop loop

**Difficulty:** Moderate

**Nat Geo Trails Illustrated Map:** Needles

**Nat Geo TOPO! Map (USGS):** The Loop

---

### FINDING THE TRAILHEAD

From the Needles entrance station, drive 6.4 miles and park on the right (north) side of the road at the Slickrock Foot Trail Parking Area, just before the end of the road. **GPS coordinates:** 38° 10' 37.428" N/ 109° 48' 52.495" W

## WHAT TO SEE

If you're a beginner or experienced hiker with a half day to spend in the Needles District, the Slickrock Foot Trail is an excellent way to enjoy it. Many hikes in the Needles follow canyon bottoms, but this trail stays high and gives an overall perspective of the entire southeastern corner of Canyonlands National Park.

The NPS suggests this trail to inexperienced hikers so they can take a look at the entire area before deciding on their next hike. On this trail beginners also learn how to follow cairns and hike on slickrock. For the beginner who has only walked well-defined dirt trails, this hike might be a little adventurous, but it certainly isn't dangerous. The trail is easy to follow, with lots of cairns marking the way. Well-placed signs mark the way to four viewpoints and the point where the lollipop loop begins.

At the trailhead, for a token fee, pick up a brochure written for this hike. It describes much of the geology of the area and is keyed specifically to the four viewpoints along the trail.

Take the hike counterclockwise as indicated by an NPS sign about a half mile up the trail where the loop section of the trail begins, which is just after the first viewpoint where you get a panoramic view of the entire region and many of the major landmarks—Six-shooter Peak, Elaterite Butte, Cathedral Butte, the La Sal Mountains, Ekker Butte, and, of course, the Needles.

Hiking the Slickrock Foot Trail

The trail stays on the ridge between Little Spring Canyon and Big Spring Canyon. At the second viewpoint you can get a good view into the upper reaches of Little Spring Canyon.

After the third viewpoint the trail turns west and then south. You can take a long look at the region's namesake, the Needles, as you walk along.

At the last viewpoint you can look down into massive Big Spring Canyon. In spring you might see a stream flowing in the distance far below. The brochure gives you a great geology lesson from this viewpoint, so plan on spending extra time here to identify all the different strata that make up the canyon's awesome cliffs.

After you leave the fourth viewpoint, it's another mile or so back to the trailhead, most of the trail following the east flank of Big Spring Canyon.

# 37. CONFLUENCE OVERLOOK

## WHY GO?
A long, strenuous day hike to a famous landmark, the confluence of the mighty Green and Colorado Rivers

### THE RUNDOWN

**See map on page 129.**

**Start:** Parking area at end of main park road at the Big Spring Canyon Overlook

**Distance:** 9.6 miles; out and back

**Difficulty:** Difficult

**Nat Geo Trails Illustrated Map:** Needles

**Nat Geo TOPO! Map (USGS):** The Loop and Spanish Bottom

### FINDING THE TRAILHEAD

From the Needles entrance station, drive 6.6 miles and park at the end of the road. **GPS coordinates:** 38° 10' 41.533" N / 109° 49' 0.983" W

## WHAT TO SEE

This is a serious hike, but the destination—a sweeping vista of the joining of two great rivers—makes up for any discomfort in getting there. Some sections go over slickrock marked with strings of cairns, but unlike most trails in the Canyonlands, most of this trail is a well-defined dirt path. The NPS has expertly routed the trail through many interesting features, taking advantage of the great scenery along the way.

Immediately after leaving the trailhead, the trail drops steeply into Big Spring Canyon. Then, after a few feet in the dry wash, the trail climbs the other side of the canyon. Be careful not to take the well-used off-trail route up the canyon and miss the cairns going off to the right, marking the ascent out of the canyon.

The climb is well marked with cairns, but footing can be a bit precarious in a few places. In one spot the NPS has installed a safety ladder. Once on top take a break in a gorgeous spot where the trail goes through a small opening between two cliffs. Looking either way through this "keyhole" gives you a great photo.

After the keyhole you stay high for about a mile. Here you can see several well-sculpted and huge "Canyonlands mushrooms" before gradually dropping into expansive Elephant Canyon. Once down in Elephant Canyon, you follow a dry wash for almost a mile, all easy walking. Then you start a gradual climb out of

The confluence of the Colorado and Green Rivers

Elephant Canyon—going by a giant red sandstone spire with no name and into another big and equally beautiful drainage called Twin Valleys. From above you can look out and see the "twins," which almost look cultivated with a light-colored grass carpeting the valley floor.

The flat bottomland of Twin Valleys is carpeted with cheatgrass, a nasty invasive species brought into the area when it was heavily grazed (before the park was designated). Cheatgrass has completely taken over the area from native species, but its light-green color contrasts nicely with the other green hues of the high desert.

Just as you get into Twin Valleys, you cross the Devils Lane four-wheel-drive road that goes north and south. The trail goes straight across the road and continues on.

After leaving the gentle grasslands of Twin Valleys, you crest a small knoll and drop into Cyclone Canyon, also invaded by cheatgrass. In Cyclone Canyon you come to the four-wheel-drive road again. This time, however, the trail becomes a road. Some maps show this as a trail, but on the ground it's a well-used road. Follow the road instead of looking around for the trail that isn't there.

Walk west 0.3 mile on the road until it ends at a vehicle turnaround with a vault toilet, a picnic table, and a sign informing you that it's still another 0.5 mile to the Confluence Overlook. It's a gradual climb to the overlook from here.

The overlook offers an incredible vista. You can see two majestic rivers, the Green and the Colorado, merging into one with the Colorado's namesake carrying on. You also get a panoramic view to the west and north into the Maze and Island in the Sky Districts with Ekker Butte highlighting the horizon. The overlook is unfenced, so don't get too close to the edge. If you have children, watch them carefully.

On the way back you'll notice that the NPS situated the parking lot in an appropriate location. You can see your vehicle from about a mile away as you come out of Elephant Canyon and head down into Big Spring Canyon.

## MILES AND DIRECTIONS

**0.0** Start at parking area at Big Spring Canyon Overlook.

**1.2** Safety ladder.

**1.5** Divide between Big Spring and Elephant Canyons.

**2.9** Four-wheel-drive road.

**3.7** Four-wheel-drive road and junction with Cyclone Canyon Trail; go straight on the road.

**4.2** End of road.

**4.8** Confluence Overlook. Retrace your steps to the trailhead.

**9.6** Arrive back at the trailhead.

# 38. **UPPER SALT CREEK**

## WHY GO?
A long hike, well suited for backpackers, through an intriguing desert valley

### THE RUNDOWN

**Start:** Outside the park at the Bureau of Land Management's Cathedral Butte Trailhead

**Distance:** 22 miles; shuttle

**Difficulty:** Difficult

**Nat Geo Trails Illustrated Map:** Needles

**Nat Geo TOPO! Map (USGS):** Druid Arch, South Six-shooter Peak, and Cathedral Butte

**Special considerations:** If you plan to stay overnight in Salt Creek or Horse Canyon, be sure to get your overnight permit at the Needles Visitor Center. You also need a day-use permit for Salt Creek.

## FINDING THE TRAILHEAD

To start at the Cathedral Butte Trailhead, drive east out of the park from the park entrance station on UT 211 for 13.7 miles and turn right (south) onto a gravel road marked Elk Mountain and Beef Basin. If you're coming from the east, the turnoff is 20 miles from US 191. Follow this well-maintained, unpaved road for 17 miles until you see the small parking area on your right (north) with a Bureau of Land Management sign that reads Bright Angel and Salt Creek. This is officially called the Cathedral Butte Trailhead. There may be a gate across the road about 9.5 miles from UT 211. You can open the gate and pass through, but be sure to close it behind you. You don't need a four-wheel-drive vehicle to get to the Cathedral Butte Trailhead unless it has rained recently, which can make the clay in the road very slippery. **GPS coordinates (Cathedral Butte):** 37° 57' 1.056" N / 109° 42' 20.996" W

For this one-way shuttle hike, park your second car (or arrange to be picked up) at Peekaboo Camp at the end of Salt Creek Road. To find Salt Creek Road, drive 0.9 mile west from the entrance station and take a left (south) onto a well-signed, paved road (marked Salt Creek) and go 0.5 mile before taking a left (east) onto an unpaved road. After 0.8 mile on the unpaved road, turn right (south) instead of going straight to the Cave Spring Trailhead and drive about a quarter mile until you reach a locked gate. This gate marks the official trailhead for Salt Creek and Horse Canyon Roads. **GPS coordinates (Salt Creek):** 38° 6' 52.931" N / 109° 45' 15.999" W. You need a high-clearance, four-wheel-drive vehicle with low-range gearing to get from here to Peekaboo Camp. Drive 2.7 miles to Horse Canyon Road; take a right and drive 1 mile more to the camp.

## WHAT TO SEE

Names can be misleading. Somehow, "Salt Creek" seems to imply a dry, harsh, and unpleasant place when quite the opposite is true. Upper Salt Creek is definitely one of the most delightful hikes in the Canyonlands, and it deserves a name like "Desert Paradise Creek."

Unlike most "creeks" in the region, this one really is a creek. A stream flows through much of the canyon for much of the year. Because of the reliable source of water, early cultures inhabited the area. Rock art and ruins can be found throughout the canyon.

This is not the typical narrow canyon common in Canyonlands. Instead it's a broad, flat, spacious valley with rich vegetative diversity ranging from cattail marshes to stately cottonwoods. And unlike many places in the park, Salt Creek has lots of wildlife—mule deer, coyotes, bobcats, black bears, and mountain lions. You might not see them, but you can see their tracks in the sand and mud.

You have at least three options for seeing Upper Salt Creek. It makes a fantastic long (22 miles!) day hike for super-fit, experienced hikers who can arrange a vehicle shuttle. If you choose this option, don't overestimate your abilities and get caught out at night.

The remoteness of this hidden corner of Canyonlands makes it a backpacking adventure, perhaps the best in the park. It can be a two- or three-day shuttle or a four- or five-day out-and-back trip starting and ending at the Salt Creek Road.

| RECOMMENDED ITINERARY | |
| --- | --- |
| First night: | SC1 or SC2 |
| Second night: | SC4 |
| Third night: | At-large camp along Salt Creek |

If you can't arrange this time-consuming shuttle (due to the driving required), you can still enjoy Upper Salt Creek by hiking out and back from Peekaboo Camp, where the Salt Creek Road ends. However, it may be too long of a day hike to reach Upper Salt Creek and return in the same day. To get as far as Upper Jump, it's a 27-mile out-and-back hike, and you'd still miss the broad expansiveness of the southernmost reaches of Salt Creek.

At-large backpacking is allowed in Salt Creek Canyon and Horse Canyon, and there are many attractive places to camp. But make sure to get a permit and camp at least a mile from the road and away from any water sources.

After studying all the options, and to fully enjoy "Desert Paradise Creek," I suggest the south-to-north backpacking option with three nights out. This allows you to hike downhill all the way. If you did the shuttle route in reverse, it would be all uphill with a very steep grade at the south end as you climb up to Cathedral Butte Trailhead.

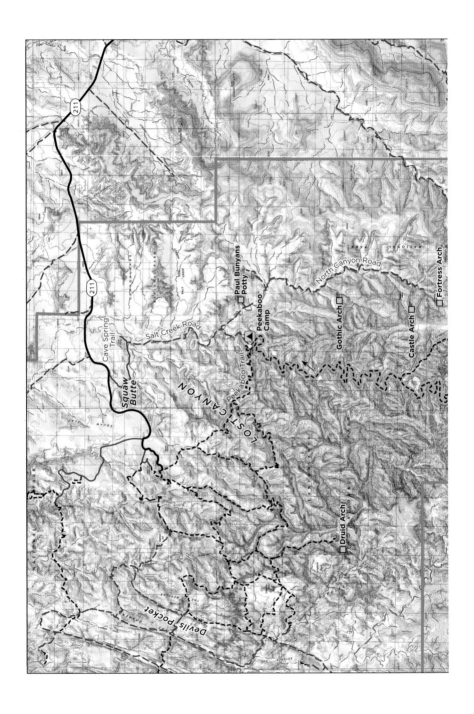

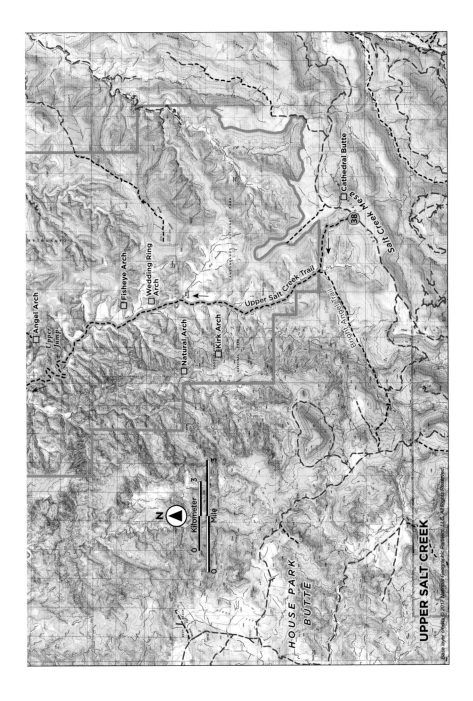

Angel Arch

Upper Jump

Fisheye Arch

Wedding Ring Arch

Natural Arch

Kirk Arch

Upper Salt Creek Trail

Cathedral Butte

38

Salt Creek Mesa

Bright Angel Trail

N

0 Kilometer 3

0 Mile 3

HOUSE PARK BUTTE

UPPER SALT CREEK

Base layer breaks © 2017 National Geographic Partners, LLC. All Rights Reserved.

Arranging a ride to the Cathedral Butte Trailhead and leaving a vehicle near Peekaboo Camp is problematic, but it's worth the effort. Leave the vehicle in the parking area near Peekaboo Camp, not in the campsites. When you get your permit, the staff at the visitor center will tell you the combination to the Salt Creek gate and whether it's scheduled to change while you're out hiking.

Water is always a big issue on such a long desert hike. Most of the time (but no guarantees) you can filter water out of Salt Creek. But storms and wind can make it too turbid to filter; carry emergency water. Discuss this thorny water issue with the visitor center staff when acquiring your backcountry permit.

From the Cathedral Butte Trailhead, the hike starts out in a juniper forest on a well-defined but rocky trail, which drops sharply for the first 1.5 miles. At the 1.5-mile mark, you'll see a big open canyon on your left, the upper reaches of Salt Creek. The rather indistinct Bright Angel Trail from the west joins the main trail after you drop into the valley. You might miss this unmarked junction, but it doesn't matter, as you're heading north.

After walking through the open canyon for about a quarter mile, you drop into the dry wash and see the park boundary signs. The NPS has put up signs on both sides of the dry wash so you won't miss them. The trail stays in the dry wash for about 100 yards before it veers left (west) at the second park boundary sign.

For the next 7 miles, the trail stays in the broad valley. It's a well-defined, packed-dirt trail all the way. It occasionally gets brushy as it weaves through sagebrush, saltbrush, and rabbitbrush. In addition to watching deer bound away, you can see four beautiful arches—Kirk and Natural on your left and Wedding Ring and Fisheye on your right. Kirk and Natural are on the skyline and easy to see, but only from a short section of trail, so be alert. Wedding Ring Arch is right by the trail but surprisingly easy to miss, so watch carefully. Fisheye is very obvious, standing out directly in front of you.

At about the 3.5-mile mark, the vegetation changes dramatically. A large spring in the area has created a series of cattail marshes and willow thickets and, in a few places, patches of green grass. After emerging from the thickets, the spring flows over some flat rocks as a full-blown stream, a great place to relax and soak in the essence of wildness. There is a large pool below the spring, but please resist the temptation to jump in. All the springs in Upper Salt Creek provide critical water supplies to wildlife and backpackers. You could contaminate them with skin oils, sunscreen, or soap. Park regulations prohibit bathing in any water sources except the Colorado and Green Rivers and in Salt Creek along the four-wheel-drive road.

About a half mile beyond the spring, you'll see Kirk Cabin and the remains of a ranching operation that predates the creation of Canyonlands National Park. This aging cabin is part of the cultural history of the park, so be careful not to artificially increase the rate of deterioration, just as you would be careful not to harm any ancient ruins or rock art.

Shortly after Kirk Cabin the trail goes by the first backcountry campsites (SC1 and SC2) on the right (east) side of the trail. SC2 is about 100 yards from the trail

The Big Ruin, a major feature along the Upper Salt Creek Trail
NPS/NEAL HERBERT

nestled in a flat open spot in the sagebrush. SC1 is farther from the trail in a juniper stand and has a slightly better view. If you're on a three-night trip, one of these sites would be the best place to stop for the first night out.

After Kirk Cabin and the first two campsites, the trail continues to wind through the open valley floor. Keep your eyes peeled for arches in this section. About a mile after Fisheye Arch, the trail goes by a famous rock art panel called All-American Man, perhaps because of its red, white, and blue pigments. Please don't climb up to the panel or touch this precious art.

Right after All-American Man, the trail goes through a narrow spot between two cliffs. It's almost like going through an arch. This is a big departure from the last 5 miles of open valley, and it's a great place for a short rest and a good view of both where you've been and where you're going. Shortly after this tight spot, you go through a big thicket with a noticeably flowing Salt Creek, which stays that way for most of the rest of the hike. Near the end of the thicket, watch for Backcountry

Campsite SC3 off to your left. If you're on a three-day trip, this campsite isn't spaced well for you, so keep hiking. If you're on a four-night trip, though, this would be a good choice for the second night.

About a half mile past the thicket, the trail passes a delightful spot where the stream falls over a rock ledge and into a gorgeous pool. This is called Upper Jump, and it seems almost tropical and out of character for this high desert environment. Again, please resist the temptation to jump into this critical water source.

After Upper Jump the canyon walls gradually close in, and Upper Salt Creek starts to resemble many other canyons in the park. The trail also starts following the wide meanders of the stream. In fact, during the next few miles of the hike, the trail winds unmercifully. It seems to turn around every bush and crosses the stream dozens of times. The result is 5 miles of hiking to go about 2 miles "as the crow flies." This section of trail also goes through several stretches of very thick brush. If you don't have long pants on, you might end up looking like a poster child for Neosporin. It's worth it to stop and switch over to long pants.

Angel Arch—a worthwhile
3-mile out-and-back sidetrip
ISTOCKPHOTO.COM

In some places the trail stays on the bench above the stream, and in other places it drops into the brushy stream bottom. When by the stream it's nice and cool, and the trail is often carpeted with cottonwood leaves.

At about the 12-mile mark, you'll see Backcountry Campsite SC4 on your right on a beautiful bench under some big cottonwoods near the stream, with a great view of a giant rock balanced on a sandstone spire. This is the last designated campsite, and a great choice for your second night out.

After going another 1.5 miles, you reach the point where Salt Creek Road (and this hike) formerly ended. Now, however, it's another 8.5 miles to Peekaboo Camp and the new terminus of Salt Creek Road. This section is open to at-large camping, so you can find a suitable campsite for your last night anywhere along this section of road-turned-to-trail.

This is also the junction with the trail to Angel Arch, a worthwhile 3-mile out-and-back side trip. The Angel Arch Trail is mostly level and easy to follow but sandy most of the way. Near the end it climbs slightly up to a small ridge that becomes a great viewing platform for this magnificent arch. However, the trail doesn't go all the way to the arch.

If you aren't interested in seeing Angel Arch, turn left and follow the abandoned road. As you hike this last section of the route, you might wonder why—environmentally and aesthetically—it was ever allowed to be a road. The scenery is fantastic, and in most cases the walking is fairly easy.

## MILES AND DIRECTIONS

0.0   Start at the Cathedral Butte Trailhead.

1.5   Junction with Bright Angel Trail, turn right.

1.8   Canyonlands National Park boundary.

3.5   Kirk Cabin.

3.6   Backcountry Campsites SC1 and SC2.

6.0   Backcountry Campsite SC3.

8.5   Upper Jump.

12.0   Backcountry Campsite SC4.

13.5   Junction with Angel Arch Trail; turn left

22.0   Peekaboo Camp and Salt Creek Road.

**Option:** For a four- or five-day out-and-back hike of up to 33 miles to Kirk Cabin, start at Peekaboo Camp at the end of the Salt Creek Road (see "Finding the trailhead" above, directions to Peekaboo Camp. Follow the hiking directions above in reverse. Turn around and head back north when you've hiked half as far as you want to go. Exploring and side trips (for instance, to Angel Arch) are not included in the trip total.

# 39. CASTLE ARCH

## WHY GO?

A short, uphill walk to a big arch accessed by a four-wheel-drive road

### THE RUNDOWN

**Start:** Castle Arch Trailhead near the end of Horse Canyon Road

**Distance:** 0.8 mile; out and back

**Difficulty:** Easy

**Nat Geo Trails Illustrated Map:** Needles

**Nat Geo TOPO! Map (USGS):** South Six-shooter Peak

### FINDING THE TRAILHEAD

From the entrance station drive 0.9 mile and turn left (south) onto a paved road (marked Salt Creek). Follow this road for 0.5 mile and then turn left (east) onto a gravel road. Follow this road for 0.8 mile until you see the sign for Salt Creek. Turn right (south) here and go about a quarter mile to the gate at the entrance to Salt Creek Road. Day-use and overnight camping permits are required; get them at the visitor center. Use the combination on your permit to open the gate and follow Salt Creek Road and then Horse Canyon Road to the trailhead near the end of Horse Canyon Road.

**GPS coordinates:** 38° 3' 47.486" N / 109° 43' 52.156" W

Sharp-leaf twinpod
NPS/NEAL HERBERT

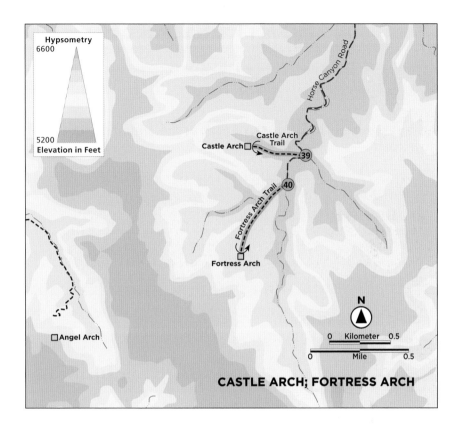

CASTLE ARCH; FORTRESS ARCH

## WHAT TO SEE

Just before the end of Horse Canyon Road is the trailhead sign for Castle Arch Trail and a spot to pull off the main road. From here the trail heads west through a heavily vegetated valley on a slightly uphill grade, nicely carpeted with oak leaves, but a bit primitive and brushy in places. It is a real treat for students of high desert vegetation. You can see the arch throughout most of the hike. However, the trail doesn't go to the arch, and in fact has no clearly definable end. Instead it just gets more and more faint, and you'll know when it's time to take one last look at the arch and head back to your vehicle.

If you're interested in more exercise after you get back to your vehicle, you can walk instead of drive about a quarter mile down the road to the Fortress Arch Trailhead.

# 40. **FORTRESS ARCH**

## WHY GO?

A short wash walk to a massive arch at the end of a four-wheel-drive road

### THE RUNDOWN

**See map on page 145.**

**Start:** Fortress Arch Trailhead at the end of Horse Canyon Road

**Distance:** 0.6 mile; out and back

**Difficulty:** Easy

**Nat Geo Trails Illustrated Map:** Needles

**Nat Geo TOPO! Map (USGS):** South Six-shooter Peak

## FINDING THE TRAILHEAD

From the entrance station drive 0.9 mile and turn left (south) onto a paved road (marked Salt Creek). Follow this road for 0.5 mile and then turn left (east) onto a gravel road. Follow this road for 0.8 mile until you see the sign for Salt Creek. Turn right (south) here and go about a quarter mile to the gate at the entrance to Salt Creek Road. Day-use and overnight camping permits are required; get them at the visitor center. Use the combination on your permit to open the gate and follow Salt Creek Road and then Horse Canyon Road to the trailhead at the end of Horse Canyon Road. **GPS coordinates:** 38° 3' 47.486" N/109° 43' 52.156" W

## WHAT TO SEE

The Fortress Arch Trail starts right at the end of Horse Canyon Road. From the parking area it heads up a dry wash and stays there for easy walking all the way. The trail ends near a big, flat rock that makes an excellent spot to relax for a few minutes while you marvel at this massive arch.

# 41. PEEKABOO

## WHY GO?

A tough day hike or moderate overnighter with lots of options and side trips

### THE RUNDOWN

**Start:** Squaw Flat Trailhead

**Distance:** 10 miles; out and back

**Difficulty:** Difficult

**Nat Geo Trails Illustrated Map:** Needles

**Nat Geo TOPO! Map (USGS):** The Loop and Druid Arch

## FINDING THE TRAILHEAD

Drive about 2.7 miles west from the Needles entrance station and turn left into Squaw Flat Campground. After entering the campground area, the road forks. Both forks go to trailheads with access to the same trails. However, the left-hand fork takes you to the trailhead with the shortest access route to the backcountry. The right-hand fork and its respective trailhead are used mostly by campers staying in the campground. **GPS coordinates:** 38° 8′ 36.487″ N/109° 48′ 13.115″ W

## WHAT TO SEE

You have several options for seeing the Peekaboo Spring area. If you're in the mood for a long, strenuous day hike, you can do 10 miles out and back. However, Salt Creek Road ends at Peekaboo Camp, so you can have less-ambitious members of your party meet you there for a quiet night in a beautiful desert campsite—if you can get a permit for this popular vehicle campsite. You can also make this an overnighter by camping at Backcountry Campsite LC1 in Lost Canyon.

Immediately after leaving the trailhead, you reach the junction with the Big Spring Canyon Trail. Go left here and head southeast toward Squaw Canyon. The first 1.1 miles of the trail are flat and easy, with the exception of several slickrock sections. The slickrock isn't dangerous, but be alert for small cairns marking the correct route.

After 1.1 miles you hit another junction, also well signed. Take the left (east) fork toward Lost Canyon and Peekaboo Spring.

The next 1.5-mile section is gorgeous. It goes over slickrock for much of the first mile or so. Then, just after climbing down a small ladder, the trail follows the north rim of a beautiful, narrow canyon before dropping into the sandy bottom of

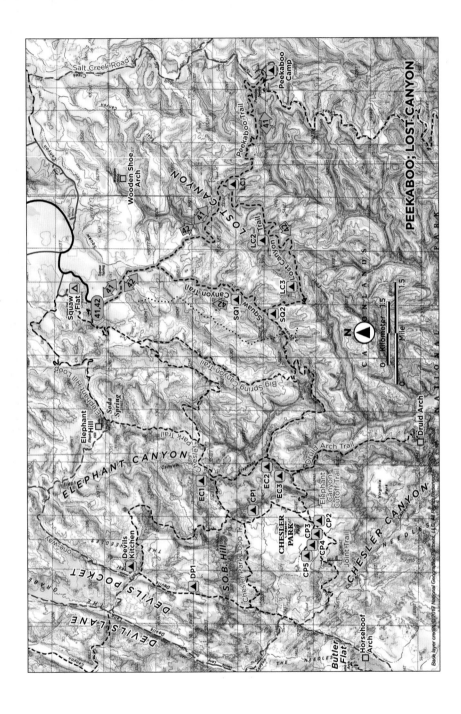

Rock art in Canyonlands
NPS/NEAL HERBERT

the canyon for the last half mile or so to the junction with the Lost Canyon Trail. If you're staying overnight, Backcountry Campsite LC1 is less than a quarter mile up the Lost Canyon Trail on your right (south).

The Lost Canyon Trail junction is in the dry wash of Lost Canyon. Go straight (east) across the wash instead of turning right (southwest) up Lost Canyon. Immediately after this junction you quickly gain about 300 feet in elevation. This part of the hike is a bit rugged but very scenic. In spring the newly emerging leaves of the deciduous trees (oaks, cottonwoods, and willows) contrast nicely with the red and white sandstone formations in this area. Also, you're up on a ridgeline, so you have great vistas in all directions. Near the end of the trail, you go right through a small arch; several other small arches are visible. Don't get too distracted by the scenery, though. You have to follow cairns most of the rest of the way to Peekaboo Camp.

Just before the end of the trail, you lose the elevation you gained coming out of Lost Canyon. It's steeper at the east end, and one spot could be dangerous if you aren't cautious. Fortunately, the NPS has installed a safety ladder to help you through this spot. After this steep section it's about a quarter mile on a well-defined, flat trail along the streambed of Salt Creek to Peekaboo Camp, which is nicely located under some stately old cottonwoods. After relaxing here for a while or staying overnight, retrace your steps to Squaw Flat Trailhead. While walking along Salt Creek, be careful not to miss the trail when it takes a sharp left up a crack in the rock to reach the ladder you climbed down on your way to Peekaboo Camp.

## MILES AND DIRECTIONS

- **0.0**  Start at the Squaw Flat Trailhead.
- **0.1**  Junction with Big Spring  Canyon Trail; turn left.
- **1.1**  Junction with Peekaboo Trail; turn left.
- **2.6**  Junction with Lost Canyon Trail; go straight.
- **5.0**  Peekaboo Camp. Retrace your steps to the trailhead
- **10.0** Arrive back at the Squaw Flat Trailhead.

*Option:* For a 5-mile shuttle hike, park a second car or arrange to be picked up at the Peekaboo Camp at the end of Salt Creek Road. To find Salt Creek Road, drive 0.9 mile west from the entrance station and take a left (south) onto a well-signed, paved road (marked Salt Creek) and go 0.5 mile before taking a left (east) onto an unpaved road. After 0.5 mile on the unpaved road, turn right (south) instead of going straight to the Cave Spring Trailhead. Drive 0.5 mile more until you see a locked gate across the road. This gate marks the official trailhead for Salt Creek and Horse Canyon Roads. Leave the vehicle in the parking area near Peekaboo Camp, but not in the campsites. When you get your permit, the staff at the visitor center will tell you the combination to the Salt Creek gate and whether it's scheduled to change while you're out hiking. **GPS coordinates (Salt Creek):** 38° 6' 52.931" N / 109° 45' 15.999" W. You need a high-clearance, four-wheel-drive vehicle with low-range gearing to get from here to Peekaboo Camp. Drive 2.7 miles to Horse Canyon Road; take a right and drive 1 mile more to the camp.

# 42. **LOST CANYON**

## WHY GO?

A spectacular loop hike through some of the best scenery in the Needles District

### THE RUNDOWN

**See map on page 148.**

**Start:** Squaw Flat Trailhead

**Distance:** 8.6 miles; lollipop loop

**Difficulty:** Moderate

**Nat Geo Trails Illustrated Map:** Needles

**Nat Geo TOPO! Map (USGS):** The Loop and Druid Arch

### FINDING THE TRAILHEAD

Drive about 2.7 miles west from the Needles entrance station and turn left into Squaw Flat Campground. After entering the campground area, the road forks. Both forks go to trailheads with access to the same trails. However, the left-hand fork takes you to the trailhead with the shortest access route to the backcountry. The right-hand fork and its respective trailhead are used mostly by campers staying in the campground.

**GPS coordinates:** 38° 8' 36.487" N / 109° 48' 13.115" W

## WHAT TO SEE

Lost Canyon is well named. It's not only the kind of place you could get lost in, it's so beautiful that it's also the kind of place you want to get lost in.

Like other loops, Lost Canyon can be done in either direction. This trail description follows the clockwise route.

The first 1.1 miles of the trail are flat and easy, with several slickrock sections. The slickrock isn't dangerous, but don't miss the sometimes small cairns that mark the correct route. The sandstone formations on the horizon along this section are marvelous. After the first 1.1 miles of easy hiking, you reach the junction with the Peekaboo Trail. Take a left (east) and head toward Lost Canyon and Peekaboo Spring.

The next 1.5-mile section is mostly slickrock. Just after climbing down a small ladder, you follow the north rim of a beautiful, narrow canyon for a short way before dropping into the canyon on a sandy trail for the last half mile to the junction with the Lost Canyon Trail, which lies in the dry wash of Lost Canyon. Take a right (southwest) here and start hiking up Lost Canyon.

Enjoying the sunrise deep
in the Needles District
NPS/NEAL HERBERT

In spring a healthy stream often flows through this lush canyon. If you're lucky enough to hike this after a rain, you might actually get your feet wet, because the trail frequently crosses the streambed. But please don't wade in the water any more than necessary to cross the stream.

Lost Canyon starts out broad and flat but gets narrow in places later on. The vegetation is more diverse than in most other canyons in the area (to the point of getting brushy in a few spots), and there are no slickrock sections. The multihued vegetation contrasts beautifully with the reddish sandstone to create some fantastic scenery.

If you plan to stay overnight, Lost Canyon has three designated campsites. The first is on your right (south) just a few yards down the trail. The second one is about a mile up the trail on your right. The third is on your right just as you start up a drainage back toward Squaw Canyon.

After hiking through Lost Canyon for 2 miles, start watching carefully for a sharp turn to the right. There is a sign (pointing to Lost Canyon Trail), but if you're pre-occupied with the scenery, you might miss it. An off-trail route continues up Lost Canyon, but at this point the official trail leaves Lost Canyon and dips into a narrow, unnamed canyon that runs north to south. If you have extra time, you can take note of this spot and then explore the upper reaches of Lost Canyon before heading back to this junction and the trailhead.

This slender, unnamed tributary is like a miniature Lost Canyon—smaller but perhaps even more stunning. After following the dry wash of the narrow gorge for about a half mile, the trail climbs a steep chute (partly on an NPS-installed ladder) to a slickrock ledge. After cautiously hiking the ledge, you climb over a ridge. You then follow a string of cairns over slickrock for another half mile or so until you drop into Squaw Canyon. This section can be hazardous, so be careful, especially if you have children along. A trail junction appears just after you cross the dry wash of Squaw Canyon. Turn right at this junction.

If you didn't make your overnight stay in Lost Canyon, you have two more choices in Squaw Canyon. One site is on your left just before the junction with the Squaw Canyon Trail, and the second is on your left less than 1 mile down the trail.

After hiking down Squaw Canyon for 1.7 miles, you hit the Peekaboo Trail again, where you turn left and retrace your steps 1.1 miles back to the Squaw Flat Trailhead.

## MILES AND DIRECTIONS

**0.0** Start at the Squaw Flat Trailhead.

**0.1** Junction with Squaw Canyon Trail; turn left.

**1.1** Junction with Peekaboo Trail; turn left.

**2.6** Junction with Lost Canyon Trail; turn right.

**2.7** Backcountry Campsite LC1.

**3.8** Backcountry Campsite LC2.

**5.1** Backcountry Campsite LC3.

**5.3** Sharp right (north) turn on Lost Canyon Trail.

**5.6** Backcountry Campsite SQ2.

**5.8** Junction with Squaw Canyon Trail; turn right.

**6.7** Backcountry Campsite SQ1.

**7.5** Junction with Peekaboo Trail; turn left.

**8.6** Arrive back at the Squaw Flat Trailhead.

# 43. LOST CANYON / ELEPHANT CANYON

## WHY GO?
A long loop hike nicely suited for backpackers

### THE RUNDOWN

**Start:** Squaw Flat Trailhead

**Distance:** 13.6 miles; loop

**Difficulty:** Moderate as a backpack; difficult as a day hike

**Maps:** Trails Illustrated Needles and USGS The Loop and Druid Arch

### FINDING THE TRAILHEAD
Drive about 2.7 miles west from the Needles entrance station and turn left into Squaw Flat Campground. After entering the campground area, the road forks. Both forks go to trailheads with access to the same trails. However, the left-hand fork takes you to the trailhead with the shortest access route to the backcountry. The right-hand fork and its respective trailhead are used mostly by campers staying in the campground. **GPS coordinates:** 38° 8' 36.487" N / 109° 48' 13.115" W

## WHAT TO SEE
If you can afford the time to make this a three-day trip, you'll have the opportunity to see most of the outstanding features of the Needles area. A three-day option provides the time for side trips to Peekaboo, Upper Lost Canyon, and Druid Arch without your overnight pack.

This trail description follows the clockwise direction. The route can, however, be hiked quite pleasantly in either direction. In either case be sure to take plenty of water and flashlights just in case you get caught out at night.

The first 1.1 miles follow a flat and easy stretch of trail with several slickrock sections. Be alert not to miss the sometimes small cairns marking the correct route over the slickrock.

After the first 1.1 miles of easy hiking, you reach the junction with the Peekaboo Trail. Take a left (east) and head toward Lost Canyon and Peekaboo Spring.

Little lizards dart everywhere along Canyon Country trails.

Most of the next 1.5-mile section is on slickrock. After climbing down a small ladder, the trail follows the north rim of a beautiful, narrow canyon for a short way before dropping into the canyon on a sandy trail for the last half mile to the junction with the Lost Canyon Trail. Take a right (southwest) here and start hiking up Lost Canyon. In spring a healthy stream often flows through this lush canyon.

Lost Canyon starts out broad and flat but gets narrow in places later on. It has more diverse vegetative growth than most canyons in the area. In a few spots it actually gets brushy. The multihued vegetation of Lost Canyon contrasts beautifully with the reddish sandstone to create some fantastic scenery.

If you're spending two nights out, you might want to camp at Backcountry Campsite LC1 or LC2 for your first night out. If you pick LC1 (on your right just past the Lost Canyon junction at the 2.7-mile mark), you can set up camp and then conveniently hike over to Peekaboo Spring and return to camp. You can also continue on to stay at LC2 (3.8-mile mark) or LC3 (5.1-mile mark). If you choose LC3, you are conveniently located to spend your extra time exploring the upper reaches of Lost Canyon and then returning to camp.

After hiking through Lost Canyon for 2 miles, start watching carefully for an

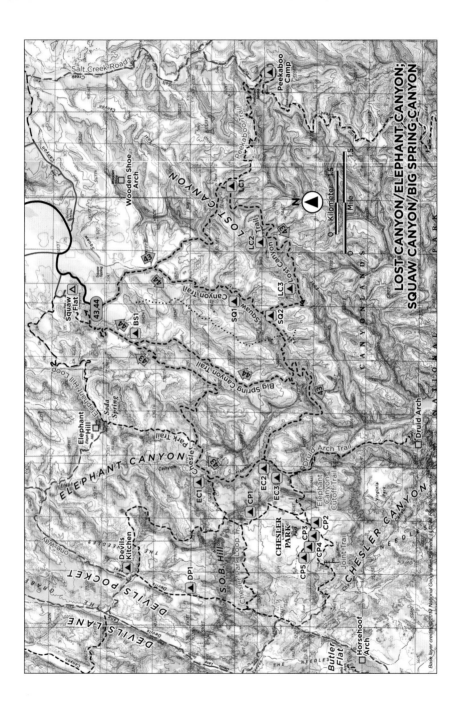

abrupt right-hand turn in the trail. There is a sign (pointing to Lost Canyon Trail), but if you're absorbed in the scenery, you might miss it. An off-trail route continues up Lost Canyon, but at this point the official trail leaves Lost Canyon and dips into a narrow, unnamed canyon that runs north to south. This small tributary is like a miniature Lost Canyon—smaller, but perhaps even more beautiful.

After following the dry wash of the narrow gorge for about a half mile, the trail climbs a steep chute to a slickrock ledge. After cautiously hiking the ledge, you climb over the ridge and then follow a trail of cairns over slickrock for another half mile or so until you drop into Squaw Canyon. This section can be hazardous, so be careful. The next trail junction is just after you cross the dry wash of Squaw Canyon.

Just before you reach the Squaw Canyon Trail, watch for Backcountry Campsite SQ2 on your left (5.6-mile mark). If you're only taking two days for this trip, this is probably your best choice for your overnight stay. However, staying out only one night results in two tough days and limits free time for side trips.

At the Squaw Canyon Trail junction, take a left and head southwest up Squaw Canyon. The trail quickly angles off to the right out of the canyon bottom onto slickrock. It stays on slickrock for most of the next 0.9-mile section to the junction with the Big Spring Canyon Trail. Take another left at this junction, continuing southwesterly, again mostly on slickrock, for 2.1 miles to the Druid Arch Trail. This is an especially scenic section of this route, and in one spot you climb over a slickrock pass with the help of a ladder on each side of a joint in the rocks.

Look for the sign at the end of this section of trail in the dry wash of Upper Elephant Canyon. If you're staying two nights, you probably want to spend the second night at Backcountry Campsite EC2 (on your right just south of the Druid Arch Trail at the 9.1-mile mark) or EC3 (on your right just down from EC2 on the Druid Arch Trail). Either campsite positions you nicely for a side trip that night or the next morning up to awesome Druid Arch.

When heading north down Upper Elephant Canyon, the trail follows the dry wash all the way. In a few places you might not be able to see the trail, but don't fret. It stays right in the canyon bottom until you reach the Chesler Park Trail junction, and you can see strategically located cairns in most cases. Turn right (east) at this junction.

From here the trail climbs out of Elephant Canyon. In 0.6 mile you see another junction with the left fork heading off to the Elephant Hill Trailhead. Unless you have arranged to leave a vehicle there (which would trim 2 miles off the hike), go to the right toward Squaw Flat.

The last 3.4 miles back to Squaw Flat alternate between flat sections with well-defined, sandy trails and small climbs over slickrock outcrops. At the 12.7-mile mark, you'll see the trail up Big Spring Canyon and Backcountry Campsite BS1 on your right and then, near the end of the trail, the junction with the spur trail to the campground.

## MILES AND DIRECTIONS

0.0  Start at the Squaw Flat Trailhead.

0.1  Junction with Squaw Canyon Trail; turn left.

1.1  Junction with Peekaboo Trail; turn left.

2.6  Junction with Lost Canyon Trail; turn right.

2.7  Backcountry Campsite LC1.

3.8  Backcountry Campsite LC2.

5.1  Backcountry Campsite LC3.

5.3  Sharp right (north) turn on Lost Canyon Trail.

5.6  Backcountry Campsite SQ2.

5.8  Junction with Squaw Canyon Trail; turn left.

6.7  Junction with Big Spring Canyon Trail; turn left.

8.8  Junction with Druid Arch Trail; turn right.

9.1  Backcountry Campsite EC2.

9.6  Junction with Chesler Park Trail; turn right.

10.2  Junction with the trail to Elephant Hill Trailhead; turn right.

12.7  Junction with Big Spring Canyon Trail; turn left.

13.1  Junction with the Loop B trail; turn right.

13.6  Arrive back at the Squaw Flat Trailhead.

# 44. SQUAW CANYON/BIG SPRING CANYON

## WHY GO?

A moderate day hike or easy overnighter capturing the essence of the Needles District

---

**THE RUNDOWN**

**See map on page 156.**

**Start:** Squaw Flat Trailhead

**Distance:** 7.1 miles; loop

**Difficulty:** Moderate

**Nat Geo Trails Illustrated Map:**
Needles

**Nat Geo TOPO! Map (USGS):**
The Loop and Druid Arch

---

## FINDING THE TRAILHEAD

 Drive about 2.7 miles west from the Needles entrance station and turn left into Squaw Flat Campground. After entering the campground area, the road forks. Both forks go to trailheads with access to the same trails. However, the left-hand fork takes you to the trailhead with the shortest access route to the backcountry. The right-hand fork and its respective trailhead are used mostly by campers staying in the campground. **GPS coordinates:** 38° 8' 36.487" N/109° 48' 13.115" W

## WHAT TO SEE

This might be the nicest, most accessible loop trail in Canyonlands National Park. It's ideal for a moderate day hike to catch the essence of the Needles landscape, and because the NPS designated four backcountry campsites along this loop trail, it can also be an easy overnighter.

Immediately after leaving the trailhead, you hit the junction between Squaw Canyon and Big Spring Canyon Trails. You can take the loop either way; one way isn't noticeably more difficult than the other. This description takes the clockwise route because it makes two confusing spots in the trail easier to follow, so turn left (southeast) at this junction.

The next mile goes through fairly flat and open country (Squaw Flats) with scattered sections of slickrock. The slickrock sections aren't steep, but stay alert and follow small cairns showing the correct route.

Mule deer
NPS/KAIT THOMAS

When you reach the junction with the Peekaboo Trail, take a right (south) and head up Squaw Canyon. This leg of the loop trail follows Squaw Canyon, which often has a flowing stream in spring. Watch for Backcountry Campsite SQ1 on your right about a mile after the junction. If you've been lucky enough to time your hike while the stream has water in it, you'll probably be treated to a chorus of spadefoot toad music. Please do not wade in the water.

The canyon narrows in places just before you hit the junction with the Lost Canyon Trail at the 2.8-mile mark. If you cross the wash, Backcountry Campsite SQ2 is down the trail about 100 yards on your right. After this junction get prepared for walking over slickrock. After a short section of well-defined, sandy trail along the streambed, the trail climbs up on the north rim of the canyon and stays on slickrock all the way to the junction with the Big Spring Canyon Trail. This is a very scenic section and a good place to have lunch if you're on a day hike.

At the junction with the Big Spring Canyon Trail, go straight and follow a string of cairns as you climb up a short but steep section to the top of a slickrock pass, where you get a great view of the surrounding landscape.

After soaking in the scenery, climb back down to the bottom of Big Spring Canyon. Even though the NPS has expertly plotted the easiest route over this slickrock pass, this section can be hazardous, especially when it's wet or you're with children, so be careful.

After you get down into beautiful Big Spring Canyon, you might see some water flowing, especially in spring. The canyon is narrow at this end but soon widens and stays that way until you get to the junction with the Chesler Park Trail. Backcountry Campsite BS2 is on your left about 1.5 miles down the canyon. BS1 is right at the junction with the Chesler Park Trail.

At this junction keep going straight (north) and head toward Squaw Flat Trailhead. Here the trail leaves Big Spring Canyon and heads across Squaw Flat. Just before you get to the trailhead, you'll see a trail going off to the left marked Campground B. If you're staying at the B Loop of the campground, take a left, but if you started at the main trailhead, take a right. From this junction it's only about a half mile to the trailhead. The NPS has nicely routed the trail through some large boulders that in one spot look almost like a tunnel.

## MILES AND DIRECTIONS

0.0   Start at the Squaw Flat Trailhead.

0.1   Junction with Squaw Canyon Trail; turn left.

1.1   Junction with Peekaboo Trail; turn right.

2.0   Backcountry Campsite SQ1.

2.8   Junction with Lost Canyon Trail; turn right.

3.7   Junction with Big Spring Canyon Trail; turn right.

5.3   Backcountry Campsite BS2.

6.2   Junction with Chesler Park Trail; turn right.

6.3   Backcountry Campsite BS1.

6.6   Junction with Loop B trail; turn right.

7.1   Arrive back at the Squaw Flat Trailhead.

# 45. BIG SPRING CANYON / ELEPHANT CANYON

## WHY GO?
A long day hike and a good choice for an overnighter

### THE RUNDOWN

**Start:** Squaw Flat Trailhead

**Distance:** 10.4 miles; lollipop loop

**Difficulty:** Difficult

**Nat Geo Trails Illustrated Map:** Needles

**Nat Geo TOPO! Map (USGS):** The Loop and Druid Arch

## FINDING THE TRAILHEAD

Drive about 2.7 miles west from the Needles entrance station and turn left into Squaw Flat Campground. After entering the campground area, the road forks. Both forks go to trailheads with access to the same trails. However, the left-hand fork takes you to the trailhead with the shortest access route to the backcountry. The right-hand fork and its respective trailhead are used mostly by campers staying in the campground.

**GPS coordinates:** 38° 8' 36.487" N / 109° 48' 13.115" W

## WHAT TO SEE

If you aren't in good physical condition, this hike might be too much for a day hike, but you have the option of making it an overnighter by staying at one of several backcountry campsites along the way. You can follow the loop in either direction, but this description follows the clockwise route.

You immediately hit the junction of Squaw Canyon and Big Spring Canyon after leaving the trailhead. Take a right (south) and head toward Big Spring Canyon, going through some large boulders just after the junction. Most of the first mile goes through flat, open country with many interesting sandstone features highlighting the horizon.

Then you drop down into Big Spring Canyon, go by Backcountry Campsite BS1 on your left, and then see a junction with the trail up the canyon. If you're following the clockwise route, go straight (south) and head up this gorgeous desert canyon. In spring the stream is often flowing. The first part of Big Spring Canyon is wide open

Big Spring Canyon in the Needles
NPS/NEAL HERBERT

(watch for Backcountry Campsite BS2 1.2 miles after this junction), but the canyon narrows in the upper reaches.

At about the 3-mile mark, the trail abruptly leaves the canyon and angles off at about 30 degrees to the left, climbing up a slickrock pass along a string of cairns. Be alert so you don't miss this spot and continue up the canyon instead.

From here the trail makes a healthy climb for about a quarter mile to the top of the pass, where you get a great vista of the surrounding country. Then the trail drops sharply down to the junction with the Elephant Canyon Spur Trail and Squaw Canyon Trail. You can see the sign from the top of the pass. The NPS has expertly plotted the climb over the ridge, but it can be hazardous, so use caution.

At this junction turn right and head southwest on slickrock for most of the 2.1 miles to the Druid Arch Trail. This is an especially scenic section of trail, and in one spot you climb over a pass with the help of a ladder on each side of a joint in the rocks.

A sign marking the end of this section of trail is in the dry wash of Upper Elephant Canyon. If you're ambitious and in good shape and have enough daylight, you can take a left (south) and head up to Druid Arch for a scenic side trip. However, if you're following the loop trail, take a right (north) where the trail closely follows the dry wash. In a few places you might not be able to see the trail, but it stays right in the canyon bottom until you reach the Chesler Park Trail junction. Turn right

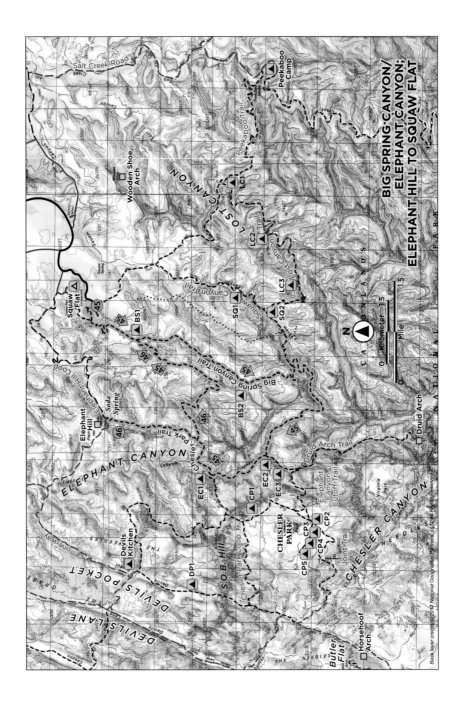

(east) at this junction. Shortly thereafter the trail climbs out of Elephant Canyon. In 0.6 mile you see another junction. The left fork goes to the Elephant Hill Trailhead. Unless you have arranged to leave a vehicle there (trimming 2 miles off the hike), go to the right toward Squaw Flat.

The last 3.4 miles back to Squaw Flat alternate between flat sections with well-defined, sandy trails and small climbs over slickrock outcrops. At the 9.5-mile mark, you'll see the trail up Big Spring Canyon that you took earlier in the trip and, shortly after that, Backcountry Campsite BS1 on your right. Then, near the end of the trail, you'll cross the scenic boulder field you walked through at the start of your hike and return on the spur trail to the campground.

## MILES AND DIRECTIONS

0.0   Start at the Squaw Flat Trailhead.

0.1   Junction with Squaw Canyon Trail; turn right.

0.6   Junction with the campground's Loop B trail; turn left

1.0   Junction with Big Spring Canyon Trail; turn left.

2.2   Backcountry Campsite BS2.

3.5   Junction with Elephant Canyon Spur Trail; turn right.

5.6   Junction with Druid Arch Trail; turn right.

6.0   Backcountry Campsite EC2.

6.4   Junction with Chesler Park Trail; turn right.

7.0   Junction with trail to Elephant Hill Trailhead; turn right.

9.5   Junction with Big Spring Canyon Trail; turn left.

9.6   Backcountry Campsite BS1.

9.9   Junction with Loop B trail; turn right.

10.4  Arrive back at the Squaw Flat Trailhead.

# 46. ELEPHANT HILL TO SQUAW FLAT

## WHY GO?

A shuttle hike through some of the best scenery in the Needles District

### THE RUNDOWN

**See map on page 164.**

**Start:** Elephant Hill Trailhead or Squaw Flat Trailhead

**Distance:** 4.9 miles; shuttle

**Difficulty:** Moderate

**Nat Geo Trails Illustrated Map:** Needles

**Nat Geo TOPO! Map (USGS):** The Loop and Druid Arch

### FINDING THE TRAILHEAD

To find the Elephant Hill Trailhead, drive 3.1 miles from the entrance station on the main park road until you see a paved road going off to the left to Squaw Flat Campground and Elephant Hill. Take this left and 0.3 mile later take a right onto another paved road. Then take another right 0.5 mile later onto the unpaved, two-wheel-drive Elephant Hill Access Road. Once on the unpaved road, it's 3 miles to the trailhead. Drive slowly on this road, especially around several blind corners. **GPS coordinates:** 38° 8' 30.272" N / 109° 49' 37.209" W

To leave a second car or be picked up at the Squaw Flat Trailhead, drive about 2.7 miles west from the Needles entrance station and turn left into Squaw Flat Campground. After entering the campground area, the road forks. Both forks go to trailheads with access to the same trails. However, the left-hand fork takes you to the trailhead with the shortest access route to the backcountry. The right-hand fork and its respective trailhead are used mostly by campers staying in the campground. **GPS coordinates:** 38° 8' 36.487" N / 109° 48' 13.115" W

## WHAT TO SEE

If your party has two vehicles, or you're staying at the Squaw Flat Campground and one member of your party volunteers to drop you off at Elephant Hill Trailhead, this is a great day hike. Although the Needles District has a great variety of quality hiking opportunities, there aren't many hikes in the moderate, 5-mile range, so if that distance suits you, this trail is an excellent choice. You can do the shuttle in reverse, but this description starts at Elephant Hill Trailhead.

Rock art in Canyonlands
NPS/NEAL HERBERT

Right after leaving Elephant Hill Trailhead, the trail climbs a steep but short hill and then goes through a small joint between two rock formations. Then the trail heads over a fairly flat stretch of slickrock with a good view of Big Spring Canyon off to the east and the Needles to the south.

At the 1.5-mile mark, you reach a junction with the Chesler Park Trail going to the right. Go left (east) and head toward Big Spring Canyon. This stretch of trail is pleasant walking as it alternates between a well-defined, packed-dirt trail and short slickrock sections. At the 4-mile mark, you'll see the Big Spring Canyon Trail coming in from the right and Backcountry Campsite BS1 straight ahead. If you want an easy backpacking trip, you could try to reserve this campsite and spend the night in the desert before covering the last mile or so back to Squaw Flat Trailhead or Campground. If you're heading for the campground, you can take a cutoff trail going off to the left just before you reach the trailhead.

## MILES AND DIRECTIONS

**0.0**  Start at the Elephant Hill Trailhead.

**1.5**  Junction with trail to Squaw Flat Trailhead; turn left.

**4.0**  Junction with Big Spring Canyon Trail; turn left.

**4.4**  Junction with the campground's Loop B trail; turn right.

**4.9**  Arrive at the Squaw Flat Trailhead.

# 47. DRUID ARCH

## WHY GO?

A scenic route to a spectacular arch

> **THE RUNDOWN**
>
> **Start:** Elephant Hill Trailhead
>
> **Distance:** 10.8 miles; out and back
>
> **Difficulty:** Difficult
>
> **Nat Geo Trails Illustrated Map:** Needles
>
> **Nat Geo TOPO! Map (USGS):** The Loop and Druid Arch

### FINDING THE TRAILHEAD

Drive 3.1 miles from the entrance station on the main park road until you see a paved road going off to the left to Squaw Flat Campground and Elephant Hill. Take this left and 0.3 mile later take a right onto another paved road. Then take another right 0.5 mile later onto the unpaved, two-wheel-drive Elephant Hill Access Road. Once on the unpaved road, it's 3 miles to the trailhead. Drive slowly on this road, especially around several blind corners.

**GPS coordinates:** 38° 8' 30.272" N / 109° 49' 37.209" W

## WHAT TO SEE

Druid Arch is one of the most popular destinations in the Needles District. In addition to seeing a spectacular arch, hikers can experience much of the special environment of the Needles area along the way. You can reach Druid Arch from several routes, but the most commonly used route is the out-and-back route from Elephant Hill Trailhead.

Shortly after leaving the trailhead, you pass through a joint between two rock formations and then go over a stretch of slickrock before reaching the first junction at the 1.5-mile mark. The left fork goes to Squaw Flat Campground. You go right (west) on the trail to Chesler Park.

In the next short (0.6-mile) stretch of trail, you pass over the small divide between Big Spring Canyon and Elephant Canyon. The trail goes through a gorgeous narrow where you get a good view in both directions of these two canyons. Then the trail drops into the dry wash of Elephant Canyon, where you see the signs for Backcountry Campsite EC1 to the right (north) and Druid Arch to the left (south).

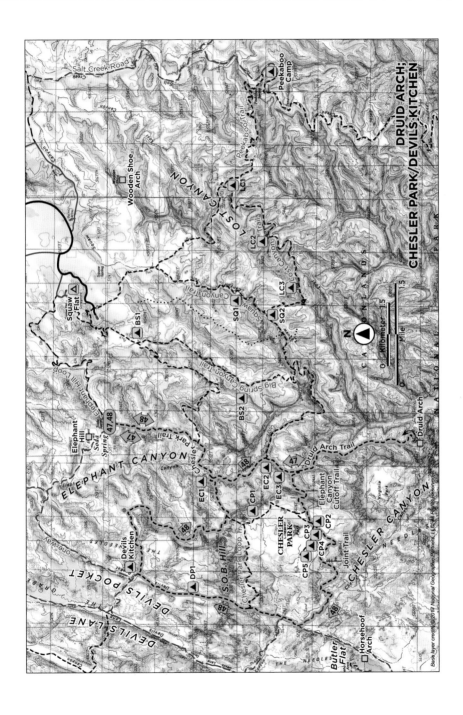

DRUID ARCH; CHESLER PARK/DEVILS KITCHEN

Druid Arch in the Needles
NPS/NEAL HERBERT

Most hikers staying overnight choose EC2 or EC3 for their night out, but EC1 is also a great campsite located on a bench on the west side of the Elephant Canyon dry wash.

From this junction the trail stays in the Elephant Canyon dry wash. You'll see the trail to Squaw Canyon going off to the left (east), between Backcountry Campsites EC2 and EC3. Keep going straight (south) up the canyon wash. Most of the last 2 miles of the trail to Druid Arch continues to stay in the dry wash of Elephant Canyon, sometimes leaving the canyon briefly on the left flank before dropping back into the dry wash again. Then, about a half mile from Druid Arch, the trail starts climbing steeply up to a bench just below the well-named arch, a delightful place to spend an hour or two before retracing your steps to Elephant Hill Trailhead or your backcountry campsite.

## MILES AND DIRECTIONS

**0.0** Start at the Elephant Hill Trailhead.

**1.5** Junction with trail to Squaw Flat Campground; turn right.

**2.1** Junction with Druid Arch Trail; turn left.

**2.2** Backcountry Campsite EC1. Turn left (south) into Elephant Canyon.

**2.7** Backcountry Campsite EC2.

**2.9** Junction with trail to Squaw Canyon; turn right.

**3.1** Backcountry Campsite EC3.

**3.4** Junction with trail to Chesler Park; turn left.

**5.4** Druid Arch. Turn around to retrace your steps back to the trailhead.

**10.8** Arrive back at the Elephant Hill Trailhead.

Juniper shrubs line the way to Druid Arch.
ISTOCKPHOTO.COM

# 48. **CHESLER PARK/ DEVILS KITCHEN**

## WHY GO?

A long day hike or backpacking trip with lots of options for camping and side trips

### THE RUNDOWN

**See map on page 169.**

**Start:** Elephant Hill Trailhead

**Distance:** 13.9 miles; lollipop loop

**Difficulty:** Difficult

**Nat Geo Trails Illustrated Map:** Needles

**Nat Geo TOPO! Map (USGS):** The Loop and Druid Arch

## FINDING THE TRAILHEAD

Drive 3.1 miles from the entrance station on the main park road until you see a paved road going off to the left to Squaw Flat Campground and Elephant Hill. Take this left and 0.3 mile later take a right onto another paved road. Then take another right 0.5 mile later onto the unpaved, two-wheel-drive Elephant Hill Access Road. Once on the unpaved road, it's 3 miles to the trailhead. Drive slowly on this road, especially around several blind corners.
**GPS coordinates:** 38° 8′ 30.272″ N/109° 49′ 37.209″ W

## WHAT TO SEE

This route is a good example of how you can craft a great loop hike out of the Needles Trails complex. The trip can vary in number of nights out, can be taken clockwise or counterclockwise, and can start and finish at any of three different trailheads: Elephant Hill, Chesler Park, or Devils Kitchen. This description takes the clockwise route from the Elephant Hill Trailhead, mainly because you can reach this trailhead with any vehicle. You definitely need a high-clearance, four-wheel-drive vehicle and be experienced driving it on rough roads to access Chesler Park and Devils Kitchen Trailheads.

This long lollipop loop goes through myriad trail junctions, so keep your map out at all times and keep your bearings lest you get on the wrong trail, which is fairly easy to do with all the junctions and trails and canyons that resemble each other.

This description covers the two-night option, but you can also do it in one night out or extend it to three. Here is a summary of options:

| LENGTH OF TRIP | BACKCOUNTRY CAMPSITE | MILES PER DAY | SIDE TRIP |
|---|---|---|---|
| One night | 1—DP1 | 1—8.4 miles<br>2—5.5 miles | Chesler Park Overlook |
| Two nights | 1—CP2, 3, 4, or 5<br>2—DP1 | 1—4.5 miles<br>2—3.9 miles<br>3—5.5 miles | Druid Arch<br>Chesler Park Overlook |
| Three nights | 1—CP2, 3, 4, or 5<br>2—same camp<br>3—DP1 | 1—4.5 miles<br>2—none<br>3—3.9 miles<br>4—5.5 miles | Big Spring Canyon<br>Druid Arch<br>Chesler Park Overlook |

**Note:** Be sure to get a map from the NPS showing exact locations of backcountry campsites.

Leaving Elephant Hill Trailhead, the trail starts out ominously, climbing a short but steep hill and then passing through a small joint between two rock formations. Then the trail levels out for a pleasant half-mile walk on slickrock, with expansive Big Spring Canyon off to the east and a good view of the Needles to the south.

At the first junction (at the 1.5-mile mark), take a right (west) and continue toward Chesler Park. The left trail goes to Squaw Flat Campground. About a quarter mile down the trail, you climb through a notch in the sandstone spires, which is the divide between Big Spring Canyon and Elephant Canyon. Take a few minutes to enjoy the view in both directions from the divide. About a quarter mile later, you reach the next junction in the dry wash of Elephant Canyon. Take the sharp left (south) onto the Druid Arch Trail, which goes directly up the dry wash. If you planned extra nights out and had a late start, you could stay at Backcountry Campsite EC1, which is just off to the right about a quarter mile north on a scenic bench on the west rim of the dry wash.

Just past the junction with the trail going to the left (east) to Squaw Canyon, you'll see EC2 off to the right, another possible campsite for hikers who started late or want to have time to do the Druid Arch side trip on the first day out. Same goes for EC3, which is 0.2 mile past the junction with the trail to Squaw Canyon, another great side trip for hikers staying at EC2 or EC3.

At the 3.4-mile mark, you reach the side trail going up to Chesler Park. If you're camping in Chesler Park (an excellent choice for the second night out) and have plenty of time, you could stash your pack here and spend a couple of hours hiking to Druid Arch.

**Chesler Park**
NPS/NEAL HERBERT

To reach Chesler Park, take a right (west) at the Druid Arch Trail junction and go 1 mile to the junction with the Joint Trail on the southeast corner of Chesler Park. If you're spending the night at Chesler Park (and you would be fortunate to have the opportunity), about 100 feet down the trail you first see the turn to the right to Backcountry Campsites CP3, CP4, and CP5. If you have a permit for CP2, it's another 50 feet down the trail on your left. All these campsites could be described as luxury suites in a five-star hotel. They're nestled among the huge sandstone boulders and spires surrounding Chesler Park, providing shade when needed and a great view out into the park. If you want to extend your trip from two nights to three nights, you might want to stay here two nights and spend the extra day taking short side trips from camp.

When you leave your camp in Chesler Park, head west on the Joint Trail for another 0.7 mile until you see a sign pointing to a side trail going left to the Chesler

Park Overlook. Although you've already seen Chesler Park, you get an especially grand view from this official overlook. You would be wise to drop your pack and hike the short trail to the viewpoint.

After you get your pack back on, you immediately drop down into the famed Joint, a long section of trail that follows a long crack in the sandstone. In places it's a tight fit getting through with a big backpack, but on a hot day it's a welcome relief from the desert sun.

After about a quarter mile in the Joint, you finally break out into the sunlight again. From here it's about a half mile on a fairly rocky trail to the Chesler Park Trailhead, where you find a vault toilet and picnic tables.

From here you have to take a short hike on a backcountry road. Walk down the road for 0.5 mile, where you see the road to Beef Basin heading off to the left (south). Go right for another 0.3 mile until you see the Devils Pocket Trail veering off to the right. There is no sign on the side of the road here. Instead it's about 30 feet down the trail, so be sure not to miss the turn and keep walking down the road.

This trail starts out through a flat, brushy meadow. After 0.8 mile you'll see the Chesler Park Loop Trail going off to the right (east). Take a left here and make a fairly serious climb through a pass in the enormous Pinnacle Formation. After the pass the trail drops into another dry, brush-covered flat called Devils Pocket.

Shortly thereafter you see the short side trail to Backcountry Campsite DP1 going off to the right. The campsite is about a quarter mile from the trail amid some large boulders and piñon pine trees. This is your best choice for your second (or third) night out, leaving a moderate 5.5 miles for the third or fourth and last day of your hike.

From DP1 it's only about a half mile to Devils Kitchen Camp, where you can find a vault toilet and picnic tables and four vehicle campsites. The Devils Pocket Trail ends right at the road in Devils Kitchen and then heads out the east side of the vehicle camp. There are several unofficial trails that have been made by visitors leaving this popular campground, so make sure you're on the right trail. Watch for the cairn-lined trail heading east near the vault toilet on the east end of the campsites. If there's any question in your mind, check the topo map and compass to make sure you don't have to backtrack to find the official trail.

After hiking 2.3 miles from Devils Kitchen, turn left (east) onto the trail to Elephant Hill Trailhead. On this short (0.6-mile) section of trail, you get some fantastic views of the Pinnacle and the Needles before dropping into the dry wash of Elephant Canyon. From here take a short trail north down the canyon to Backcountry Campsite EC1, if you've decided to camp there.

If you're heading back to your vehicle, go across the dry wash on another 0.6-mile section of trail to the junction with the Squaw Flat Trail, where you take a left (north) and go the final 1.5 miles back to Elephant Hill Trailhead.

## MILES AND DIRECTIONS

**0.0**   Start at the Elephant Hill Trailhead.

**1.5**   Junction with Squaw Flat Trail; turn right.

**2.1**   Junction with Druid Arch Trail; turn left.

**2.2**   Backcountry Campsite EC1.

**2.7**   Backcountry Campsite EC2.

**2.9**   Junction with trail to Big Spring and Squaw Canyons; turn left.

**3.1**   Backcountry Campsite EC3.

**3.4**   Junction with side trail to Druid Arch; turn right.

**4.4**   Junction with Joint Trail; turn left.

**4.5**   Backcountry Campsites CP2, CP3, CP4, and CP5.

**5.1**   Side trail to Chesler Park Overlook and start of the Joint; turn left.

**5.9**   Chesler Park Trailhead.

**6.4**   Road to Beef Basin.

**6.7**   Devils Pocket Trailhead.

**7.5**   Chesler Park Loop Trail; turn left.

**8.4**   Backcountry Campsite DP1.

**8.9**   Devils Kitchen Camp and Trailhead.

**11.2**   Junction with trail to Elephant Hill Trailhead; turn left.

**11.8**   Junction with Druid Arch Trail and spur trail to Backcountry Campsite EC2; turn left.

**12.4**   Junction with Squaw Flat Trail; turn left.

**13.9**   Arrive back at the Elephant Hill Trailhead.

# 49. THE JOINT TRAIL

## WHY GO?

Perhaps the most famous day hike in the Needles, but one of the most difficult to access

### THE RUNDOWN

**Start:** Chesler Park / Joint Trailhead

**Distance:** 2 miles; out and back

**Difficulty:** Moderate

**Nat Geo Trails Illustrated Map:** Needles

**Nat Geo TOPO! Map (USGS):** Druid Arch

### FINDING THE TRAILHEAD

You have two options for reaching this trailhead, but both require a high-clearance, four-wheel-drive vehicle with low-range gearing and the skill and experience to drive it.

The shortest but perhaps more challenging route (8 miles) leaves from the Elephant Hill Trailhead. To find the Elephant Hill Trailhead, drive 3.1 miles from the entrance station on the main park road until you see a paved road going off to the left to Squaw Flat Campground and Elephant Hill. Take this left and 0.3 mile later take a right onto another paved road. Then take another right 0.5 mile later onto the unpaved, two-wheel-drive Elephant Hill Access Road. Once on the unpaved road, it's 3 miles to this trailhead. Drive slowly on this road, especially around several blind corners. **GPS coordinates for the Elephant Hill Trailhead:** 38° 8' 30.272" N / 109° 49' 37.209" W

At the Elephant Hill Trailhead, start up the Elephant Hill backcountry road, which will challenge any four-wheel-drive enthusiast. After 1.5 miles turn left (south) onto the one-way road to Devils Kitchen. Go 0.5 mile past the spur road to Devils Kitchen Camp and turn left (south) again, then go 3.5 miles until you turn left (east) one more time and go another 0.5 mile to the Joint Trailhead.

The longer and nearly as challenging route starts from the Needles entrance station. Drive east out of the park on UT 211 for 13.7 miles and turn right (south) onto a gravel road marked Elk Mountain and Beef Basin. If you're coming from the east, the turnoff is 20 miles from US 191. Follow this unpaved road, which gets gradually worse, for 43 miles until you see the park boundary. From here drive 4.7 miles into the park until you see the junction with the road to Chesler Park Trailhead. Turn right (east) here and go 0.5 mile until the road dead-ends at the trailhead. The trailhead has a vault toilet and picnic tables. **GPS coordinates:** 38° 6' 12.854" N / 109° 51' 59.870" W

## WHAT TO SEE

The Joint Trail is an excellent choice for those who want a little adventure (but not danger), as long as somebody has the skill to drive very gnarly roads with a high-clearance, four-wheel-drive vehicle. In fact, getting to this trailhead is the hardest and most adventurous part of this trip. This route goes through some very interesting terrain, but is not long or strenuous.

The hike starts out uphill on a moderately rugged, rocky trail with cairns showing the way. In about a half mile, it dips into a long, narrow joint between two rock formations. From here it's like hiking in a narrow slot canyon for about a quarter mile. A few spots require a handhold to scramble over rocks in the Joint, and near the end you climb man-made but rustic "stairs" just before you finally emerge from the depths of the Joint.

Just as you break out into daylight, you see a sign indicating a short viewpoint trail heading right (south) from the junction. The Chesler Park Trail veers off to the left (east). The viewpoint is only about a quarter mile from the sign, but it involves a short climb onto a slickrock ledge. This might be a little nerve-racking for parents hiking with children, but it's fairly safe. The steepest spots are made easier with little steps chipped out of the solid rock. At the viewpoint you get a fantastic view of Chesler Park—the perimeter of stately, multihued sandstone formations including the Pinnacle to the north. After soaking in the view and having a pleasant rest and perhaps lunch, it's back into the "underground" of the Joint again on the way back to the trailhead.

Driving the Elephant Hill Road is for experienced four-wheelers only.
NPS/KIRSTEN KEARSE

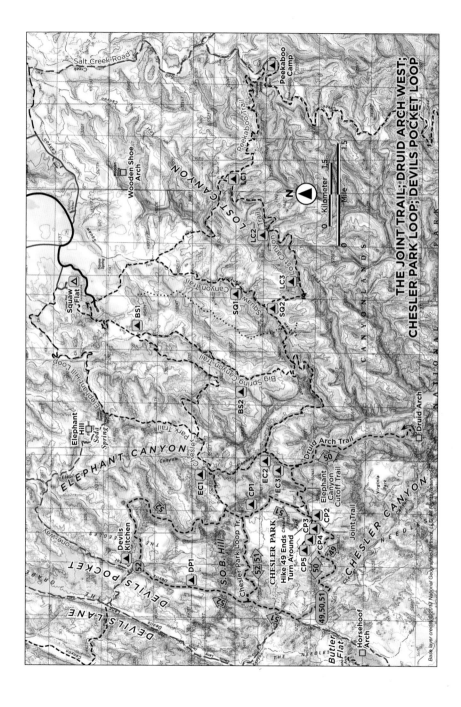

THE JOINT TRAIL; DRUID ARCH WEST;
CHESLER PARK LOOP; DEVILS POCKET LOOP

The Joint Trail
NPS/NEAL HERBERT

## MILES AND DIRECTIONS

**0.0** Start at the Chesler Park/Joint Trailhead.

**0.5** Start of the Joint.

**0.8** Side trail to Chesler Park Overlook and end of the Joint.

**1.0** Chesler Park Overlook. Retrace your steps to the trailhead.

**2.0** Arrive back at Chesler Park/Joint Trailhead.

# 50. DRUID ARCH WEST

## WHY GO?
A day hike or overnighter through the Joint and on to a majestic arch

### THE RUNDOWN

**See map on page 179.**

**Start:** Chesler Park / Joint Trailhead

**Distance:** 9 miles; out and back

**Difficulty:** Moderate

**Nat Geo Trails Illustrated Map:** Needles

**Nat Geo TOPO! Map (USGS):** Druid Arch

## FINDING THE TRAILHEAD

 You have two options for reaching this trailhead, but both require a high-clearance, four-wheel-drive vehicle with low-range gearing and the skill and experience to drive it.

The shortest but perhaps more challenging route (8 miles) leaves from the Elephant Hill Trailhead. To find the Elephant Hill Trailhead, drive 3.1 miles from the entrance station on the main park road until you see a paved road going off to the left to Squaw Flat Campground and Elephant Hill. Take this left and 0.3 mile later take a right onto another paved road. Then take another right 0.5 mile later onto the unpaved, two-wheel-drive Elephant Hill Access Road. Once on the unpaved road, it's 3 miles to the trailhead. Drive slowly on this road, especially around several blind corners. **GPS coordinates for the Elephant Hill Trailhead:** 38° 8' 30.272" N / 109° 49' 37.209" W

At the Elephant Hill Trailhead, start up the Elephant Hill backcountry road, which will challenge any four-wheel-drive enthusiast. After 1.5 miles, turn left (south) onto the one-way road to Devils Kitchen. Go 0.5 mile past the spur road to Devils Kitchen Camp and turn left (south) again, then go 3.5 miles until you turn left (east) one more time and go another 0.5 mile to the Joint Trail Trailhead.

The longer and nearly as challenging route starts from the Needles entrance station. Drive east out of the park on UT 211 for 13.7 miles and turn right (south) onto a gravel road marked Elk Mountain and Beef Basin. If you're coming from the east, the turnoff is 20 miles from US 191. Follow this unpaved road, which gets gradually worse, for 43 miles until you see the park boundary. From here drive 4.7 miles into the park until you see the junction with the road to Chesler Park Trailhead. Turn right (east) here and go 0.5 mile until the road dead-ends at the trailhead. The trailhead has a vault toilet and picnic tables. **GPS coordinates:** 38° 6' 12.854" N / 109° 51' 59.870" W

## WHAT TO SEE

The first part of the route is a gradual uphill grade on a fairly rocky trail. Watch for cairns to stay on the correct route. After about a half mile, the trails slips into a long, narrow joint—*the* Joint—between two rock formations, almost like a slot canyon, for about a quarter mile. At the end of the Joint, you climb man-made but rustic "stairs" just before you emerge from the depths of the Joint.

As you break out into daylight, a sign points to a short viewpoint trail. To take it—and you should—go right (south). The viewpoint is only about a quarter mile from the sign, a short climb onto a slickrock ledge. If you have children, watch them carefully here. The steepest spots are made easier with little steps chipped out of the solid rock. At the viewpoint you get a fantastic view of Chesler Park—the perimeter of stately, multihued sandstone formations including the Pinnacle to the north. After soaking in the view, head back to the Chesler Park Trail and take a right (east).

From the junction of the Chesler Park Overlook side trail, hike east along the south edge of majestic Chesler Park along a flat, packed-dirt, and well-defined trail.

Just before you reach the junction with the trail going south to Chesler Park, you'll see Backcountry Campsite CP2 on your right and a short trail to CP3, CP4, and CP5 on your left. If you decided to make this a moderate overnighter, any of these scenic campsites would be a great choice. If you leave early enough, you can set up camp and still have time to hike to Druid Arch. If not (and perhaps even better), get up early the next morning to take the rest of the hike.

Just beyond the campsites you reach a junction. Go right (east) here and head 1 mile down to the bottom of Upper Elephant Canyon, where you'll see the Druid Arch Trail junction in the canyon wash. Here take a right (south) to Druid Arch.

The Druid Arch Trail alternates between the dry wash and short sections on the east flank of the canyon for about 1.5 miles until it climbs steeply up to a bench below Druid Arch. This is a great place to relax for a while before returning to your campsite or the trailhead.

## MILES AND DIRECTIONS

0.0   Start at the Chesler Park / Joint Trailhead.

0.5   Start of the Joint.

0.8   Side trail to Chesler Park Overlook and end of the Joint.

1.0   Chesler Park Overlook.

1.4   Backcountry Campsites CP2, CP3, CP4, and CP5.

1.5   Junction with Chesler Park Trail; turn right.

2.5   Junction with Druid Arch Trail; turn right.

4.5   Druid Arch. Retrace your steps to the trailhead.

9.0   Arrive back at Chesler Park / Joint Trailhead.

# 51. **CHESLER PARK LOOP**

## WHY GO?
A popular, extra-scenic loop hike

### THE RUNDOWN

**See map on page 179.**

**Start:** Chesler Park / Joint Trailhead

**Distance:** 5 miles; loop

**Difficulty:** Moderate

**Nat Geo Trails Illustrated Map:**
Needles

**Nat Geo TOPO! Map (USGS):**
Druid Arch

### FINDING THE TRAILHEAD

 You have two options for reaching this trailhead, but both require a high-clearance, four-wheel-drive vehicle with low-range gearing and the skill and experience to drive it.

The shortest but perhaps more challenging route (8 miles) leaves from the Elephant Hill Trailhead. To find the Elephant Hill Trailhead, drive 3.1 miles from the entrance station on the main park road until you see a paved road going off to the left to Squaw Flat Campground and Elephant Hill. Take this left and 0.3 mile later take a right onto another paved road. Then take another right 0.5 mile later onto the unpaved, two-wheel-drive Elephant Hill Access Road. Once on the unpaved road, it's 3 miles to the trailhead. Drive slowly on this road, especially around several blind corners. **GPS coordinates for the Elephant Hill Trailhead:** 38° 8′ 30.272″ N / 109° 49′ 37.209″ W

At the Elephant Hill Trailhead, start up the Elephant Hill backcountry road, which will challenge any four-wheel-drive enthusiast. After 1.5 miles, turn left (south) onto the one-way road to Devils Kitchen. Go 0.5 mile past the spur road to Devils Kitchen Camp and turn left (south) again, then go 3.5 miles until you turn left (east) one more time and go another 0.5 mile to the Joint Trail Trailhead.

The longer and nearly as challenging route starts from the Needles entrance station. Drive east out of the park on UT 211 for 13.7 miles and turn right (south) onto a gravel road marked Elk Mountain and Beef Basin. If you're coming from the east, the turnoff is 20 miles from US 191. Follow this unpaved road, which gets gradually worse, for 43 miles until you see the park boundary. From here drive 4.7 miles into the park until you see the junction with the road to Chesler Park Trailhead. Turn right (east) here and go 0.5 mile until the road dead-ends at the trailhead. The trailhead has a vault toilet and picnic tables. **GPS coordinates:** 38° 6′ 12.854″ N / 109° 51′ 59.870″ W

## WHAT TO SEE

If you like to save the best until last, take this trail clockwise. This involves walking on a road for the first mile, but it's easy going, and you're unlikely to see any vehicles.

The road forks 0.5 mile after leaving the trailhead, with the left fork going off to Beef Basin. Take a right and walk another 0.4 mile until you see a sign for the Devils Pocket. The sign for this trail is not right along the road, so watch for it a few feet up the trail.

The next section of trail involves a gradual climb up to a junction with the trail through the Pinnacle to Devils Kitchen Camp. You turn right (east) at this junction and head for Chesler Park. You go through one rocky section with one short, steep pitch before coming out into gorgeous Chesler Park, a huge grassy flatland ringed by colorful sandstone spires. The trail goes along the north edge of the park for less than a half mile before hitting the next junction.

At this junction turn right (south) and head toward the Joint Trail. Follow the east edge of Chesler Park on a nicely defined and packed-dirt trail for 1.3 miles to the next junction. Just less than halfway through this section, you'll see Backcountry Campsite CP1 on your left. It's back from the trail about 100 yards, out of sight among several large boulders. This is a great choice if you're staying overnight. It's shady and more private than the four campsites farther down the trail.

When you reach the junction with the Elephant Canyon Cutoff Trail (which goes off to the east), go straight. In less than 50 feet, you'll see a side trail to Backcountry Campsites CP3, CP4, and CP5 off to your right and, a few steps down the trail, CP2 off to your left. CP2 and CP3 are fairly close to the trail; CP3 has the best view of Chesler Park. CP4 and CP5 are farther away from the main trail and more private. All the campsites are tucked amid gigantic boulders where you can always find shade. You also see some signs of historic ranching operations, which ran in Chesler Park before the national park was created.

From the campsites the trail is flat and easy walking. Long ago parts of this trail were a primitive road. In about a half mile you reach the start of the Joint and the side trail going to the left to the Chesler Park Overlook. Even though you've been walking through or on the edge of Chesler Park for a long time, you want to check out this viewpoint. It gives you a grand vista you don't get from the lower-elevation trails. The viewpoint is only about a quarter mile off the main trail and well worth the little climb up to a slickrock platform where you get a better-than-postcard panoramic vista of Chesler Park and the sandstone formations surrounding it.

Back at the viewpoint sign, the trail dives into the Joint, a large crack between rock formations. As you climb down man-made rock stairs to get to its depths, you might think you're not really on a trail, but you are. You stay in the Joint for another quarter mile or so. It's a tight squeeze in spots, but you shouldn't have any problems unless you're built like an NFL offensive lineman. However, you might have to push and twist to get a big backpack through the Joint. Logs placed in strategic points help you get down short drops.

**Chesler Park**
NPS/NEAL HERBERT

After you come out into sunlight again, it's less than half a mile on a fairly rocky trail down to the Chesler Park / Joint Trailhead, where you started the loop hike.

## MILES AND DIRECTIONS

0.0   Start at Chesler Park / Joint Trailhead.

0.5   Beef Basin Road junction.

0.8   Devils Pocket Trailhead.

1.3   Junction with Chesler Park Loop Trail; turn right.

2.6   Junction with Chesler Park Trail; turn right.

3.0   Backcountry Campsite CP1.

3.4   Junction with Elephant Canyon Cutoff Trail.

3.5   Junction with the Joint Trail; turn right.

3.6   Backcountry Campsites CP2, CP3, CP4, and CP5.

4.2   Chesler Park Overlook and start of the Joint.

4.8   End of the Joint.

5.0   Arrive back at Chesler Park / Joint Trailhead.

# 52. DEVILS POCKET LOOP

## WHY GO?

A great day hike for hikers with a four-wheel-drive vehicle to reach the trailhead

### THE RUNDOWN

**See map on page 179.**

**Start:** Devils Kitchen Trailhead

**Distance:** 5.3 miles; loop

**Difficulty:** Moderate

**Nat Geo Trails Illustrated Map:**
Needles

**Nat Geo TOPO! Map (USGS):**
The Loop and Druid Arch

## FINDING THE TRAILHEAD

You have two options for reaching this trailhead, but both require a high-clearance, four-wheel-drive vehicle with low-range gearing and the skill and experience to drive it.

The shortest but perhaps more challenging route (5 miles) leaves from the Elephant Hill Trailhead. To find the Elephant Hill Trailhead, drive 3.1 miles from the entrance station on the main park road until you see a paved road going off to the left to Squaw Flat Campground and Elephant Hill. Take this left and 0.3 mile later take a right onto another paved road. Then take another right 0.5 mile later onto the unpaved, two-wheel-drive Elephant Hill Access Road. Once on the unpaved road, it's 3 miles to the trailhead. Drive slowly on this road, especially around several blind corners. **GPS coordinates for the Elephant Hill Trailhead:** 38° 8′ 30.272″ N/109° 49′ 37.209″ W

From the Elephant Hill Trailhead, start up the Elephant Hill backcountry road. The first 1.5-mile stretch of this road goes over Elephant Hill, technical four-wheel-driving most of the way. At the 1.5-mile mark, turn left (south) onto the one-way road to Devils Kitchen. After 2 miles turn left (east) onto the Devils Kitchen mile-long spur road to the Devils Kitchen Camp and Trailhead.

The longer, but still difficult, option starts from the Needles entrance station. Drive east out of the park on UT 211 for 13.7 miles and turn right (south) onto a gravel road marked Elk Mountain and Beef Basin. If you're coming from the east, the turnoff is 20 miles from US 191. Follow this unpaved road, which gets gradually worse, for 43 miles until you see the park boundary.

From the south boundary drive north up Devils Lane Road for 4.7 miles to the junction with the Chesler Park Trailhead road. Continue straight (north) through the junction for another 3.1 miles, going over infamous S.O.B. Hill until you see a junction with Devils Kitchen Road. Turn right (east) here and go another mile to Devils Kitchen Camp and Trailhead, where you find four premier vehicle campsites, a vault toilet, and picnic tables. **GPS coordinates:** 38° 8′ 15.019″ N/109° 51′ 41.057″ W

Indian paintbrush

## WHAT TO SEE

If you're camped at Devils Kitchen, this is an excellent choice for a day hike. The loop can be taken from either direction, but the clockwise route is described here.

The trail starts just to the left of the sign at the south end of the campground and heads along a canyon wash for a few hundred yards. It then starts a gradual climb up toward the Pinnacle, a majestic sandstone formation and the highlight of this section of the Canyonlands. The trail alternates between slickrock and a well-defined dirt path for the entire 2.3 miles to the junction with the Chesler Park Trail.

Take a right (southwest) at this junction. You quickly start a fairly serious but short climb to a narrow "pass" in the Pinnacle. At the top of the pass, pause to look both ways for incredible views of Elephant Canyon (to the northeast) and Chesler Park (to the southwest). It's a very short section of trail, only 0.2 mile to the junction just downhill from the pass on the edge of Chesler Park. If you want to make this an overnighter, you should try to reserve Backcountry Campsite CP1, which is 0.6 mile south of this junction. The overnighter option adds about 1.2 miles to your trip.

From this junction take a right (west) and walk on a packed-dirt path along the north perimeter of Chesler Park for about a half mile before heading down a rocky section toward the next junction. Here take another right (north) and start climbing up to the second pass through the Pinnacle.

After descending from the pass, the trail goes through a series of open parks, mostly on packed dirt with a few stretches of loose sand. Less than a half mile from Devils Kitchen, you'll see Backcountry Campsite DP1 on your right. This is a lovely site about 100 yards off the trail and nestled between two big boulders under some piñon pines. The rest of the trail is flat on loose sand until you come back to Devils Kitchen right by the sign where you started.

## MILES AND DIRECTIONS

**0.0**  Start at Devils Kitchen Trailhead.

**2.3**  Junction with trail to Elephant Hill Trailhead; turn right.

**2.5**  Junction with Chesler Park Loop Trail; turn right.

**3.9**  Junction with Devils Pocket Trail; turn right.

**4.8**  Backcountry Campsite DP1.

**5.3**  Arrive back at Devils Kitchen Camp and Trailhead.

# 53. **THE BIG NEEDLES LOOP**

## WHY GO?
A major backpacking trip covering most of the outstanding features of the Needles District

### THE RUNDOWN
**Start:** Squaw Flat Trailhead

**Distance:** 21.7 miles (plus side trips); loop

**Difficulty:** Difficult

**Nat Geo Trails Illustrated Map:** Needles

**Nat Geo TOPO! Map (USGS):** The Loop and Druid Arch

### FINDING THE TRAILHEAD
 Drive about 2.7 miles west from Needles entrance station and turn left into Squaw Flat Campground. After entering the campground area, the road forks. Both forks go to trailheads with access to the same trails. However, the left-hand fork takes you to the trailhead with the shortest access route to the backcountry. The right-hand fork and its respective trailhead are used mostly by campers staying in the campground. **GPS coordinates:** 38° 8′ 36.487″ N / 109° 48′ 13.115″ W

## WHAT TO SEE
The Needles Trails backcountry zone offers many opportunities for long backpacking trips, many of them without the problematic vehicle shuttle. The following description outlines one excellent route, but you can customize your own trip by studying the map.

Although this trail description starts and ends at the Squaw Flat Trailhead, you could start or finish at three other trailheads (Elephant Hill, Devils Kitchen, or Chesler Park) and cover the same territory. However, Squaw Flat is the most accessible trailhead, and you can get there with any vehicle. This loop hike has many interesting side trips, such as Peekaboo Spring, Upper Lost Canyon, Druid Arch, Elephant Canyon, and Chesler Park Overlook.

The loop can be done in either direction with no real advantage or disadvantage, but this description follows the clockwise route. In any case, plan on a heavy pack, at least for the first two days, because of the amount of water you need to carry.

Deciding on the length of your trip depends on how much water you can carry, how many miles you can cover in a day, and how much time you have available. This description covers the three-night/four-day option, but here's a quick summary of other options:

| LENGTH OF TRIP | BACKCOUNTRY CAMPSITE | MILES PER DAY | SIDE TRIPS |
|---|---|---|---|
| Two nights | 1—SQ2<br>2—DP1 | 1—5.6 miles<br>2—8.6 miles<br>3—7.7 miles | Upper Lost Canyon<br>Chesler Park Overlook |
| Three nights | 1—LC3<br>2—CP2, 3, 4, or 5<br>3—DP1 | 1—5.1 miles<br>2—5.3 miles<br>3—3.8 miles<br>4—7.7 miles | Upper Lost Canyon<br>Druid Arch<br>Chesler Park Overlook |
| Four nights | 1—LC1<br>2—LC3<br>3—CP2, 3, 4, or 5<br>4—DP1 | 1—2.7 miles<br>2—2.4 miles<br>3—5.3 miles<br>4—3.8 miles<br>5—7.7 miles | Peekaboo Spring<br>Upper Lost Canyon<br>Druid Arch<br>Chesler Park Overlook |
| Five nights | 1—LC1<br>2—LC3<br>3—CP2, 3, 4, or 5<br>4—DP1<br>5—EC1 | 1—2.7 miles<br>2—2.4 miles<br>3—5.3 miles<br>4—3.8 miles<br>5—3.6 miles<br>6—4.1 miles | Peekaboo Spring<br>Upper Lost Canyon<br>Druid Arch<br>Chesler Park Overlook<br>Elephant Canyon |

**Note:** Be sure to get a map from the NPS showing exact locations of backcountry campsites.

The first 1.1 miles of this hike follow a flat and easy stretch of trail with several slickrock sections. Be alert not to miss the sometimes small cairns marking the correct route over the slickrock. After the first 1.1 miles of easy hiking, you reach the junction with the Peekaboo Trail. Take a left (east) and head toward Lost Canyon and Peekaboo Spring. Most of the next 1.5-mile section is slickrock. After climbing down a small ladder, the trail follows the north rim of a beautiful, narrow canyon for a short way before dropping into the canyon on a sandy trail for the last half mile to the junction with the Lost Canyon Trail. Take a right (southwest) here and start hiking up Lost Canyon. In spring a healthy stream often flows through this lush canyon.

When going through Lost Canyon, watch carefully for an abrupt right-hand turn in the trail. There is a sign pointing to Squaw Canyon Trail, but if you're absorbed in the scenery (which could easily happen), you might miss it. On the ground the trail seems to continue into Upper Lost Canyon, but at this point the official trail leaves Lost Canyon and dips into a narrow, unnamed canyon that runs north to south. If you have time, you might want to hike into Upper Lost Canyon on a side trip.

When you reach the Druid Arch Trail up Elephant Canyon at the 8.8-mile mark, you find a sign marking the junction in the dry wash. Take a left and head toward Druid Arch.

Hiking the Needles
NPS/KIRSTEN KEARSE

After a half-mile walk up Elephant Canyon, you see a junction with the trail going west to Chesler Park. If you're staying out for three or more nights, you probably have time to visit Druid Arch. If so, drop your pack somewhere around this trail junction and take a left for the scenic side trip up to awesome and well-named Druid Arch. When you get back to your pack, take the right fork (west) at this junction and go another mile to your camp at one of the four Chesler Park backcountry campsites. CP3, CP4, and CP5 are on your right just after you reach the junction with the Joint Trail, and CP2 is another 100 feet down the trail on your left. All four sites are nestled amid the large boulders surrounding Chesler Park.

After enjoying your second night out on the rim of spectacular Chesler Park, keep heading west on the Joint Trail. In another 0.6 mile you come to a junction where the Joint Trail drops down into the Joint and a side trail turns left to the Chesler Park Overlook.

If you want a short side trip, drop your pack here, grab a water bottle and a snack, and take this short trail up to the overlook. The side trail follows cairns for about a quarter mile to the top of a slickrock ledge—a great place to relax for a while and soak in the quiet beauty of the Canyonlands. From here you can see Chesler Park and the ring of sandstone spires that surround it. You've been able to see Chesler Park from your camp and from the trail, but the view is not nearly as dramatic as it is from this viewpoint.

After you return to your pack, head into the Joint—a giant crack between rock formations that goes on and on, sometimes tight enough to make getting a big pack through difficult. Several trails in Canyonlands and Arches have similar joints, but this is by far the longest.

After about a quarter mile in the Joint, you finally break out into the sunlight again. From here it's about a half mile on a fairly rocky trail to the Chesler Park Trailhead, where you'll find a vault toilet and picnic tables. From here walk down the road for 0.5 mile until you see the road to Beef Basin heading off to the left (south). You go right for another 0.3 mile until you see the Devils Pocket Trail veering off to the right.

The Devils Pocket Trail starts out through a flat, brushy meadow. After 0.8 mile you see the Chesler Park Loop Trail going off to the right (east). Take a left and make a fairly serious climb through a pass in the enormous Pinnacle Formation. After the pass the trail drops into another dry, brush-covered flat, affectionately referred to as Devils Pocket.

In less than a half mile, you see the short side trail to Backcountry Campsite DP1 going off to the right. The campsite is about a quarter mile from the trail amid some large boulders and piñon pine trees. If you're out for three nights, DP1 is probably your best choice for a backcountry campsite. This leaves a tough 7.7 miles for the fourth and last day of your hike, but your pack will be its lightest on the last day as you deplete your water supply. (However, if you would like a short hike for the last day, you can go by DP1 and on to EC1, which would mean 7.4 miles of hiking on the third day but only 4.1 miles on the last day.)

From DP1 it's only about a half mile to Devils Kitchen Camp, where you find a vault toilet and picnic tables and four vehicle campsites. Some maps might not show it exactly this way, but the Devils Pocket Trail ends right on the road in Devils Kitchen and then heads out the east side of the vehicle camp. The trail out of Devils Kitchen is confusing. There are several unofficial trails that have been made by visitors of the popular campground. Watch for the cairn-lined trail heading east from the vault toilet on the east end of the campsites. If there's any question in your mind, check the topo map and compass to make sure you don't have to backtrack to find the official trail.

After hiking 2.3 miles from Devils Kitchen, turn left (east) onto the trail to Elephant Hill Trailhead. On this short (0.6-mile) section of trail, you get fantastic views of the Pinnacle and the Needles before dropping into the dry wash of Elephant Canyon. From here take a short trail north down the canyon to EC1 if you've decided to camp there.

If you're heading back to your vehicle, go across the dry wash on another 0.6-mile section of trail to a junction where you have a choice of trailheads. If your party had two vehicles, you could have left one at Elephant Hill Trailhead and can cut 2.3 miles off your trip. If so, take a left (north) to Elephant Hill. If not, take a right (east) to Squaw Flat Trailhead.

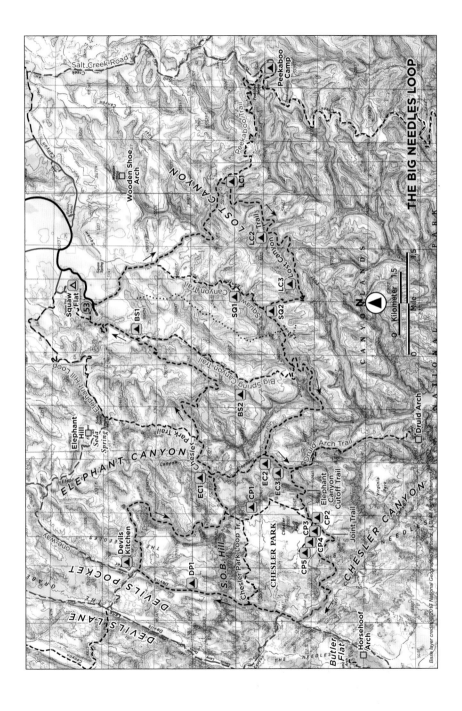

## MILES AND DIRECTIONS

**0.0** Start at the Squaw Flat Trailhead.

**0.1** Junction with Squaw Canyon Trail; turn left.

**1.1** Junction with Peekaboo Trail; turn left.

**2.6** Junction with Lost Canyon Trail; turn right.

**2.7** Backcountry Campsite LC1.

**3.8** Backcountry Campsite LC2.

**5.1** Backcountry Campsite LC3.

**5.3** Sharp right (north) turn on Lost Canyon Trail.

**5.6** Backcountry Campsite SQ2.

**5.8** Junction with Squaw Canyon Trail; turn left.

**6.7** Junction with Big Spring Canyon Trail; turn left.

**8.8** Junction with Druid Arch Trail; turn left.

**9.3** Junction with Druid Arch West Trail; turn right.

**10.3** Junction with the Joint Trail; turn right.

**10.4** Backcountry Campsites CP2, CP3, CP4, and CP5.

**11.0** Spur trail to Chesler Park Overlook and start of the Joint; turn left.

**11.8** Chesler Park Trailhead.

**12.3** Junction with road to Beef Basin; turn right.

**12.6** Trailhead for Devils Pocket Trail.

**13.4** Junction with Chesler Park Loop Trail; turn left.

**14.3** Backcountry Campsite DP1.

**14.8** Devils Kitchen Camp and Trailhead.

**17.1** Junction with trail to Elephant Hill Trailhead and Squaw Canyon; turn left.

**17.7** Junction with Elephant Hill Trail and spur trail to Backcountry Campsite EC1; turn right.

**18.3** Junction with trail to Elephant Hill Trailhead; turn right.

**20.8** Junction with Big Spring Canyon Trail; turn left.

**21.2** Junction with Squaw Flat Campground's Loop B trail; turn right.

**27** Arrive back at the Squaw Flat Trailhead.

# 54. **LOWER RED LAKE**

## WHY GO?
A difficult day hike or overnighter down to the mighty Colorado River

---

### THE RUNDOWN

**Start:** Devils Kitchen Trailhead

**Distance:** 11.8 miles; out and back

**Difficulty:** Difficult

**Nat Geo Trails Illustrated Map:** Needles

**Nat Geo TOPO! Map (USGS):** The Loop and Spanish Bottom

---

## FINDING THE TRAILHEAD

You have two options for reaching this trailhead, but both require a high-clearance, four-wheel-drive vehicle with low-range gearing and the skill and experience to drive it.

The shortest but perhaps more challenging route (5 miles) leaves from the Elephant Hill Trailhead. To find the Elephant Hill Trailhead, drive 3.1 miles from the entrance station on the main park road until you see a paved road going off to the left to Squaw Flat Campground and Elephant Hill. Take this left and 0.3 mile later take a right onto another paved road. Then take another right 0.5 mile later onto the unpaved, two-wheel-drive Elephant Hill Access Road. Once on the unpaved road, it's 3 miles to the trailhead. Drive slowly on this road, especially around several blind corners. **GPS coordinates for the Elephant Hill Trailhead:** 38° 8' 30.272" N / 109° 49' 37.209" W

From the Elephant Hill Trailhead, start up the Elephant Hill backcountry road. The first 1.5-mile stretch of this road goes over Elephant Hill, technical four-wheel-driving most of the way. At the 1.5-mile mark, turn left (south) onto the one-way road to Devils Kitchen. After 2 miles turn left (east) onto the Devils Kitchen mile-long spur road to the Devils Kitchen Camp and Trailhead.

The longer, but still difficult, option starts from the Needles entrance station. Drive east out of the park on UT 211 for 13.7 miles and turn right (south) onto a gravel road marked Elk Mountain and Beef Basin. If you're coming from the east, the turnoff is 20 miles from US 191. Follow this unpaved road, which gets gradually worse, for 43 miles until you see the park boundary.

From the south boundary drive north up Devils Lane Road for 4.7 miles to the junction with the Chesler Park Trailhead road. Continue straight (north) through the junction for another 3.1 miles, going over infamous S.O.B. Hill until you see a junction with Devils Kitchen Road. Turn right (east) here and go another mile to Devils Kitchen Camp and Trailhead, where you find four premier vehicle campsites, a vault toilet, and picnic tables. **GPS coordinates:** 38° 8' 15.019" N / 109° 51' 41.057" W

Lower Red Lake Trail
NPS/NEAL HERBERT

## WHAT TO SEE

This is a long, hot, steep trail, but it goes into one of the remotest and least-used sections of Canyonlands National Park. You stand a good chance of having the trail all to yourself.

From Devils Kitchen Camp you can drive 0.6 mile to the junction with the Devils Lane Road, where you see the trailhead for the Lower Red Lake Trail going straight off to the west. However, there is no parking area at the trailhead, so it's best to leave your vehicle in Devils Kitchen Camp and hike from there.

From the Lower Red Lake Trailhead the trail goes over a small ridge for 1 mile to the recently abandoned Cyclone Canyon Road. This is easy walking on a well-defined trail. Until 1996 hikers could cut this first mile off the trip by driving around Cyclone Canyon Road to this point, but the NPS has converted the last stretch of Cyclone Canyon Road to a trail.

Once across the abandoned road, the trail starts getting rougher and rougher as it drops into Red Lake Canyon. This is the start of an 800-foot descent to the Colorado River.

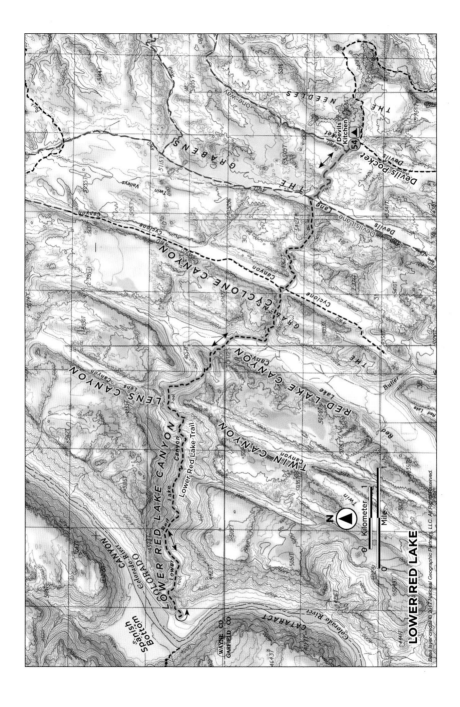

LOWER RED LAKE

Once at the bottom of Red Lake Canyon, the trail angles off to the right and more or less stays in the canyon bottom the rest of the way to the river. Less than a half mile down the trail, it turns left toward the river. A mile or so later, you'll see impressive Lens Canyon joining from the north. Lower Red Lake Canyon is steep walled and rugged the rest of the way.

The terrain flattens out somewhat when you reach the river, but regrettably the area has been burned and invaded by the evil tamarisk, which now dominates the riverbank.

You can camp at-large along Lower Red Lake Canyon, but in this steep canyon it's difficult to find a good campsite. If you're on a long day hike, take a long rest at the river. It's a steep climb back up to Devils Kitchen.

## MILES AND DIRECTIONS

**0.0**   Start at Devils Kitchen Camp.

**0.6**   Devils Lane Road.

**1.6**   Cyclone Canyon Road.

**2.8**   Lower Red Lake Canyon.

**4.0**   Lens Canyon.

**5.9**   Colorado River. Retrace your steps to the trailhead.

**11.8**   Arrive back at Devils Kitchen Camp.

# 55. **THE TUMBLEWEED LOOP**

## WHY GO?
A mostly flat day hike through little-used Cyclone Canyon, partly on backcountry roads

### THE RUNDOWN

**Start:** Devils Kitchen Trailhead

**Distance:** 9.1 miles; loop

**Difficulty:** Moderate

**Nat Geo Trails Illustrated Map:**
Needles

**Nat Geo TOPO! Map (USGS):**
The Loop

### FINDING THE TRAILHEAD

 You have two options for reaching this trailhead, but both require a high-clearance, four-wheel-drive vehicle with low-range gearing and the skill and experience to drive it.

The shortest but perhaps more challenging route (5 miles) leaves from the Elephant Hill Trailhead. To find the Elephant Hill Trailhead, drive 3.1 miles from the entrance station on the main park road until you see a paved road going off to the left to Squaw Flat Campground and Elephant Hill. Take this left and 0.3 mile later take a right onto another paved road. Then take another right 0.5 mile later onto the unpaved, two-wheel-drive Elephant Hill Access Road. Once on the unpaved road, it's 3 miles to the trailhead. Drive slowly on this road, especially around several blind corners. **GPS coordinates for the Elephant Hill Trailhead:** 38° 8′ 30.272″ N/109° 49′ 37.209″ W

From the Elephant Hill Trailhead, start up the Elephant Hill backcountry road. The first 1.5-mile stretch of this road goes over Elephant Hill, technical four-wheel-driving most of the way. At the 1.5-mile mark, turn left (south) onto the one-way road to Devils Kitchen. After 2 miles turn left (east) onto the Devils Kitchen mile-long spur road to the Devils Kitchen Camp and Trailhead.

The longer, but still difficult, option starts from the Needles entrance station. Drive east out of the park on UT 211 for 13.7 miles and turn right (south) onto a gravel road marked Elk Mountain and Beef Basin. If you're coming from the east, the turnoff is 20 miles from US 191. Follow this unpaved road, which gets gradually worse, for 43 miles until you see the park boundary.

From the south boundary drive north up Devils Lane Road for 4.7 miles to the junction with the Chesler Park Trailhead road. Continue straight (north) through the junction for another 3.1 miles, going over infamous S.O.B. Hill until you see a junction with Devils Kitchen Road. Turn right (east) here and go another mile to Devils Kitchen Camp and Trailhead, where you find four premier vehicle campsites, a vault toilet, and picnic tables. **GPS coordinates:** 38° 8′ 15.019″ N/109° 51′ 41.057″ W

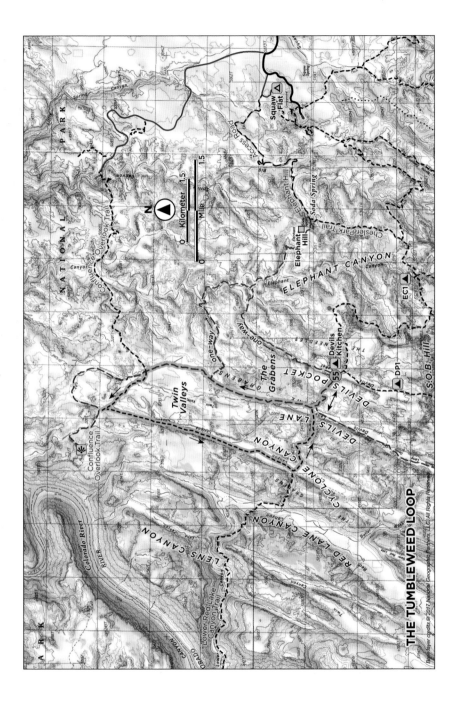

The well-named Tumbleweed Loop

## WHAT TO SEE

The route goes along the newest trail in the Needles District, the recently abandoned road through Cyclone Canyon.

From Devils Kitchen walk down the road 0.6 mile to the Devils Lane Road and take a right (north) onto the road. Stay on the road until you cross the Confluence Overlook Trail. Be alert not to miss this trail junction, which is not marked with a sign. If you miss it, you'll have to hike about another mile on Devils Lane Road before you see the Cyclone Canyon Trail junction.

After turning left (west) onto the Confluence Overlook Trail, hike 0.7 mile until you see the same road again coming in from the north. This is also the start of the new Cyclone Canyon Trail, so turn left (south) here.

From here it's a very flat hike for 2.4 miles through the scenic canyon. You'll quickly notice the predominance of tumbleweeds—hence, my name for this loop— along this section of trail, sometimes making walking difficult.

After fighting through a tumbleweed jungle, you'll cross the Lower Red Lake Trail, which drops down to the Colorado River. Turn left (east) here and hike over a small, scenic ridge and down to Devils Lane Road and then back to the Devils Kitchen Camp.

## MILES AND DIRECTIONS

**0.0**  Start at Devils Kitchen Camp.

**0.6**  Turn right onto Devils Lane Road.

**2.1**  Junction with one-way road to Elephant Hill; turn left.

**4.7**  Junction with Confluence Overlook Trail; turn left.

**5.3**  Devils Lane Road and Cyclone Canyon Trailhead; turn left.

**7.7**  Junction with Lower Red Lake Trail; turn left.

**8.6**  Devils Lane Road.

**9.1**  Arrive back at Devils Kitchen Camp.

# CANYONLANDS NATIONAL PARK: THE MAZE, ORANGE CLIFFS, AND HORSESHOE CANYON

When people use the old adage "in the middle of nowhere," they could easily be talking about **THE MAZE**, and it would be a compliment.

Most people have never been to a place as remote as the Maze, and getting there can be a great warm-up for experiencing this remote district of Canyonlands National Park. Whether you come from Hite, Hanksville, or Green River, you definitely get the feeling of being out of touch with civilization long before you reach the park boundary. Then, once you start slowly maneuvering your vehicle along the primitive roads into the Maze, you realize how vital it is to be totally self-reliant. Very few national parks can come close to the extreme remoteness of the Maze.

Self-reliance is the cornerstone of the management policy for the Maze District. This network of twisted sandstone canyons is for rugged individuals who can take care of themselves and their vehicle. There's no gas station, restaurant, or room service for 50-plus miles in any direction. And even those 50 miles don't tell the true story, because it might take half a day to cover that distance on these roads.

In many national parks, including other sections of Canyonlands, the NPS provides great "customer service." But not in the Maze. The Maze District of Canyonlands National Park combined with the Orange Cliffs Unit of Glen Canyon National Recreation Area (NRA) is larger than many national parks, but once you leave the Hans Flat Ranger Station, there are no services—no guided tours, no facilities, no toilets, not even an entrance station. You're on your own, so prepare for it.

In the Maze District you should measure roads and trails in hours instead of miles. A 1-mile trail can take 1 hour to hike; a 5-mile stretch of road can take 2 or 3 hours to drive. Under any circumstances, don't be in a hurry.

After a heavy rain the clay coating on some roads in the Maze (particularly the Flint Trail) makes them too slippery to drive. Also, in winter months, ice and snow can make the roads impassable. During winter the Flint Trail is usually closed.

Before you go to the Maze District, make sure you know where you're going, what to bring, and how to prepare. This isn't like going to other national parks. If you show up without the necessary gear to survive on your own, you won't enjoy the Maze District. Yet it happens all the time. People show up in a rented SUV that's not supposed to be driven off paved roads, and they expect to get into the Maze. A very bad idea!

Hiking into Great Gallery might be better than the art you find there (Hike 56).

Glen Canyon, including the Orange Cliffs Special Management Unit, has started charging an entrance fee. The fee is not currently required in the Orange Cliffs if you have a camping permit, but is required for day use in the Orange Cliffs.

## GETTING TO HANS FLAT RANGER STATION

From Hanksville go north 21 miles on UT 24 and turn right (east) onto a major unpaved, two-wheel-drive road marked with signs for the Glen Canyon National Recreation Area and Canyonlands National Park. From here it's 46 miles to Hans Flat Ranger Station, with a right-hand turn at the 24-mile mark; both junctions are well signed.

From Hite take UT 95 north for 2 miles and turn right (east) onto an unpaved, high-clearance, two-wheel-drive road. After 32 miles this road turns into a high-clearance, four-wheel-drive road, which includes ascending the Flint Trail (which weather conditions can make impassable) to reach Hans Flat. It's about 59 miles to the Hans Flat Ranger Station, with several junctions once you get to the park, all well signed. It takes most drivers 5 to 6 hours to drive from UT 95 to Hans Flat, depending on road conditions. Unless you have a camping reservation, you will need to pay an entrance fee at the Hite Ranger Station.

If you're coming from Green River, go to the middle of town and watch for Long Street. Turn south onto Long Street and follow it to the edge of town, following the signs to the airport. Be sure to take a gradual left turn onto an unpaved road 2 miles after passing under I-70 and stay on it for 68 miles to Hans Flat Ranger Station. At the 28-mile mark, take a left at the junction with Dugout Spring Road, and at the 46-mile mark, take another left at the Hanksville junction. This road is usually passable with a high-clearance, two-wheel-drive vehicle, but at times deep sand areas can require four-wheel-drive capability. To be safe, bring a high-clearance, four-wheel-drive vehicle. You'll need it to go into the Maze anyway.

If you want to see Horseshoe Canyon (and you'll be missing something if you don't), watch for a small sign at the 41-mile mark that says Horseshoe Canyon Foot Trail 2 Miles. If you hit the junction with the road from Hanksville, you've gone about 5 miles too far. If you're coming from Hanksville, take a left at the same junction and go 5 miles north.

You can call the Hans Flat Ranger Station (435-259-2652) for help, but only during regular office hours (8 a.m. to 5 p.m.). Do not call from 5 p.m. to 8 a.m. unless it's an emergency.

## SPECIAL REGULATIONS

In addition to park regulations, the NPS has a few special rules for the Maze, Orange Cliffs, and Horseshoe Canyon sections of the park.

- No wood fires are allowed, either in the vehicle campsites or while backpacking.

- Vehicle campers can have charcoal fires, but they must use a fire pan and remove the ashes along with other garbage. Pans can be purchased at the Hans Flat Ranger Station.

- Anybody using the vehicle campsites in the Maze District or Orange Cliffs Unit of Glen Canyon NRA must have and use a portable toilet and remove human waste along with all other garbage. An ammo can or plastic bag can be used provided the bags are specialty human waste carryout bags such as the Wag Bag or Rest Stop Two Bag. Portable toilets can be purchased at the Hans Flat Ranger Station.

- Backpackers can bury their human waste, but they must carry out their toilet paper.

- Backpack camping is at-large, but there are limits set for each backcountry zone. You don't need to get your backpacking permit until you get to Hans Flat, but you'd be wise to call in advance for a reservation. Don't make the effort to get there and then find out that you can't go backpacking because your chosen zone is full.

- Backpacking group size limit is five people.

- Vehicle permits have a limit of nine people and three vehicles, with the exception of Flint Seep, where up to sixteen people can camp.

- In Horseshoe Canyon groups larger than twenty people must be accompanied by a ranger. To arrange for a guided tour, call the Hans Flat Ranger Station between 8 a.m. and 4:30 p.m. at (435) 259-2652.

- Pets are not allowed (even in your vehicle) in the Maze District, Horseshoe Canyon, or Orange Cliffs Special Management Unit.

- Off-trail hiking in the Doll House area is prohibited.

- ATVs are not allowed in Canyonlands National Park and Glen Canyon NRA.

## WHAT KIND OF VEHICLE TO BRING TO THE MAZE

Unless you wish to hike great distances to fully experience the Maze District, you must have a high-clearance, four-wheel-drive vehicle with low-range gearing. You can see small parts of the Maze with a high-clearance, two-wheel-drive vehicle, but to see the best parts, you'll have to park it and hike long distances. A vehicle with a short wheelbase is best, but even with a long wheelbase, you can usually get through tight corners by backing up once or twice.

The roads in the Maze can deteriorate rapidly when it rains and become treacherous regardless of what kind of vehicle you have. At the same time, fortunately, they dry out relatively fast. If you get caught in a big rain, simply wait a few hours for the roads to dry.

## CALL IN ADVANCE

The staff at the Hans Flat Ranger Station is trained to help you and eager to answer your questions on the phone. That's much better for both you and the NPS because it's much more difficult to deal with lack of preparation once you're already there. Call in advance between 8 a.m. and 4:30 p.m. at (435) 259-2652. If for some reason you can't get through on the Hans Flat phone system, call the park headquarters at (435) 259-7164. For reservations for vehicle campsites in the Maze, call the park reservation office at (435) 259-4351.

## MOUNTAIN BIKING THE MAZE

Mountain biking is allowed on all designated roads (but not on trails or off-road) in the Maze District. The "Backcountry Roads" appendix has detailed descriptions for each road, including conditions for mountain biking. If you opt for a mountain-biking adventure in the Maze, carefully plan your trip. The NPS offers the following suggestions:

- Take a first-aid kit.
- Check your bike carefully before leaving, and take a bike repair kit.
- Take one gallon of water per day per biker.
- Take a lock to secure your bike if you plan to leave it to hike. This is better than riding or pushing your bike off the road to hide it.
- To avoid the intense heat of summer, try the spring and fall. Be prepared for coolish and unsettled weather.
- Wear a helmet and gloves.
- If you want solitude, avoid busy weekends and holidays.

### RECOMMENDED MOUNTAIN-BIKING ROUTES

You can take the following mountain-biking trips suggested by the NPS, or you can map out your own trip. In any case, be sure to stay on official roads. Mountain bikers can stay overnight at designated vehicle campsites, which are described as part of the road descriptions in the "Backcountry Roads" appendix, but you're required to have a portable toilet, so a support vehicle is necessary.

- East Rim of Horseshoe Canyon. Overnight trip; 44 miles round-trip from Hans Flat Ranger Station.
- Panorama Point and Cleopatra's Chair. Day or overnight trip; 20 miles round-trip from Hans Flat Ranger Station.
- Lands End and Big Ridge. Day or overnight trip; 32 miles round-trip from Hans Flat Ranger Station.
- Maze Overlook. Overnight or multi-night trip; 40 miles round-trip from the top of Flint Trail or 68 miles round-trip from Hans Flat Ranger Station.
- Land of Standing Rocks / Doll House. Multi-night trip; 50 miles round-trip from the top of Flint Trail or 78 miles round-trip from Hans Flat Ranger Station.

## GETTING THERE CAN BE HALF THE FUN

I'm not sure what the opinions of locals have to do with anything, but when I was on my way to the Maze for the first time, I started thinking that I had to drive lots of miles on backcountry roads and I might run short on gas. So I stopped in Green River to top off the tank. Somewhat foolishly, it seems, I pointed at the map and asked the gas station attendant if I could find a gas station anywhere down there. "Gas station? You'll be lucky if you find a building down there," he responded, rolling his eyes at his co-worker. He wasn't joking.

Undaunted, I later asked a waitress for directions to Hans Flat. She gave them to me but said, "There's nothing but desert out there, and if you go out there, you should have your will in order."

I was anxious to start hiking early the next morning, so I decided to drive down that night. It was a decent two-wheel-drive road all the way, but it was really lonely. For nearly 30 miles not even a light, not a sign, not another vehicle, nothing. I thought I saw a light once, but it was Venus. Shortly thereafter a jackrabbit jumped out on the road and almost gave me a heart attack.

Finally I saw a sign showing the way to Horseshoe Canyon, and then 5 miles later another sign and a junction with the left fork leading to Hans Flat Ranger Station. But there were still no lights or buildings until I reached the ranger station. That's nearly 70 miles of remoteness, quite the culture shock for people used to driving on freeways.

So if you go to the Maze, don't worry about getting caught in a traffic jam or, for that matter, seeing any sign of civilization.

# 56. **THE GREAT GALLERY**

## WHY GO?
Definitely one of the premier day hikes (closed to camping) in Canyonlands National Park, especially for hikers interested in ancient rock art

### THE RUNDOWN

**Start:** West Rim Trailhead

**Distance:** 7 miles; out and back

**Difficulty:** Moderate

**Nat Geo Trails Illustrated Map:** Canyonlands National Park

**Nat Geo TOPO! Map (USGS):** Sugarloaf Butte

## FINDING THE TRAILHEAD

There are two ways to get to Horseshoe Canyon. You can take the hike down from the west rim (as described here) or hike into the canyon from the east. To get to the West Rim Trailhead, go 5 miles north of the junction between the Hanksville and Green River access roads to the Maze and watch for a small sign on the east side of the road that says Horseshoe Canyon Foot Trail 2 Miles. From here drive 2 miles to the trailhead. **GPS coordinates:** 38° 28′ 25.601″ N / 110° 11′ 59.833″ W

## WHAT TO SEE
Although officially a detached unit of Canyonlands National Park, the Horseshoe Canyon area could be better described as a little hidden jewel lost in the desert. When you're driving toward it, you can't see it ahead and you might start to wonder if it's really out there. Then, suddenly, it drops out of the desert right in front of you.

Horseshoe Canyon is definitely worth the time it takes to get there. If you already plan on a few days in the Maze, you won't be disappointed if you spend one day of your vacation enjoying Horseshoe Canyon. If you're going to the Maze from Green River, Horseshoe Canyon is a convenient stop.

The Great Gallery is one of four major rock art sites in Horseshoe Canyon, but the fabulous rock art is only part—and perhaps not even the best part—of hiking this remote canyon. Horseshoe Canyon would be well worth the stop without seeing any rock art. It's a fantastic day hike through a secluded canyon lined with majestic cottonwoods and shaded by sheer sandstone cliffs.

Horseshoe Canyon has one other unusual trait. It's one of the few places in the Canyonlands with a fairly reliable water supply that's devoid of the evil tamarisk.

Sandstone enclaves in Horseshoe Canyon

NPS staff removed all tamarisk shrubs years ago, and now cottonwoods and other native vegetation have reclaimed the scenic canyon.

Rangers lead hikes into the canyon from the West Rim Trailhead at 9 a.m. on Saturday and Sunday during the spring and fall. Call the Hans Flat Ranger Station between 8 a.m. and 4:30 p.m. at (435) 259-2652 to verify the schedule. You can also request a guided tour during the week, but there is no guarantee that the NPS, with limited staff and funds, will be able to accommodate your party. If you have a group of twenty or more, you're required to have a ranger along.

You don't have to go with the ranger, of course, but it's the best way to get a more complete story and history of Horseshoe Canyon. The ranger stops at each of the four rock art sites to explain the history and prehistory and also comments on the natural history of the hidden canyon along the way. If you want to get good photographs of the rock art panels at the Great Gallery, early afternoon light is usually best.

The hike starts out on and follows an old road from the west rim to the canyon floor. Since it's an old road, the grade is not too steep. Nonetheless, it drops 750 feet in elevation in about 1.5 miles, which can get the heart rate up on the way back. The road is mostly slickrock at the upper end and turns to loose sand as you approach the canyon floor. This adds to the difficulty of climbing back out. Bring plenty of water.

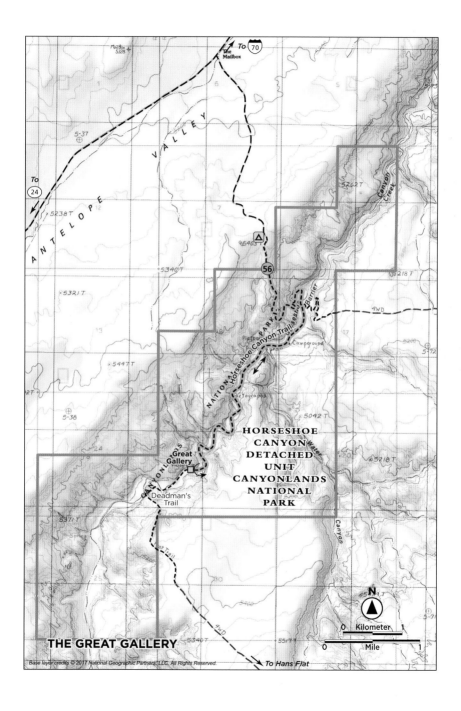

THE GREAT GALLERY

Base layer credits © 2017 National Geographic Partners, LLC. All Rights Reserved.

You'll see the remains of historic ranching operations (fences, pipes, water troughs, etc.). You can also see the old four-wheel-drive road that drops into the canyon from the east rim, which was destroyed by a big storm in 1997 and then converted to a trail. When you reach the canyon floor, the trail turns right and follows the canyon bottom for 2 miles to the Great Gallery.

A ranger often stays much of the day at the Great Gallery to answer questions. Watch for short side trails to rock art sites. If you miss them, you can catch them on the way back.

Rock art is extremely fragile and extremely precious, so don't touch any of the figures or disturb any artifacts found in the canyon. These are irreplaceable treasures. Crossing chain barriers placed around rock art by the NPS is prohibited, and this regulation is strictly enforced.

The rock art in Horseshoe Canyon is considered an example of the Barrier Canyon style, which dates back to the Late Archaic period from 2000 to 1000 BC. Later the Ancestral Puebloan cultures left their marks in the canyon but apparently stayed only briefly. These early cultures were followed by modern cultures—cattle and sheep ranchers, oil prospectors, miners, and now park visitors. Throughout all this use, however, the special character of the canyon has been wonderfully preserved. All visitors have the responsibility to do their part to keep it that way.

The Great Gallery is the last of four interpretive stops the ranger makes on the tours. It's a sprawling rock art panel with large, intricate figures, both pictographs (painted figures) and petroglyphs (figures etched in the stone with a sharp object). The NPS keeps binoculars in an ammo can so you can get a closer look at the rock art.

When you reach the Great Gallery, stop for lunch, rest a while, and marvel at a few things. For example, even though the pictographs have faded slightly through the centuries, how did the early cultures come up with a "paint" that lasted 3,000 years? What do the paintings really mean? What type of religious ceremonies might have occurred here? The ranger might toss out a few theories, but nobody really knows what went on at the Great Gallery thirty centuries ago.

On the way back, if you have the time and energy for more hiking, you can take the east-side trail up to the east rim for a different view of Horseshoe Canyon. That trail starts almost directly across from where the west-side trail hits the canyon wash and is marked by a cairn. It's about a mile to the east rim from the canyon floor.

# 57. **THE NORTH TRAIL**

## WHY GO?

A tough route into the Maze for hikers without four-wheel-drive vehicles

---

### THE RUNDOWN

**Start:** North Trail trailhead

**Distance:** 11.2 miles; out and back

**Difficulty:** Difficult

**Nat Geo Trails Illustrated Map:**
Canyonlands National Park

**Nat Geo TOPO! Map (USGS):**
Gordon Flats and Elaterite Basin

---

### FINDING THE TRAILHEAD

Drive 2.5 miles from Hans Flat Ranger Station and turn right (north) at the junction with North Point Road. Go another 0.9 mile and park on the left across from the trailhead sign. You can also park at the Panorama Point junction and hike down the road to the trailhead. **GPS coordinates:** 38° 14′ 19.223″ N / 110° 8′ 8.258″ W

## WHAT TO SEE

For hikers who don't have a four-wheel-drive vehicle or don't want to drive the Maze roads, the North Trail provides access to the Maze. It's for serious backpackers, though, since it's about 14 miles one-way to the Maze Overlook—the first 5.6 miles on designated trail (the route featured in this hike) and the rest on primitive roads. When you get to the Maze Overlook Trailhead, it's a short but tough mile-long drop into the Maze, where you can camp at-large per park regulations.

The North Trail starts out flat and well defined through junipers and piñon pines on North Point Mesa. After about a mile the trail drops into North Trail Canyon. The first part of the descent follows well-marked switchbacks. Then near the bottom there's a half-mile stretch of nearly trailless route-finding. There's no chance of getting lost, however, since the trail follows the narrow canyon.

After this one difficult stretch, the trail comes back but stays rocky and rough as it follows the dry wash of North Trail Canyon for about 2 miles. Then the valley opens up, and the trail gets easy and well defined on packed dirt, similar to the first mile up on the North Point Mesa. It stays that way over this section, about 2.5 miles, to the junction with Millard Canyon Road.

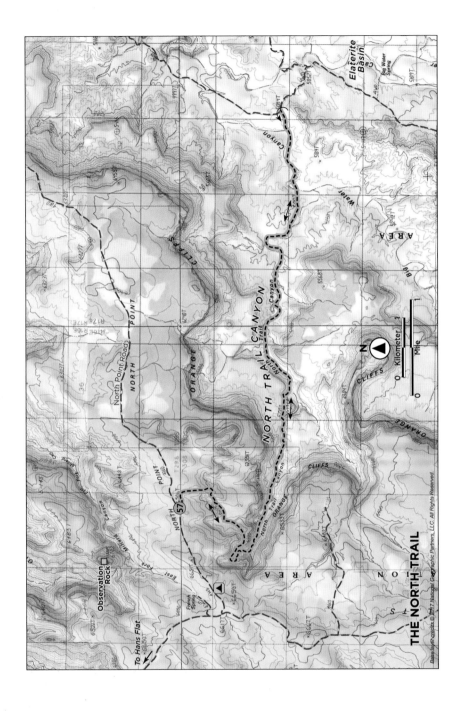

THE NORTH TRAIL

Piñon pines, like this one at Upheaval Dome, dot the landscape in Canyonlands.
ISTOCKPHOTO.COM

Near the end you cross a small ridge into the West Fork of Big Water Canyon just before the trail/road junction. You're now in Elaterite Basin. Massive Elaterite Butte dominates the horizon to the southeast, and to the north you can see equally massive Ekker Butte and Panorama Point.

If you're continuing on to the Maze Overlook, take a right (south) when you reach the road. If you're returning this way later, note the surroundings. There's no trailhead sign here.

If you plan to stay overnight and then return to the trailhead the next day, or if you started late and need a campsite for your first night on your way to the Maze Overlook, you can find many excellent choices along the easternmost 3 miles of the trail.

# 58. HAPPY CANYON

## WHY GO?

A nice day hike and a good choice for people who want to hike in the Maze District but don't have a four-wheel-drive vehicle

### THE RUNDOWN

**Start:** Trailhead at end of Happy Canyon Spur Road

**Distance:** 1.6 miles; out and back

**Difficulty:** Moderate

**Nat Geo Trails Illustrated Map:** Canyonlands National Park

**Nat Geo TOPO! Map (USGS):** Gordon Flats and Clearwater Canyon

### FINDING THE TRAILHEAD

From Hans Flat Ranger Station, drive 2.5 miles to the Panorama Point junction and take a right (south) onto Gordon Flats Road. After 12.1 miles pass by the left turn to the Flint Trail and keep going straight for another 1.3 miles until you see the right-hand turn (west) to Happy Canyon Camp. Turn here and go 0.4 mile to the camp on your left. The rest of the road has been blocked because of severe erosion. You can also park in the wide area where the road turns off to Happy Canyon Camp. **GPS coordinates:** 38° 6' 30.792" N / 110° 8' 12.261" W

Claretcup cactus

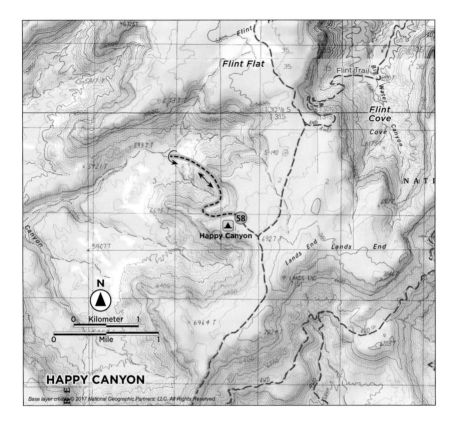

**HAPPY CANYON**

Base layer credit © 2017 National Geographic Partners, LLC. All Rights Reserved

## WHAT TO SEE

This trail is actually an abandoned jeep road. That means it has a fairly easy grade, but the road has eroded and deteriorated to make the hike tougher than it normally would be. The trail doesn't receive much use, so you'll probably have a choice piece of the Canyonlands all to yourself.

After just under a mile the trail ends as it reaches the floor of Happy Canyon. From here you can strike off in any direction to explore or set up your backpack camp. On the way down the trail, you get a sweeping view of the broad, flat Happy Canyon. You might want to take a few minutes on the way down to spot a few places to explore when you reach the end of the trail.

This hike is also a great choice for people who have only a two-wheel-drive vehicle. You can reach the end of the road without a four-wheel-drive vehicle, but there are a few rocky sections where you need to go very slowly and use great care. The NPS considers this an "overflow area" and recommends it when the Maze campsites fill up.

# 59. **THE GOLDEN STAIRS**

## WHY GO?

A delightful short day hike, especially if you're staying at Golden Stairs Camp

### THE RUNDOWN

**Start:** Golden Stairs Camp

**Distance:** 2.6 miles; out and back

**Difficulty:** Moderate

**Nat Geo Trails Illustrated Map:** Canyonlands National Park

**Nat Geo TOPO! Map (USGS):** Elaterite Basin

### FINDING THE TRAILHEAD

From Hans Flat Ranger Station, drive 2.5 miles to the Panorama Point junction and take a right (south) onto Gordon Flats Road. After 12.1 miles turn left (east) and head down the Flint Trail switchbacks for 2.8 miles to Maze Overlook Road, where you take a left (north). About 2.6 miles down this road, watch for a sign indicating a right turn (east) to the Golden Stairs Camp. In 2 miles this spur road dead-ends at the Golden Stairs Camp, a parking area, and the trailhead. The trailhead is on the east side of the camp, not at the parking area where you might expect to find it. The trailhead does not have a sign, so watch for a No Bicycles sign and a string of cairns heading off to the east.
**GPS coordinates:** 38° 8′ 39.938″ N / 110° 4′ 59.086″ W

## WHAT TO SEE

If you're staying at the Golden Stairs Camp, you'll want to take a delightful evening or early morning walk down the Golden Stairs. For those who don't have the high-clearance, four-wheel-drive vehicle necessary to make it over the Teapot Rock section of Doll House Road, this trail also can be used as a way to backpack into Ernie's Country.

From the trail you get an expansive view of much of the Maze District, including the sprawling Ernie's Country and the Fins, and even a distant glimpse of the Land of Standing Rocks. You can also see the road to the Doll House as it passes through the rugged Teapot Rock Country.

For the first half mile, the trail passes through junipers and piñon pines on a mesa. Shortly after leaving the trailhead, you pass over China Neck, a narrow "bridge" between two sections of the mesa with steep cliffs on both sides. If you have children with you, watch them carefully.

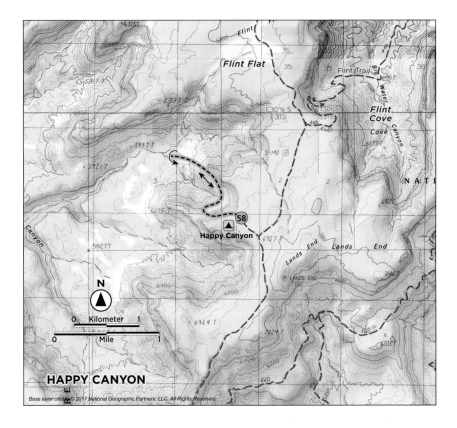

Soon after crossing the narrow section, the trail drops off the mesa and takes a big curve to the right, gradually descending. The grade is fairly mild as the trail traverses along the face of the cliff where it drops sharply down to the road. During this short steep section, you go through a series of gold-colored sandstone ledges commonly referred to as the Golden Stairs. It's difficult to see them while hiking down, but on the way back they're much more visible. Also on the way back, you get a great view to the north of the Mother and Child.

Although it's difficult to imagine when you're hiking this trail, it actually follows a historic route once used by ranchers to get their stock up to the mesa to graze. The trail goes over slickrock or loose rock most of the way. It isn't suited for fast hiking, but it's well marked and easy to follow.

At the east end of the trail where it meets the road, there is no sign. Instead, a huge cairn marks the trailhead.

# 60. **MAZE OVERLOOK**

## WHY GO?
A short but steep drop into the Maze, often the first leg of longer day hikes or backpacking trips

### THE RUNDOWN

**Start:** Maze Overlook Trailhead and Parking Area

**Distance:** 1.6 miles; out and back

**Difficulty:** Difficult

**Nat Geo Trails Illustrated Map:** Canyonlands National Park

**Nat Geo TOPO! Map (USGS):** Elaterite Basin and Spanish Bottom

## FINDING THE TRAILHEAD
From Hans Flat Ranger Station, take a right (south) onto Gordon Flats Road at the Panorama Point junction at the 2.5-mile mark. At the 12.1-mile mark, turn left (east) and head down the Flint Trail. At the 14.9-mile mark, you hit the junction with Maze Overlook Road. Take a left (north) and go another 8.1 miles to the junction with Millard Canyon Road. Take a right here and go 5 miles to the Maze Overlook. **GPS coordinates:** 38° 14' 4.687" N / 110° 0' 4.469" W

The view from Maze Overlook
NPS/NEAL HERBERT

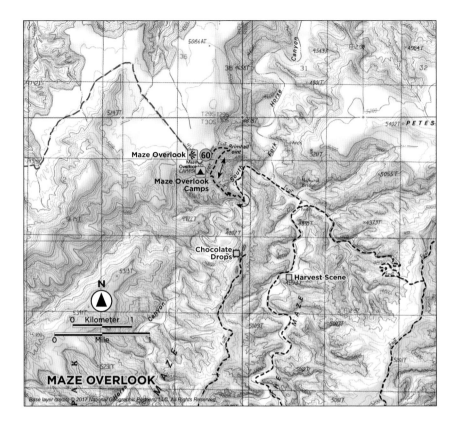

## WHAT TO SEE

Before you head down the trail, take a few minutes to survey the landscape. They call this place the Maze Overlook because you get a great overview of the well-named Maze. The magnificent Chocolate Drops highlight the southern horizon, and you can see Standing Rock, Chimney Rock, Lizard Rock, and many other famous landmarks of the Maze District from here.

The Maze Overlook Trail is not for beginners or hikers afraid of heights. It's short, but it drops 600 feet in elevation in about a mile and is steep and exposed in places, requiring you to use your hands for safety.

Over the first part of the trail, try not to get too absorbed by the scenery and miss the next cairn. The trail meanders back and forth, using ledges as a safe route to the canyon bottom. Then the trail strikes off across the slickrock. It goes through two tight joints, which might be too narrow for an overstuffed backpack. In two or three places, you might want to use a rope to lower your backpack to be safe. Slickrock steps, chipped out of solid rock, help you get down the steepest parts of the trail.

Even though the trail seems rough, it's actually expertly constructed to get down a difficult route to the floor of the Maze. With a little care the Maze Overlook Trail can be perfectly safe.

Once you get to the bottom, you'll see a major seep where, if necessary, you can get water. However, be sure to purify it before drinking. From this point you can head off in several directions to add distance to your hike, following canyons through the Maze.

# 61. **HARVEST SCENE**

## WHY GO?
A rare loop trail that's the longest day hike in the Maze

---

### THE RUNDOWN

**Start:** Chimney Rock Trailhead

**Distance:** 8.7 miles; loop

**Difficulty:** Difficult

**Nat Geo Trails Illustrated Map:**
Canyonlands National Park

**Nat Geo TOPO! Map (USGS):**
Spanish Bottom

---

### FINDING THE TRAILHEAD

From Hans Flat Ranger Station, drive 2.5 miles to the Panorama Point junction and take a right (south) onto Gordon Flats Road. After 12.1 miles turn left (east) and head down the Flint Trail switchbacks for 2.8 miles to Maze Overlook Road, where you take a right (south). Follow this road through Waterhole Flat for 3.5 miles to a four-way junction with Doll House Road. Turn left (northeast) and head for the Doll House and Land of Standing Rocks. Some maps might show a cutoff trail where it looks like you can save some time, but this is deceptively incorrect. You actually can make faster time on the longer route because of the excellent roads in this section. Once on Doll House Road, stay on it for 17.1 miles to Chimney Rock Camp. At the east end of the camp, you find a parking area and a major trailhead. The trails aren't signed, but watch for strings of cairns heading off on each side of Chimney Rock, which mark the two trails you want for the Harvest Scene loop. **GPS coordinates:** 38° 11' 11.109" N / 109° 58' 27.962" W

## WHAT TO SEE

This trail is not only a rare loop (most Maze trails are out and back), but it's also the longest designated trail in the Maze. If you're in the vicinity with an extra day at your disposal, you can reward yourself by spending that time on this long day hike. You can also backpack and camp at-large in the area, which has several great campsites.

The trail goes to one of the most famous rock art sites in the world, Harvest Scene. Plus it passes through two beautiful canyons indicative of the hiking terrain that has made the Maze so popular. The difference is that you're on designated routes instead of off-trail canyon routes.

Although the routes are designated and marked by cairns, this hike is not for beginners. It has some steep climbs and requires experience in following routes

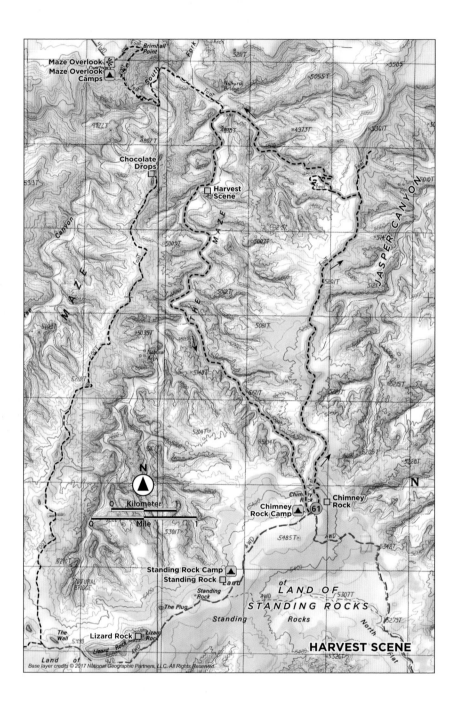

The Chocolate Drops are visible from several roads and trails in the Maze District.
NPS/NEAL HERBERT

marked only (and sometime sparsely) with cairns. Most of the trail goes over slick-rock or follows canyon washes, and there are several side canyons quite capable of confusing the hiker. Cairns mark the trail, but backpackers sometimes set up unofficial cairns to mark the location of their camp and cairns sometimes fall down, so you must be able to find the correct way on your own. Keep your topo map in hand all the way, constantly noting your location.

This trail description follows the counterclockwise route, not because it's easier but because it's slightly less confusing at one critical spot where you turn out of one canyon and into another. To take the counterclockwise route, start on the trail just east of Chimney Rock. Be careful not to start on a trail on the far east end of the parking area. This is an off-trail route up Shot and Water Canyons.

The first section of trail stays on top of a slickrock ridge between two unnamed canyons. In some sections the cairns are sparse, so stay alert. To your right you can see into precipitous Jasper Canyon, which is closed to all entry to preserve a unique biological resource.

At the 3.5-mile mark, the trail takes a sharp left and makes a steep but safe descent into the dry wash of an unnamed canyon. This is the most confusing stretch of the hike, so keep the topo map out and note your progress carefully. There are at least three side canyons that could get you lost.

After a mile walk in this canyon, you reach a major junction of canyons. It's not an exaggeration to say that canyons head off in every direction. You need to take the sharp left into an unnamed canyon and head for the Harvest Scene (named on most maps). If there's any doubt in your mind, backtrack or take the extra time to make sure you're headed in the right direction.

Any doubts you have will be erased after about a half mile, when you see the spectacular Harvest Scene rock art panel on your right. (Just before you get to Harvest Scene, you get a good view of the massive Chocolate Drops formation on the canyon rim near the Maze Overlook Camps.)

Like other rock art panels, the Harvest Scene is an extremely precious treasure, so don't touch or damage the rock art in any way. It has lasted 3,000 years, and if all park visitors treat it with exceptional care, it might last another 3,000.

After taking a break at Harvest Scene, continue south down the unnamed Maze canyon, a side canyon to sprawling Horse Canyon. Again, keep the topo map out to make sure you don't accidentally get in the wrong canyon.

Both canyons you follow on this hike have intermittent and unreliable water sources. On many spring hikes you can see little gemlike pools with their biotic communities of snails, worms, and water striders.

After a pleasant 3-mile walk up Petroglyph Fork, you climb up to the canyon rim. This is a fairly steep but short climb. From this point it's an easy mile or so on slickrock back to Chimney Rock.

# 62. COLORADO / GREEN RIVER OVERLOOK

## WHY GO?

Perhaps the most spectacular hike in the Doll House area of the Maze

### THE RUNDOWN

**Start:** Trailhead just before turn to Doll House 1 Camp

**Distance:** 7.4 miles; out and back

**Difficulty:** Moderate

**Nat Geo Trails Illustrated Map:** Canyonlands National Park

**Nat Geo TOPO! Map (USGS):** Spanish Bottom

### FINDING THE TRAILHEAD

From Hans Flat Ranger Station, drive 2.5 miles to the Panorama Point junction and take a right (south) onto Gordon Flats Road. After 12.1 miles turn left (east) and head down the Flint Trail switchbacks for 2.8 miles to Maze Overlook Road, where you take a right (south). Follow this road along an exposed ledge and down a steep dugway for 3.5 miles to a four-way junction with Doll House Road. Turn left (northeast) and head for the Doll House and Land of Standing Rocks. Some maps might show a cutoff trail that looks like it can save some time, but this is deceptively incorrect. You can actually make faster time on the longer route because of the excellent roads in this section. Once on Doll House Road, stay on it for 20.8 miles to the Doll House Camps. When you get to the Doll House area, the road forks, with Doll House 3 Camp on the right and Doll House 1 and Doll House 2 Camps on the left. Take a left; the trailhead is on your left about 100 yards before you turn again to Doll House 1 Camp.
**GPS coordinates:** 38° 9' 18.350" N / 109° 56' 56.004" W

## WHAT TO SEE

This is the longest and perhaps most spectacular of the three designated hikes in the Doll House area. It traverses all types of terrain—canyon wash, open parks, narrow joints, slickrock. It even goes by massive Beehive Arch on its way to lofty overlooks where you can see the mighty Colorado River absorbing the equally mighty Green River and heading south to Cataract Canyon.

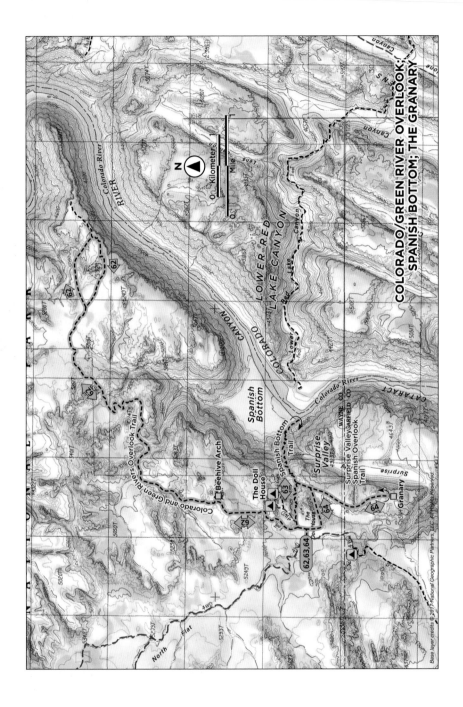

COLORADO/GREEN RIVER OVERLOOK; SPANISH BOTTOM; THE GRANARY

Green River sunset
NPS/NEAL HERBERT

If you have time for only one day hike during your stay in the Doll House area, this is a great choice. If you're in the mood to backpack, you can find many excellent at-large campsites along this route.

The first mile or so of the trail wanders its way through the spires of the Doll House, going right by Beehive Arch. If you're only interested in a short, flat day hike, you can turn around after investigating the massive arch.

After you leave the Doll House area, the trail drops into the dry wash of an unnamed canyon, which forks once, with the trail going right. Watch for cairns here; if you aren't paying attention, you could go straight and get off the trail. After about 2.5 miles you climb out of the dry wash. The trail goes through several open parks with sandstone spires on the horizon.

Next you pass through two narrow canyons between the sandstone formations before reaching the beginning of a small loop. The little loop trail at the end of this hike might not be marked with a sign, and it can be confusing. Get your map out and check it carefully. Along the loop you can strike off to the southeast or northeast along slickrock ledges to get magnificent views of the Colorado and Green Rivers.

On the way back don't miss the spot where the trail leaves the dry wash and goes off to the left. It would be relatively easy to keep going straight and be temporarily lost.

# 63. **SPANISH BOTTOM**

## WHY GO?
A short, steep hike down to the Colorado River

### THE RUNDOWN
**See map on page 228.**

**Start:** Trailhead just before turn to Doll House 1 Camp

**Distance:** 3 miles; out and back

**Difficulty:** Moderate

**Nat Geo Trails Illustrated Map:** Canyonlands National Park

**Nat Geo TOPO! Map (USGS):** Spanish Bottom

## FINDING THE TRAILHEAD
From Hans Flat Ranger Station, drive 2.5 miles to the Panorama Point junction and take a right (south) onto Gordon Flats Road. After 12.1 miles turn left (east) and head down the Flint Trail switchbacks for 2.8 miles to Maze Overlook Road, where you take a right (south). Follow this road along an exposed ledge and down a steep dugway for 3.5 miles to a four-way junction with Doll House Road. Turn left (northeast) and head for the Doll House and Land of Standing Rocks. Some maps might show a cutoff trail that looks like it can save some time, but this is deceptively incorrect. You can actually make faster time on the longer route because of the excellent roads in this section. Once on Doll House Road, stay on it for 20.8 miles to the Doll House Camps. When you get to the Doll House area, the road forks, with Doll House 3 Camp on the right and Doll House 1 and Doll House 2 Camps on the left. Take a left; the trailhead is on your left about 100 yards before you turn again to Doll House 1 Camp.
**GPS coordinates:** 38° 9' 18.350" N / 109° 56' 56.004" W

## WHAT TO SEE
The Spanish Bottom Trail drops steeply from the trailhead all the way down to the Colorado River, hitting the river just after the Colorado has absorbed the Green River. Even though the trail drops about 1,100 feet in about a mile, it's still the easiest way to get to the Colorado River from the Doll House area. The well-constructed trail with frequent switchbacks partly mitigates the steepness. The trail is well defined and marked the entire way.

The first quarter mile of the trail is nice and flat as it curves between the stunning sandstone towers of the Doll House. Then, shortly after you take a left at the junction with the Granary Trail, the Spanish Bottom Trail starts descending.

Spanish Bottom in the Maze
District of Canyonlands
NPS/NEAL HERBERT

For most of the way down, you can see the large and extremely flat Spanish Bottom and the Colorado River flowing by it. You might see some campers, too, since this is a popular campsite for people floating the river. They like to camp here to gather their courage for the thunderous Cataract Canyon just around the bend in the river.

When you get to the bottom, take a break and relax for a while—and, of course, amass your strength for a steep climb back up to the Doll House. The sharp incline makes this a great trail to hike in the coolish temperatures of the early morning or early evening.

# 64. **THE GRANARY**

## WHY GO?

A short hike with some stunning scenery and cultural history

**THE RUNDOWN**

See map on page 228.

**Start:** Trailhead just before turn to Doll House 1 Camp

**Distance:** 1.6 miles; loop

**Difficulty:** Easy

**Nat Geo Trails Illustrated Map:** Canyonlands National Park

**Nat Geo TOPO! Map (USGS):** Spanish Bottom

## FINDING THE TRAILHEAD

From Hans Flat Ranger Station, drive 2.5 miles to the Panorama Point junction and take a right (south) onto Gordon Flats Road. After 12.1 miles turn left (east) and head down the Flint Trail switchbacks for 2.8 miles to Maze Overlook Road, where you take a right (south). Follow this road along an exposed ledge and down a steep dugway for 3.5 miles to a four-way junction with Doll House Road. Turn left (northeast) and head for the Doll House and Land of Standing Rocks. Some maps might show a cutoff trail that looks like it can save some time, but this is deceptively incorrect. You can actually make faster time on the longer route because of the excellent roads in this section. Once on Doll House Road, stay on it for 20.8 miles to the Doll House Camps. When you get to the Doll House area, the road forks, with Doll House 3 Camp on the right and Doll House 1 and Doll House 2 Camps on the left. Take a left; the trailhead is on your left about 100 yards before you turn again to Doll House 1 Camp.

**GPS coordinates:** 38° 9′ 18.350″ N / 109° 56′ 56.004″ W

## WHAT TO SEE

The first part of the hike (which follows the same route as the Spanish Bottom Trail) is actually part of a small loop. After less than a half mile of flat, easy hiking through the Doll House towers, you reach a junction. Take a right (southwest) and head to the Granary instead of dropping off the edge of the plateau to Spanish Bottom.

After another quarter mile of easy walking, you reach yet another junction, with the Granary Trail going to the left. The right fork takes you back to the trailhead, and you will take this path after you visit the Granary and see Surprise Valley.

Just before you reach the Granary, look for an overlook on your left only a few feet off the trail. From here you get a spectacular vista of Surprise Valley, a classic

Ancestral Puebloan granary
NPS/NEAL HERBERT

graben and a gorgeous one at that. About another 100 yards up the trail is the Granary, a typical storage place used by the Ancestral Puebloans to hide grain for the lean winter months.

On the way back be sure to take the left fork at the first junction. This follows a well-laid-out route through the Doll House, including a long stretch through joints in the sandstone formations. The entire trail is well defined, mostly packed dirt, and easy to follow.

# CANYONLANDS NATIONAL PARK BACKCOUNTRY CAMPSITE GPS COORDINATES

| NAME OF CAMPSITE | TYPE OF CAMPSITE | LAT_D | LONG_D |
|---|---|---|---|
| SC1 | Designated backcountry campsite | 37° 59' 3.942" N | 109° 44' 32.148" W |
| SC2 | Designated backcountry campsite | 37° 59' 8.271" N | 109° 44' 28.831" W |
| SC3 | Designated backcountry campsite | 38° 2' 19.475" N | 109° 45' 44.564" W |
| SC4 | Designated backcountry campsite | 38° 3' 18.498" N | 109° 46' 16.068" W |
| LC1 | Designated backcountry campsite | 38° 7' 14.913" N | 109° 46' 38.918" W |
| LC2 | Designated backcountry campsite | 38° 6' 59.828" N | 109° 47' 10.300" W |
| LC3 | Designated backcountry campsite | 38° 6' 34.783" N | 109° 47' 42.045" W |
| SQ1 | Designated backcountry campsite | 38° 7' 18.832" N | 109° 48' 0.005" W |
| SQ2 | Designated backcountry campsite | 38° 6' 47.350" N | 109° 48' 18.017" W |
| BS2 | Designated backcountry campsite | 38° 7' 33.578" N | 109° 48' 49.584" W |
| BS1 | Designated backcountry campsite | 38° 8' 10.948" N | 109° 48' 36.245" W |
| EC3 | Designated backcountry campsite | 38° 6' 47.428" N | 109° 50' 14.082" W |
| EC2 | Designated backcountry campsite | 38° 6' 52.693" N | 109° 50' 13.406" W |
| EC1 | Designated backcountry campsite | 38° 7' 28.712" N | 109° 50' 23.841" W |
| CP1 | Designated backcountry campsite | 38° 6' 50.361" N | 109° 50' 46.705" W |
| CP3 | Designated backcountry campsite | 38° 6' 23.487" N | 109° 51' 2.249" W |
| CP2 | Designated backcountry campsite | 38° 6' 19.235" N | 109° 51' 0.375" W |

| NAME OF CAMPSITE | TYPE OF CAMPSITE | LAT_D | LONG_D |
|---|---|---|---|
| CP4 | Designated backcountry campsite | 38° 6' 26.948" N | 109° 51' 2.841" W |
| CP5 | Designated backcountry campsite | 38° 6' 35.612" N | 109° 51' 7.921" W |
| DP1 | Designated backcountry campsite | 38° 7' 47.190" N | 109° 51' 48.613" W |
| Syncline | Designated backcountry campsite | 38° 26' 50.381" N | 109° 57' 16.180" W |
| Shafer | Backcountry vehicle campsite | 38° 28' 2.716" N | 109° 46' 33.592" W |
| White Crack | Backcountry vehicle campsite | 38° 15' 32.269" N | 109° 52' 8.388" W |
| Potato Bottom C | Backcountry vehicle campsite | 38° 25' 45.059" N | 110° 0' 34.292" W |
| Potato Bottom B | Backcountry vehicle campsite | 38° 25' 38.970" N | 110° 0' 31.625" W |
| Potato Bottom A | Backcountry vehicle campsite | 38° 25' 20.706" N | 110° 0' 20.322" W |
| Hardscrabble A | Backcountry vehicle campsite | 38° 27' 10.722" N | 110° 0' 32.018" W |
| Hardscrabble B | Backcountry vehicle campsite | 38° 27' 0.772" N | 110° 0' 33.255" W |
| Labyrinth A | Backcountry vehicle campsite | 38° 28' 30.060" N | 109° 59' 59.556" W |
| Labyrinth B | Backcountry vehicle campsite | 38° 28' 28.571" N | 110° 0' 1.777" W |
| Taylor | Backcountry vehicle campsite | 38° 28' 35.123" N | 109° 55' 39.385" W |
| Bobby Jo | Backcountry vehicle campsite | 38° 5' 49.809" N | 109° 52' 42.817" W |
| Horsehoof Arch | Backcountry vehicle campsite | 38° 5' 43.382" N | 109° 52' 52.807" W |
| Peekaboo Camp | Backcountry vehicle campsite | 38° 6' 45.004" N | 109° 45' 8.254" W |
| The Wall | Backcountry vehicle campsite | 38° 10' 17.862" N | 110° 1' 8.290" W |
| Standing Rock | Backcountry vehicle campsite | 38° 10' 48.175" N | 109° 59' 14.812" W |
| Chimney Rock | Backcountry vehicle campsite | 38° 11' 8.083" N | 109° 58' 41.518" W |

| NAME OF CAMPSITE | TYPE OF CAMPSITE | LAT_D | LONG_D |
|---|---|---|---|
| New Bates Wilson | Backcountry vehicle campsite | 38° 9' 44.999" N | 109° 51' 34.023" W |
| Millard Canyon | Backcountry vehicle campsite | 38° 23' 25.420" N | 110° 2' 9.068" W |
| Willow Flat | Frontcountry campsite | 38° 22' 58.140" N | 109° 53' 14.967" W |
| Squaw Flat | Frontcountry campsite | 38° 8' 53.640" N | 109° 48' 7.039" W |
| Horseshoe Canyon | Backcountry vehicle campsite | 38° 28' 17.567" N | 110° 12' 1.308" W |
| Devils Kitchen | Backcountry vehicle campsite | 38° 8' 15.019" N | 109° 51' 41.057" W |
| Dollhouse 3 | Backcountry vehicle campsite | 38° 8' 59.271" N | 109° 57' 10.301" W |
| Dollhouse 2 | Backcountry vehicle campsite | 38° 9' 16.525" N | 109° 56' 51.492" W |
| Dollhouse 1 | Backcountry vehicle campsite | 38° 9' 18.350" N | 109° 56' 56.004" W |
| Maze Overlook 2 | Backcountry vehicle campsite | 38° 13' 55.002" N | 110° 0' 13.335" W |
| Maze Overlook 1 | Backcountry vehicle campsite | 38° 14' 2.075" N | 110° 0' 3.739" W |
| Murphy C | Backcountry vehicle campsite | 38° 19' 26.988" N | 109° 54' 43.488" W |
| Murphy B | Backcountry vehicle campsite | 38° 19' 24.883" N | 109° 54' 26.493" W |
| Murphy A | Backcountry vehicle campsite | 38° 19' 19.268" N | 109° 54' 27.949" W |
| Gooseberry A | Backcountry vehicle campsite | 38° 19' 58.681" N | 109° 49' 40.031" W |
| Gooseberry B | Backcountry vehicle campsite | 38° 19' 54.873" N | 109° 49' 48.608" W |
| Airport D | Backcountry vehicle campsite | 38° 23' 20.222" N | 109° 48' 4.408" W |
| Airport C | Backcountry vehicle campsite | 38° 23' 22.760" N | 109° 47' 58.865" W |
| Airport B | Backcountry vehicle campsite | 38° 23' 30.814" N | 109° 47' 42.238" W |
| Airport A | Backcountry vehicle campsite | 38° 23' 37.807" N | 109° 47' 48.720" W |
| Candlestick | Backcountry vehicle campsite | 38° 22' 18.917" N | 109° 57' 45.607" W |

# BACKCOUNTRY ROADS

In many cases, hikers have to navigate backcountry roads to reach trailheads in both **ARCHES AND CANYONLANDS NATIONAL PARKS**, so here is a brief summary of the road conditions, including vehicle requirements.

## Arches National Park

### WILLOW FLATS

**Start:** Willow Flats turnoff on the main park road

**Distance:** 4 miles from paved road to park boundary

**Maps:** Trails Illustrated Arches National Park and USGS Arches National Park

**Permits:** No permit required

**Minimum vehicle requirements:** Low-clearance, four-wheel-drive

**Difficulty:** Easy

**Road conditions:** Smooth driving on unpaved surfaces, packed dirt most of the way with a few short rocky sections and possible washouts after rains

**Suitability for mountain biking:** Moderate; the road can get seriously washboarded

**Vehicle campsites:** None

### SALT VALLEY

**Start:** Salt Valley turnoff on the main park road

**Distance:** 9.6 miles from the paved road to park boundary

**Maps:** Trails Illustrated Arches National Park and USGS Arches National Park

**Permits:** No permit required

**Minimum vehicle requirements:** Low-clearance, two-wheel-drive

**Difficulty:** Easy unless road surface is wet, which makes the road impassable

**Road conditions:** Smooth driving on unpaved, packed-dirt surface

**Suitability for mountain biking:** Excellent, although the road can get seriously washboarded

**Vehicle campsites:** None

**Special precautions:** Avoid this road after it rains. Sections of clay become seriously slippery when wet.

## FOUR-WHEEL-DRIVE ROAD

**Start:** Salt Valley turnoff on the main park road

**Distance:** 16.6 miles for entire loop, not including a 3-mile round-trip to Tower Arch

**Maps:** Trails Illustrated Arches National Park and USGS Arches National Park

**Permits:** No permit required

**Minimum vehicle requirements:** High-clearance, four-wheel-drive with low-range gearing

**Difficulty:** Easy to moderate with one difficult stretch between Salt Valley Road and the Tower Arch turnoff

**Road conditions:** The road conditions on Salt Valley and Willow Flats Roads are easy, but the connecting road has some difficult stretches. Shortly after turning off the Salt Valley Road, the road goes over a ridge with several tight turns, small ledges, and long rocky sections. Drive this section slowly and carefully.

**Suitability for mountain biking:** Excellent on Salt Valley Road, but only fair on the four-wheel-drive road and difficult during one long section of loose sand at the 12-mile mark

**Vehicle campsites:** None.

**Special attractions:** Tower Arch and the view of the Marching Men from the junction of the four-wheel-drive road and the spur road to Tower Arch

**Special precautions:** It's better to drive this loop in a counterclockwise direction so you can go downhill on one long section of loose sand. In fact, in summer months, park regulations prohibit driving on this road in a clockwise direction.

## MILES AND DIRECTIONS

0.0   Start at Salt Valley turnoff.

7.1   Left turn at sign marked Four-Wheel-Drive Road.

9.9   Spur road to Tower Arch.

12.0   Difficult stretch of loose sand.

14.0   Eye of the Whale Arch.

16.1   Willow Flats Road.

16.6   Main park road.

**HOW TO DRIVE**

Of course you know how to drive, right? Driving some of the roads in Arches and Canyonlands National Parks might make you wonder about your ability. The most critical advice given out by the NPS is "Don't be in a hurry." If you're on a tight schedule, you probably won't have much fun. You might wreck your vehicle, too, and the towing fee might bankrupt you.

Stay on the designated road and don't widen the road just to miss a mud puddle, small rock, or little ledge. If the road goes over a ledge, that's probably the best route and has been used by thousands of drivers who have gone before you. If each visitor widened the road a few inches, it would soon have a major negative impact on the fragile high desert environment.

Watch ahead for vehicles coming your way, especially in narrow sections or on switchbacks. If you see another vehicle coming, pull over at the first convenient spot. Don't assume the other driver has seen your vehicle or that there will be another good spot to pull off before your vehicles meet.

# Canyonlands National Park: Island in the Sky

## GREEN RIVER OVERLOOK

**Start:** Turnoff on Upheaval Dome Road

**Distance:** 1.3 miles (one-way)

**Maps:** Trails Illustrated Island in the Sky and USGS Upheaval Dome

**Permits:** No permit required

**Minimum vehicle requirements:** Low-clearance, two-wheel-drive

**Difficulty:** Easy

**Road conditions:** Paved road

**Suitability for mountain biking:** Excellent

**Vehicle campsites:** Road goes by entrance to Willow Flat Campground

**Special attractions:** Great vista of White Rim country and, in the background, the Maze District. A skyline locator at the overlook helps you identify the major landmarks. The interpretive display at the overlook explains how John Wesley Powell explored the Green River country and found "cathedral-like buttes towering hundreds or thousands of feet and cliffs that cannot be scaled and canyon walls that shrink the river into insignificance." Today you can float through this section of the Green River and still see the same thing— and be as impressed as Powell was.

**Special precautions:** Although the overlook is partially fenced, watch children carefully.

Heading down Shafer Trail
to the White Rim Road

## SHAFER TRAIL

**Start:** About a quarter mile south of the Island in the Sky entrance station

**Distance:** 6.6 miles (one-way) to the park boundary

**Maps:** Trails Illustrated Island in the Sky and USGS Musselman Arch

**Permits:** Vehicle camping or backcountry permit required. Free day-use permit required. Get one at the visitor center. People driving up the Shafer Trail from Moab must stop at the park entrance station and pay the park entrance/exit fee.

**Minimum vehicle requirements:** High-clearance, four-wheel-drive with low-range gearing. Carry chains in winter.

**Difficulty:** Moderate

**Road conditions:** Fairly easy driving with the exception of a few short rocky spots in the last 2 miles

**Suitability for mountain biking:** Excellent, but be careful going down switchbacks. There is a steep grade coming back up to the entrance station.

**Vehicle campsites:** Shafer Camp (one campsite)

**Special precautions:** Be alert driving or mountain biking down the steep switchbacks in the first mile. Watch ahead and pull over if you see another vehicle coming up the switchbacks. Road conditions change if it rains or snows. When wet you need a four-wheel-drive vehicle with chains.

## MILES AND DIRECTIONS

0.0   Start south of Island in the Sky entrance station.

4.5   Bottom of switchbacks.

5.1   Left turn to Moab and Potash; vault toilet.

6.1   Shafer Camp.

6.6   Park boundary.

## THE WHITE RIM

**Start:** About a quarter mile south of the Island in the Sky entrance station

**Distance:** 72.2 miles within the park, plus another 24.6 miles to get back to your starting point

**Maps:** Trails Illustrated Island in the Sky and USGS Musselman Arch, Monument Basin, Turks Head, Horsethief Canyon, and Upheaval Dome

**Permits:** Vehicle camping and backcountry permit required. Free day-use permit required. Get one at the visitor center.

**Minimum vehicle requirements:** High-clearance, four-wheel-drive with low-range gearing

**Difficulty:** Moderate

**Road conditions:** When dry it's fairly easy four-wheeling most of the way, primarily on a packed-dirt road surface with intermittent rocky sections. The section of road around

Musselman Arch gets very rocky, and the sections over Murphy Hogback and between Potato Bottom and Hardscrabble Camps are steep and hazardous when wet.

**Suitability for mountain biking:** Excellent conditions most of the way, with the exception of numerous but short rocky sections. Steep upgrades going up to Fort Bottom, Murphy Hogback, Shafer Trail, and near the end of the trip at Mineral Bottom. Also, some deep sandy stretches, especially on the west side, can make mountain biking difficult. Remember that bicycles stay on the roads just as motorized vehicles do.

**Vehicle campsites:** All campsites along White Rim Road have NPS-maintained vault toilets. Reservations are highly recommended, as sites may be booked up to one year in advance. The campsites include the following:

**Airport**—Four campsites. Fairly exposed. Conveniently located for first night out on a multiday mountain-biking trip. In the shadow of Airport Tower. About 100 yards west of road.

**Gooseberry**—Two campsites. Exposed. About 100 yards west of road.

**White Crack**—One campsite. Exposed. Private (about 1.4 miles from White Rim Road). Great view into Colorado River Basin.

**Murphy**—Three campsites. Right along road. Great view into Green River Basin.

**Candlestick**—One campsite. Exposed. Great view of Candlestick Tower.

**Potato Bottom**—Three campsites. Right along road. Short level walk to Green River.

**Hardscrabble**—Two campsites. Private. Short walk to Green River.

**Labyrinth**—Two campsites. At junction with Taylor Canyon Road. Exposed. Short walk to Green River.

**Taylor**—One campsite. Private. Great view of Moses and Zeus and Trail Canyon.

**Special attractions:** The White Rim Road is, for most people, a multiday adventure. It has incredible scenery and world-famous mountain biking. The most popular way to see the White Rim Road is on a mountain bike, usually supported by a four-wheel-drive vehicle. Most people spend at least three days here to enjoy camping and hiking and to take spur roads into Lathrop and Taylor Canyons.

**Special precautions:** Unlike many park roads, the White Rim Road gets extensive use during peak seasons. The NPS limits the amount of overnight use with the permit system, but currently day use is not limited. Watch carefully for other vehicles (especially on the steep sections on the Shafer Trail, on the Murphy Hogback, and on Hardscrabble Hill near Fort Bottom) and for mountain bikers and hikers on the road. When wet, road conditions can dramatically worsen (especially around Fort Bottom). If you get caught in a rain, it might pay to wait 4 to 5 hours to let the road dry out. Also, be cautious around unfenced overlooks at the Gooseneck Overlook, Musselman

Arch, and Colorado River Overlook. The NPS recommends that you carry chains and a shovel as well. Be sure to take adequate water supplies. Store water in multiple containers—just in case one springs a leak.

## MILES AND DIRECTIONS

**0.0** Start south of Island in the Sky entrance station.

**4.5** Bottom of switchbacks.

**5.1** Turnoff to Moab and Potash.

**6.4** Gooseneck Trailhead.

**8.2** Colorado River Overlook.

**8.4** Musselman Arch.

**16.2** Lathrop Trail.

**16.3** Turnoff to Lathrop Canyon.

**17.3** Airport Tower Camp.

**27.2** Gooseberry Trail.

**27.7** Gooseberry Camp.

**35.7** Turnoff to White Crack Camp (1.4 miles off White Rim Road).

**42.1** Murphy Wash Trail.

**43.3** Murphy Camp.

**43.4** Murphy Hogback Trail.

**53.5** Candlestick Camp.

**55.7** Wilhite Trail.

**63.5** Potato Bottom Camp (A).

**64.7** Potato Bottom Camp (B and C).

**66.1** Fort Bottom Trail.

**67.8** Turnoff to Hardscrabble Camp (A and B).

**69.1** Upheaval Canyon Trail.

**69.7** Turnoff to Taylor Canyon (5 miles to Taylor Canyon Camp).

**69.8** Labyrinth Camp.

**72.2** Park boundary.

**76.0** Junction with Mineral Bottom Trail and spur road to Mineral Bottom Launch.

**77.5** Top of switchbacks and parking area.

**90.4** UT 313 and parking area.

**96.8** Island in the Sky entrance station.

## LATHROP CANYON

**Start:** Junction of White Rim Road and Lathrop Canyon, 16.3 miles from the Island in the Sky entrance station

**Distance:** 4 miles (one-way) from White Rim Road to Colorado River

**Hiking time:** About 30 to 60 minutes

**Maps:** Trails Illustrated Island in the Sky and USGS Musselman Arch and Monument Basin

**Permits:** At-large backpacking permit required. (Must be obtained at the visitor center.) Day use allowed without a permit.

**Minimum vehicle requirements:** High-clearance, four-wheel-drive with low-range gearing

**Difficulty:** Difficult

**Road conditions:** Extremely steep at head of canyon near White Rim Road, a few short slickrock sections and sandy conditions near the bottom.

**Suitability for mountain biking:** Mostly good, with a few short stretches of loose sand

**Vehicle campsites:** None; day use only. During high water this area can be inaccessible.

**Special attractions:** At the end of the road, where it runs into the Colorado River, you'll find a great place for a picnic or lunch break, with picnic tables, a vault toilet, and the shade of sprawling cottonwood, tamarisk, and willow trees.

**Special precautions:** The potential for flash floods is extremely high when it's raining. Road conditions can change rapidly. You might be tempted to jump in the river, but this is not a swimming pool. It's a big, powerful river.

## TAYLOR CANYON

**Start:** Junction between White Rim Road and Taylor Canyon Road, 2.5 miles from the north boundary of the park

**Distance:** 5 miles (one-way)

**Hiking time:** About 30 to 60 minutes

**Maps:** Trails Illustrated Island in the Sky and USGS Upheaval Dome

**Permits:** Vehicle camping or backpacking permit required, which can be obtained at the visitor center. Day use allowed without a permit.

**Minimum vehicle requirements:** High-clearance, four-wheel-drive with low-range gearing.

**Difficulty:** Moderate

**Road conditions:** Excellent conditions with a few rocky sections. Road conditions can change rapidly when wet, with flash flooding potential. Deep sand exists when conditions are very dry.

**Suitability for mountain biking:** Excellent conditions usually. Road conditions can change rapidly when wet, with flash flooding potential. Deep sand exists when conditions are very dry.

**Vehicle campsites:** Taylor Camp (one campsite) is at the end of the road in the shadow of the magnificent Moses formation.

**Special attractions:** The famous Moses and Zeus spires make Taylor Canyon particularly popular with rock climbers.

**Special precautions:** Don't try climbing the spires in the area without the proper training, equipment, and experience.

# Canyonlands National Park: The Needles

## SALT CREEK

**Start:** Salt Creek Trailhead at the locked gate

**Distance:** From the locked gate it's 3.7 miles (one-way) to Peekaboo Camp and the end of the road.

**Maps:** Trails Illustrated Needles and USGS The Loop, South Six-shooter Peak, and Druid Arch

**Permits:** The first step on your trip is a stop at the Needles Visitor Center to get a permit, needed for overnight or day use. Salt Creek has only two vehicle campsites (both at Peekaboo Camp), so overnight permits are often difficult to get. To improve your chances, use the park's reservation system. You can reserve a day-use permit in advance just like you do overnight permits. If you feel lucky, you can go to the visitor center and hope all permits aren't taken for that day. Try to get to the visitor center early in the day. When you get your permit, a ranger gives you the combination (changed daily) to the locked gate at the trailhead. Listen carefully to how to use the combination lock. It can be tricky.

**Minimum vehicle requirements:** High-clearance, four-wheel-drive with low-range gearing

**Difficulty:** Moderate

**Road conditions:** The first 2.5 miles are the most difficult part of the road because you pass through several sections of very loose sand where you must keep your speed up. The rest of the road is easy going with the exception of frequent stream crossings. In spring some of the water stretches can go on for 100 yards or more.

**Suitability for mountain biking:** The NPS does not recommend mountain biking in Salt Creek. Loose sand in the first 2.5 miles and frequent stream crossings along the road make mountain biking marginal at best.

**Vehicle campsites:** Peekaboo Camp (two campsites) is on your right about a mile after the junction with Horse Canyon Road. It's a lovely site under some huge cottonwood trees but quite close to the road, making privacy during midday difficult.

**Special attractions:** Besides being a gorgeous high desert canyon, Salt Creek attracted many early residents because of its reliable water sources. As a result, the canyon has numerous ruins and rock art panels.

**Special precautions:** Salt Creek is subject to flash floods. To be safe, take sleeping bags; water filter, water purification tablets, or extra water; and emergency food for two or three days. And, of course, keep your eye on the weather conditions.

## MILES AND DIRECTIONS

**0.0**  Start at the locked gate.

**2.5**  Junction with Horse Canyon Road.

**3.7**  Peekaboo Camp.

Camping at the Horseshoe
Canyon Trailhead

**BE OBSERVANT**

A wealth of rock art panels lies hidden in the overhanging cliffs and high alcoves of Salt Creek and Horse Canyon. Mainly because of the reliable water sources, Archaic and Ancestral Puebloan Indians inhabited this area over a span of at least 200 years. These early residents used the area extensively for farming, which explains the large number of granaries found in the canyon.

The National Park Service has designated the area the Salt Creek Archeological District. In 1975 the district was placed on the National Register of Historic Places. Be extremely careful not to disturb any ruins, granaries, or rock art. If you observe anybody else disturbing these fragile resources, please report it to a ranger.

## HORSE CANYON

**Start:** Salt Creek Trailhead at the locked gate

**Distance:** From the locked gate it's 8.9 miles (one-way) to the end of the road, plus the 0.5-mile (one-way) road to the Tower Ruin Viewpoint.

**Maps:** Trails Illustrated Needles and USGS The Loop, North Six-shooter Peak, and South Six-shooter Peak

**Permits:** Overnight and day-use permits required. Check at the Needles Visitor Center.

**Minimum vehicle requirements:** High-clearance, four-wheel-drive with low-range gearing

**Difficulty:** Moderate

**Road conditions:** Although Horse Canyon is, for the most part, easy four-wheeling, you must go through the first 2.5 miles of Salt Creek to get there. This stretch has several sections of loose sand where you must keep your speed up. Just before the Castle Arch Trailhead, there's one tight spot between a boulder and a cliff where you could leave some paint on a rock if you aren't careful.

**Suitability for mountain biking:** The NPS does not recommend mountain biking in Horse Canyon. Some parts of Horse Canyon would be fair for mountain biking, but several stretches of loose sand would be difficult. Getting through the first 2.5 miles of Salt Creek would make the area marginal at best for mountain biking.

**Vehicle campsites:** No vehicle campsites, but the parking area for Paul Bunyan's Potty has a vault toilet.

**Special attractions:** Paul Bunyan's Potty is an unusual (but well-named) pothole arch. Also, be sure to take the spur road to see Tower Ruin, among the most spectacular anywhere. It's in an alcove high above the valley floor. Don't climb up to this fragile site. Instead, just look and marvel about what it must have been like to build it, get water up there, or even live there.

## MILES AND DIRECTIONS

**0.0** Start at the locked gate.

**2.7** Junction with Salt Creek Road.

**3.7** Paul Bunyan's Potty.

**4.7** Tower Ruin Road.

**8.7** Castle Arch Trailhead.

**8.9** Fortress Arch Trailhead and end of Horse Canyon Road.

## COLORADO OVERLOOK

**Start:** Needles Visitor Center
**Distance:** From the visitor center it's 7 miles (one-way) to the overlook parking area.
**Maps:** Trails Illustrated Needles and USGS The Loop
**Permits:** No permit required
**Minimum vehicle requirements:** High-clearance, four-wheel-drive with low range gearing. Two-wheel-drive vehicles are not allowed.
**Difficulty:** Moderate
**Road conditions:** The first 3 miles are packed dirt and easily passable with a two-wheel-drive vehicle. Then the road gets rocky as it goes over several slickrock sections. The last mile is the toughest—it's mostly slickrock with several significant ledges.
**Suitability for mountain biking:** Excellent mountain biking
**Vehicle campsites:** None
**Special attractions:** Note the incredible canyon gouged out by Salt Creek on its way to the Colorado River.
**Special precautions:** This is an unfenced overlook with very steep cliffs, so be careful not to get too close to the edge. Keep the kids by your side.

## LAVENDER CANYON

**Start:** Locked gate at park boundary
**Distance:** From UT 211 it's 13.9 miles (one-way) to the park boundary. From the park boundary it's 4.1 miles (one-way) to the end of the main road or 3 miles (one-way) to the end of the west fork road of the West Fork of Lavender Canyon.
**Maps:** Trails Illustrated Needles and USGS South Six-shooter Peak and Hans Point
**Permits:** Day-use permit required, which is available at the Needles Visitor Center. At the park boundary you'll find a locked gate that opens with the combination the ranger writes on your permit. The combination changes every day, so you must come in and out on the days designated on the permit.
**Minimum vehicle requirements:** High-clearance, four-wheel-drive with low-range gearing
**Difficulty:** Moderate
**Road conditions:** The condition of the unpaved road to the park boundary is good. Inside the park the roads are mostly packed dirt with frequent sections of loose sand and a few short rocky sections. The road up the West Fork of Lavender Canyon (not shown on some maps) is more narrow and difficult than the main road. Some maps show the main road splitting again near the end of the road, but the right-hand fork only goes about 100 yards from the main road.
**Suitability for mountain biking:** Difficult mountain biking (both inside and outside the park) because of the abundance of loose sand
**Vehicle campsites:** No vehicle camping is allowed in Lavender Canyon. At-large backpacking with a permit is allowed, but you must leave your vehicle at the park boundary.

**Special attractions:** Under the right light conditions, the canyon walls such as those to the east dropping down from Bridger Jack Mesa really do take on a beautiful lavender color. In the first 0.5 mile after entering the park, watch for two beautiful but easy-to-miss arches on the western rim of the canyon. The first is Natural Arch. About 200 yards later you can see the second, Caterpillar Arch. Most maps note only one or the other of these two arches, but not both. Cleft Arch at the end of the main road is also an awesome sight.

**Special precautions:** The road to the park boundary goes through ranching operations on private land and through leased Bureau of Land Management land, so watch carefully for cattle (especially in spring, when calves are running around carefree) and respect private property in the area. Be sure to close all gates behind you.

## MILES AND DIRECTIONS

0.0   Start at locked gate.

0.1   First gate.

0.7   Left turn at an unsigned junction.

0.8   Wooden gate.

3.0   Right turn at a signed junction.

13.9   Locked gate at park boundary.

14.4   Split in road.

17.4   Cleft Arch.

18.0   End of main road.

## DEVILS LANE / CONFLUENCE OVERLOOK

**Start:** Park boundary

**Distance:** From UT 211 it's 42.8 miles (one-way) to the park boundary. From the park boundary it's 12.3 miles (one-way) to the Confluence Overlook Trailhead.

**Maps:** Trails Illustrated Needles and USGS Cross Canyon, Spanish Bottom, Druid Arch, and The Loop.

**Permits:** No permit necessary for day use, but overnight vehicle camping or at-large backpacking permits are required.

**Minimum vehicle requirements:** High-clearance, four-wheel-drive with low-range gearing

**Difficulty:** Difficult

**Road conditions:** With the exception of three technically difficult sections (South Boundary Hill, S.O.B. Hill, and Silver Stairs), the road is easy four-wheeling, mostly packed dirt with a few short rocky sections and some loose sand.

**Suitability for mountain biking:** Moderate mountain biking with a few sections of loose sand

**Vehicle campsites:** Bobby Jo (two campsites), Horsehoof (one campsite), and New Bates Wilson Camp (two campsites)

**Special attractions:** Confluence Overlook and challenging sections for experienced four-wheelers

**Special precautions:** The Confluence Overlook is unfenced, so please be careful, especially with kids.

## MILES AND DIRECTIONS

**0.0**  Start at park boundary.

**0.5**  South Boundary Hill (short rocky section).

**3.8**  Road to Bobby Jo and Horsehoof Camps.

**4.7**  Road to Chesler Park Trailhead.

**5.0**  Devils Pocket Trailhead.

**6.6**  S.O.B. Hill.

**7.8**  Road to Devils Kitchen Camp, Lower Red Lake Trailhead.

**8.4**  Silver Stairs.

**8.7**  One-way road to Elephant Hill.

**9.1**  New Bates Wilson Camp.

**11.4**  Confluence Overlook foot trail.

**12.0**  Junction with roads to Confluence Overlook (west) and Cyclone Canyon Trail.

**12.3**  Confluence Overlook Trailhead.

## ELEPHANT HILL / DEVILS POCKET LOOP

**Start:** Elephant Hill Trailhead

**Distance:** 9.4 miles (loop)

**Maps:** Trails Illustrated Needles and USGS The Loop

**Permits:** Day-use and overnight camping permits required. Get them at the visitor center.

**Minimum vehicle requirements:** High-clearance, four-wheel-drive with low-range gearing

**Difficulty:** Difficult

**Road conditions:** Starting right at the trailhead, Elephant Hill is extremely technical four-wheeling, as is the Silver Stairs section about halfway around the loop. Plus, there are a few more difficult sections. Between these rocky, technical spots, however, the road is easy driving on packed dirt with some loose sand. Keep in mind that this one-way loop can only be done in a clockwise direction.

**Suitability for mountain biking:** Fair to good, with slow going in technical sections over Elephant Hill and Silver Stairs and through some short sections of loose sand

**Vehicle campsites:** Devils Kitchen (four campsites), nestled amid large boulders and narrow spots between rock formations

**Special attractions:** Definitely challenging for the experienced four-wheeler

**Special precautions:** Be sure to check which sections of the loop are one-way travel only.

## MILES AND DIRECTIONS

0.0   Start at Elephant Hill Trailhead.

1.5   Junction with one-way road.

3.5   Devils Kitchen Camp, Devils Pocket Trailhead.

4.5   Junction with Devils Lane Road, Lower Red Lake Trailhead.

5.1   Silver Stairs.

6.1   Junction with one-way road.

8.3   Junction with Elephant Hill Road.

9.4   Elephant Hill Trailhead.

Driving the White Rim Road is not for the faint-hearted.

Most people see the White Rim Road from a mountain bike saddle.

# Canyonlands National Park: The Maze

The backcountry roads of **THE MAZE** should probably be viewed as trails that vehicles and mountain bikes use instead of as roads. The conditions are primitive, so be prepared—both mentally and with the right vehicle in excellent condition.

## HORSESHOE CANYON

**Start:** Hans Flat Ranger Station

**Distance:** From Hans Flat 20 miles (one-way) to the bottom of Horseshoe Canyon

**Maps:** Trails Illustrated Canyonlands National Park and USGS Head Spur and Sugarloaf Butte

**Permits:** Permit required for vehicle camping at the High Spur campsite. Camping is not permitted in Horseshoe Canyon.

**Minimum vehicle requirements:** First 5 miles, low-clearance, two-wheel-drive to rim of canyon; high-clearance, four-wheel-drive with low-range gearing on Deadman's Trail and on the side road to High Spur Camp

**Difficulty:** Moderately difficult to canyon rim

**Road conditions:** Excellent the first 5 miles, then conditions worsen significantly: It's packed dirt and loose sand with many long rocky sections all the way to the rim of Horseshoe Canyon.

**Suitability for mountain biking:** Flat, easy going in most places with a few stretches of loose sand in the first 10 miles and near the canyon rim. Side roads to High Spur Camp and up Deadman's Trail are also excellent for mountain biking.

**Vehicle campsites:** High Spur Camp on east side of road 10 miles north of Hans Flat, 1 mile off the main road and in the shadow of a huge sandstone formation that rises abruptly out of the mesa. Get a great view of Cleopatra's Chair, which really looks like a chair from here.

**Special attractions:** Horseshoe Canyon

### MILES AND DIRECTIONS

0.0 Start at Hans Flat Ranger Station.

10.0 Turnoff to High Spur Camp.

12.0 Leave Glen Canyon NRA.

12.6 Turnoff to Deadman's Trail.

20.0 Rim of Horseshoe Canyon.

### NORTH POINT

**Start:** Hans Flat Ranger Station

**Distance:** From Gordon Flats Road 7 miles (one-way) to where road splits to Cleopatra's Chair and Panorama Point

**Maps:** Trails Illustrated Maze District/Northeast Glen Canyon and USGS Elaterite Basin and Cleopatra's Chair

**Permits:** Vehicle camping or at-large backpacking permit required. Day use allowed with no permit.

**Minimum vehicle requirements:** High-clearance, four-wheel-drive with low-range gearing

**Difficulty:** Moderate

**Road conditions:** Mostly through junipers and piñon pines on the mesa. Several long, very steep, rocky sections intermingled with smooth sections of packed dirt. There is some loose sand with a 1-mile-long smooth section through a big open park.

**Suitability for mountain biking:** Mostly excellent conditions—flat terrain, packed dirt with a few rocky sections and some loose sand

**Vehicle campsites:** None

**Special attractions:** Good scenery most of the way.

### PANORAMA POINT

**Start:** End of North Point Road

**Distance:** From end of North Point Road, 2 miles (one-way) to Panorama Point overlook and camp

**Maps:** Trails Illustrated Maze District/Northeast Glen Canyon and USGS Cleopatra's Chair

**Permits:** Vehicle camping or at-large backpacking permit required. Day use allowed with no permit.

**Minimum vehicle requirements:** High-clearance, four-wheel-drive with low-range gearing

**Difficulty:** Moderate

**Road conditions:** Packed dirt with frequent rocky sections and ledges and a long stretch of solid slickrock near the end of the road.

**Suitability for mountain biking:** Excellent conditions

**Vehicle campsites:** Panorama Point is probably the most scenic campsite in the Maze—or anywhere else! There's a great vista down into Elaterite Basin with the Maze in the distance to the east, Ekker Butte to the north, and Elaterite Butte to the south. The camp is right at the end of the road in junipers and piñon pines and just a few feet from the edge of the cliff, so if you have children, watch them carefully. Panorama Point may be closed to camping in the spring due to nesting peregrine falcons, so be sure to check with a ranger before making your final plans.

**Special attractions:** Truly spectacular scenery from Panorama Point at end of road

**Special precautions:** Extremely steep cliff at end of road and near camp. Very exposed and windy.

## CLEOPATRA'S CHAIR

**Start:** End of North Point Road

**Distance:** From end of North Point Road, 3 miles (one-way) to end of road and Cleopatra's Chair Camp

**Maps:** Trails Illustrated Maze District / Northeast Glen Canyon and USGS Cleopatra's Chair

**Permits:** Vehicle camping or at-large backpacking permit required. Day use allowed with no permit.

**Minimum vehicle requirements:** High-clearance, four-wheel-drive with low-range gearing

**Difficulty:** Moderate

**Road conditions:** Mostly packed dirt with a few short rocky sections

**Suitability for mountain biking:** Excellent conditions

**Vehicle campsites:** Cleopatra's Chair Camp is at the end of the road in the south shadow of massive Cleopatra's Chair and about 100 feet from a great overlook into sprawling Millard Canyon.

**Special precautions:** Be extra cautious around the steep cliff at the end of the road and near camp.

## GORDON FLATS

**Start:** Hans Flat Ranger Station

**Distance:** From Hans Flat Ranger Station, 12.1 miles (one-way) to the fork; the left-hand fork goes down Flint Trail and the right-hand fork to Big Ridge

**Maps:** Trails Illustrated Maze District / Northeast Glen Canyon and USGS Gordon Flats

**Permits:** Vehicle camping or at-large backpacking permit required. Day use allowed without a permit.

**Minimum vehicle requirements:** Low-clearance, two-wheel-drive

**Difficulty:** Moderate

**Road conditions:** One of the best roads in the Maze / Orange Cliffs area; mostly packed dirt. It can be driven with almost any vehicle.

**Suitability for mountain biking:** Excellent conditions

**Vehicle campsites:** Flint Seep Camp is about 100 yards west of the Gordon Flats Road nestled in a grove of junipers and piñon pines. This camp has been established as a group site with a limit of sixteen people and five vehicles. Call the park reservation office to reserve.

## MILES AND DIRECTIONS

0.0   Start at Hans Flat Ranger Station.

2.2   French's Cabin.

2.4   French's Spring.

2.5   North Point Road.

9.1   Bagpipe Butte Overlook.

11.1   Flint Seep Camp.

11.9   Flint Trail Overlook.

12.1   Flint Trail / Big Ridge junction.

## THE BIG RIDGE

**Start:** Flint Trail junction

**Distance:** 8 miles (one-way) from Flint Trail junction to Glen Canyon NRA boundary

**Maps:** Trails Illustrated Maze District / Northeast Glen Canyon and USGS Gordon Flats and Clearwater Canyon

**Permits:** Vehicle camping or at-large backpacking permit required. Day use allowed with no permit.

**Minimum vehicle requirements:** High-clearance, four-wheel-drive with low-range gearing

**Difficulty:** Moderate

**Road conditions:** Rockier than most roads in the area, but not extreme. Mostly flat as it stays on top of the Big Ridge Mesa. Gets worse after the Neck—even rockier with some bad gullies. Goes through junipers and piñon pines most of the way. About 3 miles past the park boundary (around the old Simplot Landing Strip), the road becomes impassable.

**Suitability for mountain biking:** Flat, mostly packed dirt, with minimal loose sand and frequent short rocky sections

**Vehicle campsites:** The Neck Camp is just off the west side of the road where the mesa narrows into a narrow "neck" like a similar spot in the Island in the Sky. Good scenery from the campsite. To get to Happy Canyon Camp, take the side road heading west off the main road about a mile past the Flint Trail junction and follow it for about 0.4 mile until you see the camp on your left. The road continues on for another 100 yards, where it ends at the trailhead for the Happy Canyon Trail and a good view of the Henry Mountains to the south.

## MILES AND DIRECTIONS

0.0   Start at Flint Trail junction.

0.9   Turnoff to Happy Canyon.

2.3   The Neck Camp.

8.0   Glen Canyon NRA boundary.

## THE FLINT TRAIL

**Start:** Gordon Flats Road

**Distance:** From Gordon Flats Road 2.8 miles (one-way) to Maze Overlook Road

**Maps:** Trails Illustrated Maze District/Northeast Glen Canyon and USGS Clearwater Canyon and Teapot Rock

**Permits:** Vehicle camping or at-large backpacking permit required. Day use allowed without a permit.

**Minimum vehicle requirements:** High-clearance, four-wheel-drive vehicle with low-range gearing. A short wheelbase is best for the tight turns on the switchbacks.

**Difficulty:** Difficult

**Road conditions:** The first part of the road is a very steep series of switchbacks from the Big Ridge down the Orange Cliffs to another small mesa. When dry, the switchbacks are easily passable with extra attention from the driver. But when wet, the clay gets too slippery to drive. If you get caught in a rainstorm, wait until the clay dries out before attempting the Flint Trail.

**Suitability for mountain biking:** Conditions are good when dry, but use extreme caution and keep the speed down when going down the switchbacks.

**Special precautions:** Go slowly on switchbacks; avoid them when wet. Chains are required for all four wheels in winter when snow is on the ground.

## MAZE OVERLOOK

**Start:** Hans Flat Trailhead

**Distance:** From Hans Flat 27.5 miles (one-way) to the Maze Overlook Camps; from the junction with Flint Trail, 15.4 miles to the Maze Overlook Camps

**Maps:** Trails Illustrated Maze District/Northeast Glen Canyon and USGS Elaterite Basin and Teapot Rock

**Permits:** Vehicle camping or at-large backpacking permit required. Day use allowed with no permit.

**Minimum vehicle requirements:** High-clearance, four-wheel-drive with low-range gearing

**Difficulty:** Difficult

**Road conditions:** Some sections are easy going, but most of the road is rocky (both loose rock and slickrock), with some steep sections and several ledges where clearance is critical. You'll want to get out of your vehicle at times to carefully check the route. Probably the toughest section is just past the Golden Stairs turnoff, as you drop off the mesa into Big Water Canyon. Great scenery all the way, with the Orange Cliffs on the western horizon as you make a big turn around Elaterite Butte.

**Suitability for mountain biking:** Mostly good conditions with frequent rocky sections and minimal loose sand. Conditions turn to excellent after the junction with the Millard Canyon Road.

**Vehicle campsites:** Both Maze Overlook 1 and Maze Overlook 2 are gorgeous campsites in the shadow of the fabulous Chocolate Drops towers, which are sculpted from Organ Rock shale. You can see it all from these camps: the Maze, Elaterite Butte, Ekker Butte, Panorama Point, the Land of Standing Rocks, and even the mighty La Sal Mountains serving as a backdrop to the east. The camps are quite exposed, however, so they can be unpleasant on a windy day. The camps also are extremely popular, so get your reservation in early.

**Special attractions:** Outstanding scenery along the road and from Maze Overlook Camps

## MILES AND DIRECTIONS (FROM FLINT TRAIL JUNCTION)

0.0   Start at Flint Trail junction.

2.6   Golden Stairs turnoff.

10.2  Millard Canyon junction.

11.8  Canyonlands National Park boundary.

15.4  Maze Overlook Camps, trailhead, and parking area.

## GOLDEN STAIRS

**Start:** Maze Overlook Road

**Distance:** From Maze Overlook Road 1 mile (one-way) to Golden Stairs Camp and parking area

**Maps:** Trails Illustrated Maze District / Northeast Glen Canyon and USGS Elaterite Basin

**Permits:** Vehicle camping or at-large backpacking permit required. Day use allowed with no permit.

**Minimum vehicle requirements:** High-clearance, four-wheel-drive with low-range gearing

**Difficulty:** Difficult

**Road conditions:** Mostly rocky with ledges

**Suitability for mountain biking:** Slightly rough conditions

**Vehicle campsites:** Golden Stairs Camp sits up high on a 6,000-foot mesa crowned with junipers and piñon pines. The view right from camp is not great, but a short walk gives you superb vistas in several directions.

## MILLARD CANYON

**Start:** Hans Flat Ranger Station
**Distance:** From Hans Flat Ranger Station 50 miles (one-way) to the Green River
**Maps:** Trails Illustrated Maze District/Northeast Glen Canyon and USGS Turks Head, Cleopatra's Chair, and Horsethief Canyon
**Permits:** Vehicle camping or at-large backpacking permit required. Day use allowed with no permit.
**Minimum vehicle requirements:** High-clearance, four-wheel-drive with low-range gearing
**Difficulty:** Moderate
**Road conditions:** Conditions vary on this long stretch of road. Many sections are rocky and slow going, but nothing extreme. Just before you reach Millard Canyon Camp and the Green River, the road gets very rocky.
**Suitability for mountain biking:** Good to excellent most of the way, with a few rocky sections, especially near the end where the road heads down to the river.
**Vehicle campsites:** Ekker Butte is not one of the prime campsites in the area. It's mostly slickrock, and tent camping is marginal. The NPS considers it an overflow site, so it's usually available. The Millard Canyon Camp is right on the Green River and is one of the nicest campsites in the Maze.
**Special attractions:** Great campsite on the Green River, and you probably will have the area to yourself.

## MILES AND DIRECTIONS

0.0   Start at Hans Flat Ranger Station.

0.3   North Trail Trailhead.

2.0   Canyonlands National Park boundary (no sign).

9.2   Ekker Butte Camp.

23.0 Millard Canyon Camp.

## SUNSET PASS

**Start:** Waterhole Flat junction

**Distance:** From Waterhole Flat junction 4.5 miles (one-way) to Glen Canyon NRA boundary

**Maps:** Trails Illustrated Maze District / Northeast Glen Canyon and USGS Clearwater Canyon

**Permits:** Vehicle camping or at-large backpacking permit required. Day use allowed without a permit.

**Minimum vehicle requirements:** High-clearance, four-wheel-drive with low-range gearing

**Difficulty:** Moderate

**Road conditions:** Packed dirt most of the way, with a few short rocky sections and one long rocky section just on the east side of the pass, which is actually a gap in the Orange Cliffs

**Suitability for mountain biking:** Excellent conditions with a moderately steep climb to the pass

**Vehicle campsites:** Sunset Pass Camp is in a grove of junipers and piñon pines on the south side of the road just as it goes through the gap in the Orange Cliffs. It's exposed to the wind and rain, but not nearly as much as popular campsites such as Maze Overlook or Standing Rock.

### MILES AND DIRECTIONS

0.0   Start at Waterhole Flat junction.

2.5   Sunset Pass Camp.

4.5   Glen Canyon NRA boundary.

## WATERHOLE FLAT

**Start:** Flint Trail junction

**Distance:** 6.5 miles (one-way) to Waterhole Flat junction

**Maps:** Trails Illustrated Maze District / Northeast Glen Canyon and USGS Clearwater Canyon and Teapot Rock

**Permits:** Vehicle camping or at-large backpacking permit required. Day use allowed with no permit.

**Minimum vehicle requirements:** From Hite, high-clearance, two-wheel-drive; from Hans Flat Ranger Station, high-clearance, four-wheel-drive with low-range gearing

**Difficulty:** Moderate

**Road conditions:** From the Flint Trail junction to the Waterhole Flat junction, it's packed dirt with a few short rocky sections but easy going all the way, especially the southernmost half of this section of road, where it gets so good that you might have to be careful not to exceed the 15 mph speed limit. The north half goes between precipitous Red Cove on the east and the massive Orange Cliffs on the west, both well named for their color, and the south half goes across the broad, mostly flat terrain of Waterhole Flat. On some older maps you may see a road heading west over to Sunset Pass, but that road has been recently abandoned. The same old map might show a road heading south down a wash to Doll House Road. This looks like a shortcut, but it isn't an official road and probably takes longer than driving the long way around. The long route is easy driving, and you can make great time compared to driving through the narrow, rocky wash.

**Suitability for mountain biking:** Excellent road for mountain biking

## THE ROAD TO THE DOLL HOUSE

**Start:** Waterhole Flat junction
**Distance:** 21 miles (one-way)
**Maps:** Trails Illustrated Maze District/Northeast Glen Canyon and USGS Teapot Rock, Elaterite Basin, and Spanish Bottom
**Permits:** Vehicle camping or at-large backpacking permit required. Day use allowed without a permit.
**Minimum vehicle requirements:** High-clearance, four-wheel-drive with low-range gearing
**Difficulty:** Difficult
**Road conditions:** From the Waterhole Flat junction, the road starts out smooth and stays that way for about 3 miles. Then it gradually gets rougher as you approach the Teapot Rock Camp. After passing by the campsite, you face a 5-mile section of road that is probably the worst in the Maze District—you probably can walk it faster than you can drive it. You must get out of your vehicle frequently to check routes over ledges and in rocky sections. Use extreme caution all the way unless you want to seriously damage your vehicle and get stranded in the Maze. After you reach the Wall Camp, the road gets better, turning into mostly packed sand with a few rocky sections. From Chimney Rock to the Doll House, the road has sections of loose sand and gets seriously rocky just before the Doll House.

**Suitability for mountain biking:** Conditions may be better for mountain biking than they are for driving, especially in the section from Teapot Rock Camp to the Wall Camp. After the Chimney Rock Camp, the road has some sections of loose sand. The loose sand and rocky sections may prove difficult for novice riders, but for the most part this is a fantastic mountain-biking road.

**Vehicle campsites:** Vehicle camps in the Maze do not have vault toilets. You are required to have a portable toilet with you.

**Teapot Rock**—The road goes right by this camp, so privacy can be a problem. Plus, it's very rocky and exposed, but it does have a great view of Teapot Rock. Also, if you don't have a high-clearance, four-wheel-drive vehicle, you can camp here and hike or mountain bike into the Maze area.

**The Wall**—On the north side of the road about 100 yards off the road. Very scenic campsite with great view of the Maze, Chocolate Drops, Standing Rock, and many other famous formations. Very exposed, so it can be unpleasant on a windy day.

**Standing Rock**—Right in the shadow of awesome Standing Rock, so you can sit in camp for hours and wonder how this smokestack-like sandstone spire survived the power of nature. Like the Wall Camp, this camp is about 100 yards north of the road and is quite exposed.

**Chimney Rock**—Following the trend set by the Wall and Standing Rock Camps, this camp is just north of the road and very exposed but has incredible scenery. It has the attraction of being right by a major trailhead for trails and off-trail routes into the Maze and serves as a base camp for hikers who like day hiking instead of backpacking.

**Doll House 1**—Semiprotected between two massive sandstone towers, but still with a good view off to the east and close to the trailheads for designated trails leaving the Doll House area. This camp, along with the other two Doll House camps, has the advantage of privacy, since all are located at the end of spur roads.

**Doll House 2**—Like Camp 1, Camp 2 is tucked amid the Doll House towers. More exposed than Camp 1, which can be a problem on windier days, but less exposed than Camp 3.

**Doll House 3**—Unlike Camps 1 and 2, you can get a great view of the Doll House itself from Camp 3. It's in an open area on the southwest edge of the famous sandstone formation. This can be the least desirable of the three on a windy day but the most desirable in good weather. Also, Camp 3 is farther from the official trailheads for the three designated trails leaving the Doll House area.

**Special attractions:** Truly spectacular scenery and the aura of remoteness and self-reliance

**Special precautions:** Hazardous road

## MILES AND DIRECTIONS

**0.0** Start at Waterhole Flat junction.

**3.6** Teapot Rock Camp.

**9.2** Golden Stairs Trailhead.

**10.3** Canyonlands National Park boundary.

**13.8** The Wall Camp.

**15.8** Standing Rock Camp.

**17.1** Chimney Rock Camp.

**17.2** Harvest Scene Trailhead.

**20.6** Turn to Doll House 3 Camp.

**20.7** Colorado/Green River Overlook Trailhead.

**20.8** Spanish Bottom and Granary Trailhead.

**21.0** Doll House 1 and 2 Camps.

## HITE

**Start:** Waterhole Flat junction

**Distance:** 32 miles (one-way) to Hite

**Maps:** Trails Illustrated Maze District/Northeast Glen Canyon and USGS Clearwater Canyon and Bowdie Canyon West

**Permits:** No permit required outside the park boundary.

**Minimum vehicle requirements:** High-clearance, four-wheel-drive with low-range gearing

**Difficulty:** Moderate

**Road conditions:** With the exception of a few rocky sections near the Waterhole Flat junction, this is a good four-wheel-drive road all the way to the paved road just before Hite.

**Suitability for mountain biking:** Excellent conditions for mountain biking, but not quite as scenic as many other roads in the Maze

# TRAIL FINDER

## EASY DAY HIKES
**Arches:** Park Avenue, Windows, Landscape Arch, Sand Dune Arch, Double Arch, Balanced Rock, Skyline Arch
**Island in the Sky:** Mesa Arch, Grand View, White Rim Overlook, Murphy Point, Lathrop (to canyon rim), Gooseneck
**Needles:** Roadside Ruin, Pothole Point, Castle Arch, Fortress Arch
**Maze:** The Granary

## MODERATE DAY HIKES
**Arches:** Delicate Arch, Fiery Furnace, Tower Arch, Windows Primitive Loop
**Island in the Sky:** Aztec Butte, Neck Spring, Whale Rock, Fort Bottom, Moses, Upheaval Canyon, Upheaval Dome Overlook
**Needles:** Cave Spring, Slickrock Foot Trail, Lost Canyon, Squaw Canyon / Big Spring Canyon, Big Spring Canyon / Elephant Canyon, Elephant Hill to Squaw Flat, Druid Arch, Druid Arch West, The Joint Trail, Chesler Park Loop, Devils Pocket Loop
**Maze:** The Great Gallery, Happy Canyon, The Golden Stairs, Colorado / Green River Overlook, Spanish Bottom

## DIFFICULT DAY HIKES
**Arches:** Devils Garden Primitive Loop
**Island in the Sky:** Syncline Loop, Lathrop, Gooseberry, Murphy Loop, Alcove Spring, Lathrop (to White Rim Road), Wilhite
**Needles:** Confluence Overlook, Peekaboo, Lost Canyon / Elephant Canyon, Chesler Park / Devils Kitchen, Lower Red Lake
**Maze:** The North Trail, Maze Overlook, Harvest Scene

## MULTIDAY HIKES
**Island in the Sky:** Alcove Spring / Syncline Loop
**Needles:** Upper Salt Creek, Lost Canyon / Elephant Canyon, Chesler Park / Devils Kitchen, The Big Needles Loop

# AUTHOR'S FAVORITES

## REALLY EASY DAY HIKES
**Arches:** Sand Dune Arch, Park Avenue, Landscape Arch
**Island in the Sky:** Mesa Arch, Aztec Butte, Whale Rock, White Rim Overlook, Grand View, Upheaval Dome Overlook
**Needles:** Pothole Point, Cave Spring, The Joint Trail
**Maze:** The Granary, Colorado / Green River Overlook (to Beehive Arch)

## EASY DAY HIKES, BUT NOT TOO EASY
**Arches:** Broken Arch, Tower Arch
**Island in the Sky:** Murphy Point, Moses, Fort Bottom
**Needles:** Slickrock Foot Trail
**Maze:** Spanish Bottom

The most famous arch on earth, Delicate Arch in Arches National Park
COURTESY DAI HIROTA/ IMPACT PHOTOGRAPHICS

## MODERATELY DIFFICULT HIKES, BUT NOT TOO DIFFICULT
**Arches:** Delicate Arch, Devils Garden (to Double O Arch), Fiery Furnace
**Island in the Sky:** Neck Spring, Lathrop (to canyon rim)
**Needles:** Squaw Canyon / Big Spring Canyon, Chesler Park Loop, Devils Pocket Loop
**Maze:** The Great Gallery, Maze Overlook, Colorado / Green River Overlook

## LONG, HARD DAY HIKES SO HIKERS CAN EAT ANYTHING THEY WANT FOR DINNER AND NOT FEEL GUILTY
**Arches:** Devils Garden Primitive Loop
**Island in the Sky:** Syncline Loop, Murphy Loop, Alcove Spring
**Needles:** Lost Canyon, Lost Canyon / Elephant Canyon, Druid Arch, Confluence Overlook, Upper Salt Creek
**Maze:** Harvest Scene

## FIRST NIGHT IN THE WILDERNESS
**Island in the Sky:** Murphy Loop, Upheaval Canyon
**Needles:** Upper Salt Creek (out-and-back option), Squaw Canyon / Big Spring Canyon, Elephant Hill to Squaw Flat, Chesler Park Loop
**Maze:** Happy Canyon, Colorado / Green River Overlook

## FOR PHOTOGRAPHERS
**Arches:** Devils Garden, Park Avenue, Fiery Furnace, Delicate Arch
**Island in the Sky:** Murphy Point, Moses, White Rim Overlook, Grand View
**Needles:** The Joint Trail, Peekaboo, Lost Canyon, Confluence Overlook, Devils Pocket Loop
**Maze:** Maze Overlook, Harvest Scene, Colorado / Green River Overlook

## MULTIDAY BACKCOUNTRY ADVENTURES
**Island in the Sky:** Alcove Spring / Syncline Loop
**Needles:** The Big Needles Loop, Chesler Park / Devils Kitchen, Upper Salt Creek
**Maze:** Harvest Scene

## FOR TRAIL RUNNERS AND POWER HIKERS
**Island in the Sky:** Neck Spring, Lathrop (to canyon rim), Upheaval Canyon
**Needles:** Squaw Canyon / Big Spring Canyon, Lost Canyon / Elephant Canyon

# CANYONLANDS
## Natural History Association

Canyonlands Natural History Association (CNHA) was established in 1967 as a not-for-profit organization to assist the scientific, educational, and visitor service efforts of the National Park Service (NPS), the Bureau of Land Management (BLM), and US Forest Service (USFS).

CNHA's goals include enhancing each visitor's understanding and appreciation of public lands by providing a thorough selection of quality educational materials for sale in its bookstore outlets. A portion of CNHA's proceeds, including profit from this publication, are returned directly to our public land partners to fund their educational, research, and scientific programs. Bookstore sales support the agencies' programs in various ways, including free publications, outdoor education programs for local school districts, equipment and supplies for ranger/naturalists, exhibits, and funds for research. Since its inception in 1967, CNHA has donated over $13 million to its public land partners.

## THE DISCOVERY POOL

CNHA established the Discovery Pool in 2006 to provide its federal partners with financial support for eligible scientific studies conducted within their administrative boundaries. The goals for use of the Discovery Pool grants are:

- Encourage the scientific research that makes up the backbone of interpretive and educational programs, including resource management or protection surveys and monitoring.

- Provide matching funds that may assist federal partners in obtaining larger grants.

- Promote an understanding of the intricate cultural and natural resource complexities found on federally administered lands.

Since its inception, the CNHA Discovery Pool has awarded over $350,000 in grants to all of our federal partners! The wide range of projects includes but is not limited to the following studies.

- Goodman Point Archaeological Project
- Bighorn Sheep Collaring

- Multi-Spectral Imaging of Rock Art in Canyonlands National Park
- Alpine Habitat Baseline Study
- Cedar Mesa Building Murals and Social Identities Project
- Paleontological Investigations of Comb Ridge, Utah

For a complete listing and description of all the Discovery Pool projects and for the guidelines to apply for a grant, please visit www.cnha.org/discovery-pool. You can be a part of the Discovery Pool by becoming a Discovery member.

## CNHA MEMBERSHIP

People protect that which they understand. With visitor use demands escalating and agency funding declining, CNHA's role in assisting in the agencies' educational efforts will continue to expand. Those wishing to support CNHA and its mission are invited to join the association's membership program.

Through your membership donation, CNHA is able to fund educational projects and programs such as Canyon Country Outdoor Education, Night Sky programs at Arches and Canyonlands National Parks, Junior Ranger Programs, Student Conservation Association volunteers, and much more. Membership dues and other contributions are tax deductible to the extent provided by law.

For more information about CNHA, the Discovery Pool, its membership program, or its products, please visit online at www.cnha.org or call (435) 259-6003.

The exteriors of several of the rooms of this well-preserved pueblo were decorated with rare examples of both incised and painted plaster decorations. With the help of the CNHA Discovery Pool grant funding, archaeologists are investigating the distribution, dating, and role of this and other styles of building decorations in the region during the AD 1200s.
BEN BELLORADO/COURTESY CNHA

# HIKE INDEX

# ACKNOWLEDGMENTS

For twenty years this trail guide has been a cooperative effort between the National Park Service staff at Canyonlands and Arches National Parks and the staff of the Canyonlands Natural History Association. It would be most appropriate to say that it would not have happened without them.

A lot of people have helped me with this book and its revisions, too many to list here, but I would especially like to thank these NPS employees who helped coordinate, research, and review the original guidebook, which was released in 1997—Larry Frederick, Bruce McCabe, Aneth Wight, Mary Beth Maynard, Karen Schlom, Gary Cox, Diane Allen, and Fred Patton. Jim Blazak helped make sure we had all updates in the first revision. On the third edition, thanks to Stephen Allen, Cynthia Beyer, Sierra Coon, Dick Toll, and Laura Lusk for helping update the book. And for this, the fourth edition, additional thanks to Nathaniel Clark, Keri Nelson, Will Leggett, and Karen Garthwait.

Also, special thanks to Canyonlands Natural History Association, a wonderful partner. Jean Treadway, Brad Wallis, Gloria Brown, Cindy Hardgrave, and Sam Wainer all helped make this a real partnership in publishing.

For the first edition the staff at Falcon, as always, deserves a big thank-you for putting up with my distractions while researching and writing the book, with special thanks to Randall Green, our guidebook editor; Marita Martiniak, the graphic artist who laid out the book; Noelle Sullivan, the copy editor; and Tony Moore, who did the original maps. For finishing the first revision, thanks to FalconGuides staffers Gillian Belnap, Scott Adams, and Erin Joyce. For this revision, thanks to John Burbidge and the rest of the crew at FalconGuides and Globe Pequot.

## BOOKS IN PRINT BY BILL SCHNEIDER

*Backpacker Magazine's Bear Country Behavior*
*Backpacking Tips* (coauthor)
*Bear Aware, A Quick Reference Bear Country Survival Guide*
*Best Backpacking Vacations Northern Rockies*
*Best Easy Day Hikes Absaroka-Beartooth Wilderness*
*Best Easy Day Hikes Canyonlands and Arches*
*Best Easy Day Hikes Grand Teton*
*Best Easy Day Hikes Yellowstone*
*Best Hikes on the Continental Divide* (coauthor)
*Hiking Canyonlands and Arches National Parks*
*Hiking Carlsbad Caverns and Guadalupe Mountains National Parks*
*Hiking Grand Teton National Park*
*Hiking Montana* (coauthor)
*Hiking Montana, Bozeman*
*Hiking the Absaroka-Beartooth Wilderness*
*Hiking Yellowstone National Park*
*The Tree Giants*
*Where the Grizzly Walks*